Governments and Politics of the German-Speaking Countries

Governments and Politics of the German-Speaking Countries

Walter S. G. Kohn

Nelson-Hall nh Chicago

Library of Congress Cataloging in Publication Data

Kohn, Walter, S G
    Governments and politics of the German-speaking
countries.

    Bibliography: p.
    Includes index.
    1. Germany—Politics and government. 2. Austria—
Politics and government. 3. Switzerland—Politics
and government. 4. Liechtenstein—Politics and
government. I. Title.
JN3221.K58   320.3′094   79–16859
ISBN 0–88229–262–5

Contents

The idea for this book was first conceived when I was teaching Central European government to a group of students from Northern Illinois University and Illinois State University who were spending a semester in Salzburg, Austria, during the fall of 1971. I am grateful for their inspiration. I am also grateful for the co-operation and understanding shown by various administrators at Illinois State University, especially by the chairman of the Political Science Department, Professor Hibbert R. Roberts.

A number of people in the countries here under discussion have been more than helpful. They are too numerous to mention individually; however, I want to assure each how much the assistance is appreciated. Writing a book always entails sacrifices on the part of one's immediate family and a special thank you is due to my children for putting up with me during all that time and especially to my wife, Rita, without whose encouragement, criticism and assistance in so many different ways this book could never have been finished.

Map of Modern Europe

1

Introduction

Winston Churchill once remarked that the British and the Americans have everything in common except language. A "lorry" in one country is called a "truck" in the other; a "lift," an "elevator"; and a "wireless," a "radio." Nevertheless, many institutions, principles, beliefs, and customs are shared by the two nations. This is particularly true in the fields of law and politics where the concepts of Magna Charta and the Bill of Rights, extended and modernized, became an integral part of government, not only in Britain but throughout the English-speaking democracies.

Of those countries where German is spoken, on the other hand, one could maintain that they have little in common except language. The dialect used in Cologne differs vastly from that of Leipzig, and the speech of a native of Bern cannot possibly be mistaken for that of a native Viennese, let alone a Berliner. However, Johann Wolfgang Goethe and Immanuel Kant, Gottfried Keller and Sigmund Freud stem from the same *Kultur*—that is, civilization—held together by a common language. Of course, this is also true of William Shakespeare and Walt Whitman, Stephen Leacock and Alan Paton. But while English-speaking peoples are all branches of the same tree, a similar common political and philosophic heritage is difficult to detect among citizens of German-speaking countries.

1

This book will discuss the varying political developments in those German-speaking lands and show how they are governed at the present time. Although a rather large variety of studies of comparative government has appeared in print, they have concentrated either on individual countries or on specific problems. Some books deal with regional groupings, such as the Scandinavian or Benelux nations. Others discuss a few countries having little in common except that, for some reason or another, they struck the author's fancy. The "big four," i.e., Britain, France, Germany, and the Soviet Union, is probably the most favored combination.

This volume is a study of the governments and politics of a highly important region. It stretches from the Atlantic Ocean to the Alps and from the Rhine to the Oder and Neisse rivers and includes five countries, with five distinctly different forms of government. They vary in size from ninety-six thousand square miles to a mere sixty-two, and in population from more than sixty million inhabitants to twenty-one thousand. One of them became independent almost seven hundred years ago; two others took their present forms only in the midtwentieth century. We can observe several distinct constitutions and governmental institutions, including Western democracies and a communist regime. Federalism is very highly developed in Switzerland, but is practically nonexistent in the German Democratic Republic. There are examples of multiparty, two-party, and one-party systems. Political coalitions govern in some countries. One party rules alone in others. Where there are presidents they vary in power and authority. They may be elected directly or indirectly or chosen annually from among the ministers on a rotating basis. In one instance, monarchy still prevails.

The differing political and governmental practices across the region have one thing in common: the use of the same written language. Even here, however, some distinctions must be made. On the one hand, German is the native tongue of the overwhelming majority of the population of Switzerland, but there are three other official languages, French, Italian, and Romanche, which are spoken by 30 percent of the Swiss. On the other hand, German is probably used by a larger percentage of natives in Luxemburg than in Switzerland, but the principality is economically, militarily, and politically so much a part of the Benelux "trinity" that its inclusion here might seem anachronistic.

Of the major language areas in Europe, German is least confined within the borders of one country. English is spoken throughout Great Britain; with some relatively minor exceptions the French language coincides with the territory of France; Italian is pretty much restricted to its political frontiers and to one Swiss canton. The German language, however, is as dispersed throughout Europe as Germany, as a national, historically identifiable entity, was fragmented before Napoleon. Napoleon, incidentally, did more for German unification than any other individual, including Bismarck. When he came to power the Habsburg emperors lived in Vienna although that city was not thought of as the capital of Germany. Parliament sat in Regensburg and the Court of Justice at Wetzlar; however, neither Parliament nor the Court was of much practical significance. The king of Prussia was not a prince of the empire as such; he participated in its councils only in his capacity as elector of Brandenburg. In contrast, the king of Sweden held enough German territory to be a member of the empire. As late as the post-Napoleonic period, the monarchs of Denmark, Holland, and even England belonged to the German confederation because of certain lands they owned.

During the war of liberation against Napoleon the German poet Ernst Moritz Arndt asked the question, "What is the German's Fatherland?" Through a number of verses he enumerated Prussia, Swabia, and the Rhineland. He also included Austria and the Danube Valley, the "Belt" (narrow stretches of sea, separating several parts of Denmark), and Switzerland. Finally he came to the conclusion that Germany extends "As far as German tongues do sound," an area where each Frenchman was a foe and each German a friend.

Under Prussian leadership, several successful wars in the second half of the nineteenth century were followed by two unsuccessful ones in the first half of the twentieth. The ultimate result was the almost complete elimination of non-German-speaking elements from the countries where German is the official language. Apart from such small and isolated regions as the Austrian Burgenland, where there are about twenty-eight thousand Croatians, the single major exception is Switzerland. However, four hundred years ago Switzerland ceased to pursue an aggressive foreign policy, and its territory has been virtually unchanged since that time. Because German is the native language of the majority of the Swiss, Switzerland is included here, even though the use of German there has declined slightly over the past few decades.

Switzerland is the oldest independent country among the five under discussion, and one of the oldest existing republics in the world. Small and decentralized, it possesses a strongly developed federal system. Sworn to neutrality even in an era of supposed collective security, the country demonstrates its fiercely democratic character by frequent use of the referendum on various levels. Yet its women were not enfranchised until 1971. Switzerland clings to a number of other political practices that are quite unusual in modern democracies. It has a permanent coalition government in which even the ratio of the four participating parties is rapidly becoming a tradition; an annually rotating presidency; and a citizen army composed of all able-bodied men between the ages of twenty and fifty.

Austria is another small, neutral country, but its neutrality dates only to 1955 and its size to 1919. When Austria's present boundaries were established in that year, they enclosed a sorry remainder of what had been one of Europe's major powers. With hardly enough economic strength to exist independently, yet prevented by its former enemies from establishing close ties with Germany, Austria became the scene of vicious internal strife which eventually paved the way for conquest by Adolf Hitler. Only after experiencing union with Nazi Germany, occupation by the Allies and, finally, liberation from both, did the Austrian people really begin to support independence, neutralism, and democracy.

Another consequence of the Second World War was the division of Germany. Although unification is still high on the publicly proclaimed agenda of almost every German politician, the realization seems to be growing that at best it is a long way off. West Germany has managed thus far to steer clear of the disastrous course of the Weimar Republic. A sound constitutional system has been developed; peaceful governmental changes based on election results have taken place. Extremists on the Right and on the Left, with minor temporary exceptions, have been quite unsuccessful. Political maturity has been further demonstrated by the evolution from thirty or more political parties in the pre-Hitler era to one-tenth of that number today.

While the German Federal Republic in the west is a member of NATO, the eastern part is allied with the Soviet Union and other Communist countries in Eastern Europe by the Warsaw Pact. Officially known as the German Democratic Republic (its German initials are DDR), this country interprets *democratic* as *anti-Fascist, anticapitalist,* and *pro-Communist.* Here we find the same political and economic arrangements as in the Soviet Union and its other satellites, and proof that beautifully worded constitutions, by themselves, do not necessarily guarantee anything; in practice, they may be quite meaningless.

Finally, by way of contrast, there is little Liechtenstein, the only remaining monarchy of the old Holy Roman Empire of the German nation. It has an area equivalent to that of the District of Columbia but only one-fortieth of the District's population. It is thus not only the smallest of the countries under discussion but also one of the tiniest in all Europe. However, miniscule Liechtenstein is virtually independent. Its sovereignty was demonstrated when its head of government addressed the historic Helsinki conference in the summer of 1975, on the same day as United States President Gerald Ford. Because Liechtenstein's official language is German, even if what is actually spoken is a dialect based on German, it deserves inclusion in the present volume.

Table 1. The German-Speaking Countries

Country	Area in Square Miles	Population in 1,000s
German Federal Republic (West Germany)	95,975	61,195
German Democratic Republic (East Germany) (DDR)	41,722	17,075
Austria	32,366	7,074
Switzerland	15,941	5,429
Liechtenstein	62	21

2

Geography and National Identity

Each of the five countries under discussion has its own characteristics and peculiarities within its own political and constitutional system. These differences did not develop overnight but are, at least in part, the result of historic experiences that have varied from area to area. The first problem to be dealt with, therefore, is how each of the five countries came to take on its present dimensions, and how geography has affected history.

Of all the German-speaking countries, only Switzerland is recognizable in its present boundaries on a three-hundred-year-old map. The Swiss achieved their independence several centuries ago. Like the other countries discussed in this book, they were part of the Holy Roman Empire of the German nation in its early days. That empire, however, was anything but a coherent unit. It consisted of a variety of territories, large and small. Some areas were ruled by worldly lords, others by bishops or abbots, but the citizens of some towns governed themselves, just as in certain rural districts the wishes of the local peasantry prevailed. These were instances where no overlord was acknowledged except the emperor himself. During the Middle Ages, more and more of these Free Imperial Territories lost this status. They passed into the hands of overlords who became the ruling middlemen between the emperor and his subjects. Such lords were eager to enlarge their possessions and accumulate more land; their aim was to gain more power and with it more strength to resist the emperor. Some of the emperors in turn wanted to safeguard the freedom and independence of particular areas. This was done by issuing the inhabitants of such areas a *Freibrief,* a document confirming their freedom directly under the imperial crown with the emperor as their only worldly ruler. The alpine communities of Uri, Schwyz, and Unterwalden possessed such independence. The villagers held annual meetings to decide political and economic questions and to elect their highest official, who represented the emperor and acted as judge over disputes.

With the spread of feudalism, these local rights were challenged. The House of Habsburg was expanding, and it cast a longing eye on the *reichsfreie* villages in the Alps. The situation was complicated when in 1273 the imperial crown passed to the Habsburgs and the threat to the villages' independence and their supposed defender became one and the same. The story of William Tell may be merely a legend, but it is historically true that the three forest communities did get together in 1291 and formed a united front against any infringements of their age-old rights. They expressed strong determination to defend their freedom, with their lives if necessary. This fraternity based on a solemn oath *(Eidgenossenschaft)* was the beginning of Switzerland: to this day the term is part of the official name of the country, just as 1291 is celebrated as the nation's year of birth.

Switzerland thus began as a defensive alliance between three rather insignificant villages. Armed clashes occurred, and the Austrians were decisively defeated at Morgarten in 1315. Sporadic fighting continued during the next few centuries. The three forest communities did not remain alone in their perpetual league and alliance. In time, they were joined by others, including Luzern, Zürich, and Bern. Together they were sometimes able to inflict heavy losses on the Habsburgs. In 1499, in the Treaty of Basel, Emperor Maximilian I in effect guaranteed the Swiss complete freedom, not within the empire but from it. This independence was reaffirmed and formally recognized by the Peace of Westphalia in 1648. Schwyz, one of the original forest communities, gave its name to the new country. Within the Swiss confederation, the individual cantons were autonomous, at times even warring among themselves. Today Switzerland still practices individualism and localism to the greatest possible degree.

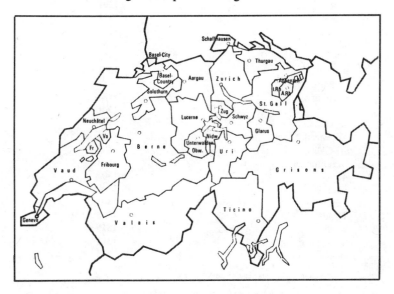

Switzerland

Until modern artillery techniques provided an effective answer to their infantry, the Swiss were an important power in Europe. But a series of military defeats, beginning with Marignano in 1515, brought an end to any grandiose designs Switzerland might have harbored. Henceforth it no longer participated in the game of power politics. This lack of an aggressive foreign policy is to a large extent responsible for the fact that the borders of the Swiss confederation have remained virtually unchanged since the end of the sixteenth century (except for a brief interlude at the time of Napoleon). Although six new cantons were created in 1803, these were merely part of a reorganization of existing Swiss territory. The three cantons added in 1815 were French-speaking areas Napoleon had taken from Switzerland that were now reincor-

Table 2. The Swiss Cantons and the Confederation

Canton	Joined Confederation
Uri	1291
Schwyz	1291
Unterwalden*	1291
Luzern	1331
Zürich	1351
Glarus	1352
Zug	1352
Bern	1353
Freiburg	1481
Solothurn	1481
Basel**	1501
Schaffhausen	1501
Appenzell***	1513
St. Gallen	1803
Graubünden	1803
Aargau	1803
Thurgau	1803
Tessin	1803
Waadt	1803
Wallis	1815
Neuenburg	1815
Genf	1815

*Now two half-cantons, Nidwalden and Obwalden
**Now two half-cantons, Basel-Stadt and Basel-Land
***Now two half cantons, Inner Rhoden and Ausser (Outer) Rhoden
Source: The basis for this table, as well as much of the detail on the preceding pages, was taken from Ulrich im Hof, *Vom Bundesbrief zur Bundesversammlung,* 1948. In order to avoid unnecessary confusion, the German names of the cantons are used throughout this book.

porated into the *Eidgenossenschaft,* this time with the full status of cantons.

The second country to achieve independence within its present boundaries was the principality of Liechtenstein. Its birth can be attributed not to the national aspirations of its people but to the ambitions of its rulers. As a geographic entity the principality was nonexistent until the early eighteenth century. At that time, two small *reichsfreie* alpine areas passed into the hands of the Liechtenstein family. Over the years members of the family had endeared themselves to the Austrian court by service in diplomatic and military capacities. They had been rewarded with rich gifts of lands and titles; they built beautiful palaces and acquired priceless art treasures. In 1608, they were elevated to the ranks of princes, but one of their ambitions remained unfulfilled: a seat in the *Reichsfürstentag,* the Imperial Council of Princes. To gain this, not even their extensive land holdings in Bohemia, Silesia, and elsewhere were sufficient. What was needed was ownership of land that was *reichsfrei,* directly under the Imperial crown. The Liechtenstein family was interested in obtaining free imperial territory but faced the difficulty that such real estate was obviously not often for sale.

However, a rare opportunity presented itself after the Thirty Years War. This conflict had devastated large areas of Europe, ostensibly because the forces of the Reformation were engaged in a life-and-death struggle with Catholicism. Two free imperial territories, the *Grafschaft* Vaduz and the *Herrschaft* Schellenberg, had been part of the theatre of war. They had been invaded and occupied repeatedly, experiencing plunder and theft, murder and rape. In addition, pestilence took its toll. What war and the plague had not touched was taken by the self-inflicted punishment of witch-hunting that claimed perhaps 10 percent of the total population of three thousand. No wonder that the two tiny territories were completely impoverished and their rulers quite willing to sell them.

A prince of Liechtenstein purchased Schellenberg in 1699 and Vaduz in 1712. The two were united in 1719 by imperial edict and became the *Reichsfürstentum* Liechtenstein, the three hundred forty-third member state of the Holy Roman Empire of the German nation. The house of Liechtenstein had at long last obtained a seat in the Imperial Council of Princes.

Several rather unique features of the origin of Liechtenstein should be briefly noted.[1] First, it is unusual for a family of nobles to give its name to a land; customarily a territory lends its name to that of its ruling prince. Secondly, there was a complete absence of the causes usually responsible for the creation of a new country: war, revolution, or unification for some historic or dynastic reason. Certainly the population had no say whatsoever in the establishment of the state; its creation was attributable merely to the ambitions and aspirations of its new rulers.

That the princes were not particularly interested in the principality but merely in its ownership can be seen from the fact that it was more than a century later, in 1842, before a reigning prince first bothered to visit his little land. Not until the present monarch, Franz Josef II, ascended the throne in 1938 did a princely ruler make Liechtenstein his permanent place of residence.

As remarkable as the account of its creation is the history of the little country's survival. When Napoleon redrew the map of Europe in the early nineteenth century, the more than three hundred member states of the Holy Roman Empire were greatly reduced in number. Smaller ones in particular were forced out of existence, but Liechtenstein survived. In 1806 it became one of the sixteen members of the *Rheinbund,* Napoleon's satellite Confederation of the Rhine, despite the prince of Liechtenstein's loyalty to the house of Habsburg, on whose behalf he negotiated with the French emperor. If being an esteemed adversary saved the prince's little realm from extinction by Napoleon, his faithful services to the Austrian court assured the survival of the principality after the French were defeated. Liechtenstein then became one of the thirty-nine member states of the German League with representation in the loosely constructed Diet. In 1852, Liechtenstein concluded a customs union with Austria, but this did not mean loss of independence. Despite repeated declarations of neutrality in World War I, Liechtenstein was subjected to the same Allied blockade as Austria, causing much hardship. In 1919, the principality renounced its economic ties with Austria. After a brief attempt to go it alone, a customs union with Switzerland went into effect in January 1924 and is still in force today.

At present the principality is economically connected with Switzerland. It shares Swiss currency. Swiss diplomats care for the interests of the little country. But there are many indications that Liechtenstein is independent and not part of the *Eidgenossenschaft.* Liechtensteiners working as foreigners in Switzerland during the Great Depression were discriminated against. After the Austrian *Anschluss,* local Nazis attempted a coup that was foiled by a number of factors, including Liechtenstein's internal resistance, but certainly not by Swiss protection. Liechtenstein brought a case against Guatemala before the International Court of Justice, a right conceded only to independent sovereign states. Today, Liechtenstein's membership in such international organizations as UNICEF, EFTA, the International Court of Justice, and the International Atomic Energy Agency evidences its independence. Unlike Switzerland, Liechtenstein has a monarchy and an election system which still excludes women. There is little doubt that the customs union with Switzerland could be renounced at any time by either of the two contracting parties.

Austria today is a small country whose present boundaries date back to the end of World War I. Until then Austria, as part of the Austro-Hungarian monarchy, was one of the major powers in the world. As already indicated, the house of Habsburg had gradually accumulated more and more land in Europe. At one time it ruled over territories as far apart as Spain and the Netherlands. Although many of these areas were connected with the Austrian Habsburgs for only a brief time, Vienna was the center of enormous possessions in central Europe. After the imperial crown of the Holy Roman Empire was bestowed upon the Habsburgs by election in the fifteenth century,[2] it remained with them on a hereditary basis until the empire itself ended in 1806. For the next century, the Habsburgs concentrated on the Austrian empire, which had been put together over many generations through diplomacy and clever marriages, rather than through military exploits.

The glory of Austria did not often stem from the battlefield. It is no coincidence that the man who was perhaps its greatest general was a Frenchman, Prince Eugene of Savoy. But military defeats like those repeatedly inflicted on the Austrians by such adversaries as Frederick the Great of Prussia or Napoleon could not diminish the power and luster of the Habsburgs. When the old order was restored in Europe after the upheaval of the French Revolution and Napoleon's conquests, Austria, together with Britain, France, Russia, and Prussia was one of the Great Powers. Its chancellor, Metternich, dominated the continent.

Hegemony over Germany's loosely organized confederation was jointly exercised by Austria and Prussia. Step by step, however, Prussia seized leadership, particularly through the *Zollverein,* a customs union it first established with a tiny neighbor and gradually extended to all other German states. In the process, Prussia

Map of the Principality of Lichtenstein

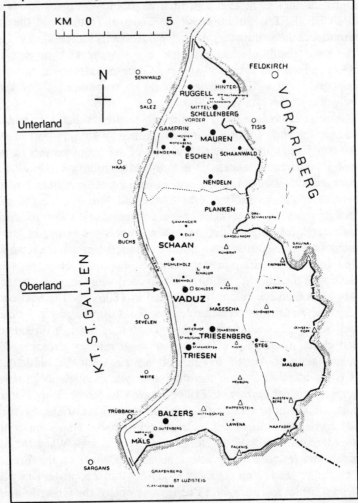

Source: Hubert d'Havrincourt, *Lichtenstein*
Editions Rencontre, (Lausanne: 1964), p. 164

waged three successful wars: the first with Austria against Denmark; the second against Austria and the southern German states; and the third against France. In this war, Austria remained neutral, and southern Germany fought on Prussia's side. The net result of these conflicts was the unification of Germany under Prussian auspices and the exclusion of Austria from German affairs. Bismarck's diplomacy avoided any permanent hard feelings between Vienna and Berlin. Instead, he created a military alliance between the two capitals.

The unification of Germany left Austria neither small nor helpless. The countries that we know today as Czechoslovakia, Hungary, Poland, Rumania, and Yugoslavia were either partially or completely dominated by Vienna. When we remember that modern states like Czechoslovakia and Yugoslavia are composed of a number of different nationality groups, each with a different language and a different culture and often hostile to its ethnic neighbors, we begin to appreciate the multitude of tongues and peoples that a hundred years ago owed allegiance to "His Imperial Majesty, by the Grace of God, Emperor of Austria."

This complexity was a constant source of friction, and it eventually destroyed the entire imperial structure. The French Revolution had kindled two flames across Europe which no efforts could extinguish. One was the desire for some kind of constitutional government. The other was an increasing nationalism, manifested by opposition to being governed by a foreign ruler in a foreign capital. In recognition of such opposition Hungarians were granted equality with the German-speaking Austrians in 1867. Henceforth the empire was known as Austria-Hungary. Although this *Ausgleich* brought satisfaction to the Hungarians, or at least to their ruling circles in Budapest, it did nothing for the Czechs, Slovaks, Croats, Slovenes, and other minorities. However, Emperor Franz Joseph, who, like Queen Victoria of Great Britain, came to be regarded almost as a permanent fixture through the last half of the nineteenth century, provided stability for the uneasy structure of the empire, even though the violent death of several members of his family indicated the precariousness of the situation.

When the emperor died in 1916, an epoch ended. A major war was in progress that was certain to lead to drastic changes, no matter what the outcome might be. The year 1918 brought military defeat, and with it the dissolution of the empire. The various non-German-speaking peoples withdrew. The new Austria was simply a tiny area which nobody claimed. It had an area slightly larger than Maine or South Carolina. "*L'Autriche c'est qui reste*" is the way the French statesman Clemenceau phrased it: "Austria is what is left over."

What was left over was a very small country within a huge and vulnerable border, and with a capital city far too large for such a little state. To call the new Austria Vienna plus a few thousand square miles of scenery was perhaps not too great an exaggeration. Industrialization had not penetrated deeply into the hinterlands, and Vienna was full of the administrators and professionals of a huge empire, whose services were no longer needed. It was doubtful whether Austria was economically able to stand on its own feet. Because the inhabitants almost all regarded German as their mother tongue, and because of the strong historic and cultural ties with whatever might be considered Germany, political union between Austria and post-World War I Germany appeared to be a plausible and logical solution to Austria's problems.

There is little doubt that such an *Anschluss* would have met with the overwhelming approval of the people in both countries at that time. Austria's first official name in 1918/19 was *Deutschösterreich,* or German Austria, spelled as one word. Germany was a struggling democracy that, like Austria, was undergoing severe hardships. Deprived of much territory and suffering under huge reparation payments, its economic and political problems were enormous in a world with little sympathy for the sufferings of the vanquished. We will never know whether Germany and Austria, united in the 1920s under a parliamentary system, would together have been strong enough to overcome the grave difficulties of the postwar era. The eventual triumph of right-wing extremism might have been avoided. Any such thought is, of course, merely idle speculation. The victorious Allies, in their attempt to keep Germany as weak as possible, forbade *Anschluss*. Even economic cooperation—the customs union that was agreed upon between Berlin and Vienna in 1931—met with strong French objections. The proposed union was taken to the League of Nations, referred to the Permanent Court of International Justice, and there rejected by a vote of eight to seven as contrary to the Geneva Protocol of 1922.

It must be emphasized that this association with Germany was at that time desired by most Austrians, of all classes, groups, and parties with few exceptions. But they desired association with a Germany governed by democratic principles and the rule of law. After Hitler's assumption of power in 1933, any such wish ceased to prevail among the Social Democrats, the Jews, and the many adherents of the governing Christian Social party. This reversal was especially evident after the Nazis had assassinated Austrian Chancellor Engelbert Dollfuss. Even before that assassination, however, bitter conflicts had developed between the two major political forces in Austria, the Social Democrats and the Christian Socials, culminating in a brief but bloody civil war. This conflict led to the suspension of parliamentary democracy, the elimination of the Social Democratic party as a legal factor in the decision-making process, and the establishment of a semi-Fascist clerical regime.

With large parts of Austrian society dissatisfied and disenfranchised, it was not difficult for Adolf Hitler to encourage discontent and unrest by increasing his demands for a dominant role for the Nazis in Austrian affairs. In March, 1938, German troops marched into Austria without a shot being fired. They were greeted by genuine enthusiasm on the part of huge crowds, led by the princes of the church. Foreign powers, especially France, now only issued weak, meaningless diplomatic protests.

However, thousands of Austrians were sent to concentration camps, the church itself came under increasing attack by the new rulers, and the country was reduced to being merely Germany's eastern province, the *Ostmark*. As World War II demanded more and more sacrifices from the population, the remark by the Viennese proprietress of a small shop, "this is not at all what I expected,"[3] came to reflect the views of most of the nation. Those bitter enemies in the pre-Hitler era, Social Democrats and Christian Socials, learned to overlook political differences and gained respect for one another as together they suffered the physical and mental torments of Nazi concentration camps.

Thus, before 1933, close cooperation and even political union with Germany was the wish of the majority of Austrians. When annexation did come in 1938, it was welcomed by most. Some years later, any such feeling had evaporated. Seven years of Nazi rule, wartime suffering on the battlefronts and at home, followed by a decade of military occupation by the victorious Allies, cured almost all Austrians of any wish for unification with Germany. National consciousness and the recognition of an Austrian nation independent from Germany, although speaking the German language, may be only a few decades old; nevertheless, it is accepted today by practically everyone throughout Austria. Even the most right-wing party no longer clamors for *Anschluss*. In the final analysis it was Hitler who established Austrian nationalism on a firm foundation.

In another respect Hitler's activities had ironic consequences. Unification had eluded the German people for centuries. Then Hitler united within his domain every area that poet Ernst Moritz Arndt had named, with the exception of Switzerland. But not for long. When in April of 1945 the *Führer* committed suicide amidst the ruins of Berlin, all of Europe was in ruins and Germany was about to be divided into four occupation zones. Eventually the three Western zones became one political entity, the present German Federal Republic. The former Russian zone became the German Democratic Republic. Today there are two Germanys rather than a Germany divided. The two German states are now internationally recognized. Both have become members of the United Nations. However, the border of barbed wire and cement blocks that separates them makes the frontiers of old seem like matchsticks and cardboard.

In 1806, the thousand-year-old Holy Roman Empire was quietly laid to rest. It had long since fully deserved Voltaire's description of being neither holy nor Roman nor an empire. It had not been much more than an empty shell until Napoleon eliminated the majority of the more than three hundred local units that had claimed independence and sovereignty. Despite hostility toward the French emperor after his defeat, no one suggested putting the clock back entirely to prerevolutionary times—except the French Bourbon kings who had "learnt nothing and forgotten nothing." The thirty-odd independent political units which formed the German Confederation after 1815 differed considerably in size and population. To a large extent they were dominated by Austrian Chancellor Metternich, who saw to it that liberal movements throughout Europe were suppressed. At the same time, Prussia quietly and effectively built up its customs union. In 1866 came the Prussian-Austrian showdown that removed Vienna once and for all from German affairs and established Berlin as the center of the new Germany. This was officially recognized on January 18, 1871, in the Hall of Mirrors of the palace of Versailles, when the king of Prussia was proclaimed hereditary German emperor.

German unification was thus finally achieved. A diverse group of principalities of various dimensions was now a cohesive entity.

It still contained non-German-speaking minorities: Poles in the east, Danes in Holstein to the north, and Frenchmen in newly acquired Alsace-Lorraine in the west. Nevertheless, Germany came close to being a modern nation-state for the first time. True, the minorities were to contribute to eventual destruction of what so often is called the Second German Empire. The country sadly lacked practice in the application of some of the basic democratic principles. The people themselves and their elected representatives had little influence on policy-making. Prussian predominance was especially unfortunate in view of the strongly pronounced peculiarities, based on centuries of independence, of the individual member states. However, the downfall of the empire was due not to these constitutional defects or even to dissatisfaction within its borders but rather to ill-fated military and foreign policies. These eventually led to war, four years of slaughter and bloodshed, and to defeat.

The emperor fled to neutral Holland, and a democratic republic was established that tried desperately to pick up the pieces. This was far from easy. At the mercy of its conquerors, the new government had to assume responsibility for the preceding disaster. In addition to being forced to pay huge reparations, Germany lost all its colonies, its foreign minorities, and large areas inhabited by Germans. This was especially true in the east, where a Polish state was recreated. Neighboring countries were forced to make sizable contributions of land, people, and raw materials. Democratic Germany was thus beset by many woes, domestic and foreign, from the outset, and when a major economic crisis developed in the early 1930s, the republic was unable to survive.

Cleverly playing on the discontent created by a harsh peace treaty, crippling inflation, and disastrous unemployment, Adolf Hitler made spectacular gains. Having received only 2.6 percent of the popular vote in the parliamentary elections of 1928, his party obtained 18.3 percent two years later, and 37.4 percent by 1932. As leader of the largest party in the *Reichstag* he was called upon by the aged and probably half-senile president, Paul von Hindenburg, to assume the leadership of the nation on January 30, 1933. Hitler claimed that he would rehabilitate Germany and restore the honor allegedly lost through the actions of domestic traitors while German armies remained unconquered on the battle-field. These claims fell on sympathetic ears. Hitler tore up the peace treaty clause by clause. He reintroduced conscription, re-militarized the Rhineland, and pursued a policy of rearmament more and more openly. The cosigners of the Versailles Treaty confined their protests to ineffective diplomatic notes.

When Hitler annexed Austria in 1938, he used the pretext of uniting German-speaking people. These nationals, he claimed, were being kept apart by force, violence, and shameful suppres-sion. A similar argument was advanced in connection with the so-called Sudeten region of Czechoslovakia, an area inhabited by 3.5 million German-speaking people. This territory had never been part of Germany proper although before the First World War it had belonged to Austria. The native population had had some genuine grievances which the Prague government eventually tried to resolve. Any wish to be reunited with Germany, however, was quite recent, historically incorrect, and originally not widespread. Hitler's henchmen created an atmosphere of terror. The Czech administration resisted Nazi demands in full realization of the strategic and economic importance of their mountain region, which also contained Europe's second-largest armament factory. But with war threatening, Czechoslovakia's pledged allies abandoned her. At Munich British Prime Minister Chamberlain agreed to give Hitler everything he wanted—in return for a piece of paper promising "peace in our time."

The German chancellor showed his true intentions a few months later. Under the threat of military invasion he forced the aging president of the now defenseless Czechoslovakia to surrender the remainder of his country. Czechoslovakia thereby became a Ger-man "protectorate." Once again Berlin controlled large numbers of people whose native tongue was not German.

The next victim was Poland. The Poles fought back when at-tacked in September of 1939, and their struggle signalled the out-break of the Second World War. Hitler was able to conquer the western half of Poland within a few weeks despite fierce resistance, while his former archenemy and apparently newly found friend Stalin marched into the eastern part. The following spring, Hitler attacked and defeated Denmark, Norway, Holland, Belgium,

Luxemburg, and France in quick succession. The next year he conducted a lightning campaign across the Balkans, and then he began his invasion of the Soviet Union. His armies reached the outskirts of Moscow and Leningrad and were almost in possession of Stalingrad on the Volga River by the following summer. But these cities did not fall. As that year and the next progressed the Russians first stopped the Germans and then pushed them back. On the western front, Britain, which had held out alone against Hitler for an entire year, and the United States, which had entered the conflict in 1941 after being attacked by the Japanese at Pearl Harbor, mounted an invasion of the European continent in June of 1944 by landing in Normandy in northern France.

German armies were now confronted by what German generals for generations had regarded as the greatest nightmare of them all: a land war to be fought on two fronts in Europe (not to mention the African-Italian campaign). Despite Hitler's desperate orders to his troops to defend every town, village and hamlet, the Allied forces pressed forward relentlessly. By October 1944, American troops had captured Aachen in west Germany and the Russians were fighting on east Prussian soil. Six months later, American troops joined with the Russian forces at Torgau on the Elbe River. Hitler committed suicide while street fighting went on in Berlin. By May 1945 all German armies had surrendered unconditionally. Unlike World War I, when no German territory was occupied by enemy soldiers until after the Armistice, every square mile of Germany was now controlled by Allied forces. The German government ceased to exist; the conquering forces possessed all of its territory.

At several high-level conferences prior to the end of the war, representatives of the United States, Britain, and the Soviet Union had made plans for the postwar period, dividing Germany into zones of occupation. They had reached an understanding about who was to administer what area. Military campaigns had brought the Americans deep into central Germany; and the Russians had gained full control over what was left of Berlin. Consequently, in order to comply with the earlier agreements, military adjustments had to be made. The former capital, like Germany itself, was divided into American, British, Russian, and French sectors. France, though not a participant at conferences of Yalta and Potsdam, was given a zone of occupation in southwestern Germany made up of territories originally allocated to the United States and Great Britain, respectively.

None of Hitler's conquests were allowed to remain. Austria's independence was restored, although the four powers occupied the country for a decade. The Sudeten area was reunited with the rest of Czechoslovakia; however, the invalidity of the Munich Agreement remained a legal bone of contention between Bonn and Prague until the early 1970s. Since a number of the German-speaking inhabitants of Czechoslovakia had shown themselves disloyal to the Prague government when Hitler threatened, many were expatriated to Germany proper, often at the cost of human suffering not unlike that inflicted on victims of Nazism a few years earlier.

A similar transfer of people occurred in restored Poland, but here the problem was even more complicated. Russia had occupied eastern Poland after the Stalin-Hitler Pact in 1939. That area fell approximately within a line suggested by the British statesman Lord Curzon in 1919 as the boundary between Russia and Poland. This territory was inhabited by a population whose cultures resembled those of the adjoining Soviet provinces. There was, then, some justification in Moscow's claim to those regions. That claim was powerfully reinforced by the presence of Russian armies. The Allies had agreed in principle that the Poles should be compensated for the loss of those lands to the USSR at the expense of Germany. On the basis of military rather than historic arguments, German territory east of a line formed by the rivers Oder and Neisse was put under Polish administration and immediately cleared of Germans. The American Secretary of State James Byrnes later said that the final disposition of these areas and the drawing of permanent boundaries would await the signing of a peace treaty with Germany. To date, no such treaty has been signed, nor is any likely to be signed. A number of agreements between various countries, including the Thirty-Five Nations Declaration at Helsinki in 1975, all seem to underwrite the *status quo* despite occasional denials that this has actually been done.

The Oder-Neisse frontier has been a *fait accompli* for more than a quarter of a century. The West German government under Willy Brandt finally acknowledged this fact in the face of strong and vocal opposition at home.

The Allies had little difficulty in agreeing that Germany should be confined to her borders of 1937, that is, those existing before Hitler began his territorial conquests. Three modifications of this principle were made, however. The first, as indicated above, dealt with Poland. The second concerned the area of East Prussia centered around the city of Königsberg which, under the name of Kaliningrad, became part of the Soviet Union. The third modification affected the small but economically important Saar Valley in the western part of Germany

After World War I, France was interested in separating the coal-rich Saar region of some one thousand five hundred square miles from Germany. For fifteen years the area was independently ruled by the League of Nations and economically exploited by France. In 1935, a plebiscite showed the inhabitants' overwhelming desire to be returned to Germany. Hitler regarded this as one of his first great successes. However, there is no doubt that the population of the Saar Valley would have wanted to be part of Germany under any government and under any conditions. This lesson apparently had not been learned a decade later, when the territory was again separated from Germany proper and given political autonomy within a customs and currency union with France. In 1954, France and West Germany negotiated a European status for the region. In a plebiscite the following year, the inhabitants turned down the proposal by a two-thirds majority. More talks were held, and France and Germany, in a rather startling show of good will, agreed to accept the verdict of the populace. The area was united with Germany, first politically, then economically. As a result, the Saarland no longer poisons Franco-German relations. Instead the area has become a vital link between two countries who are now partners of the European community.

One question that did not cause much dissension among the Allies was the dismemberment of Prussia. That state had been the dominant factor in the life of Germany in the recent past. In 1933,

Prussia's population accounted for forty out of Germany's 65 million, its area, 293,000 out of 469,000 square miles. Although only one of seventeen states, Prussia's influence was obviously great indeed.

The events leading up to World War I were to some extent attributable to what was called Prussian militarism. It was that same Prussian militarism which many people thought had led to Adolf Hitler and all the excesses of World War II. Historically such a picture is not entirely correct; Hitler formed his party and staged his first *putsch* in Bavaria, not in Prussia. In the days of the Weimar Republic, "Prussia was strongest among the German states in her anti-Fascist measures for law enforcement."[4] In March of 1933 the capital city of Berlin gave the newly appointed Chancellor Hitler less than 30 percent of its vote, as compared with a national average of 43.9 percent. Nevertheless, at the end of World War II, Prussia was wiped from the map. This was not too difficult to do because large areas in the east found themselves under Polish jurisdiction, in any case.

A series of states was now established. Bavaria had approximately its historic boundaries, but the previously Bavarian Palatinate, together with parts of Hesse and the Prussian Rhine province, became the new state of Rhineland-Palatinate. The old Hanse cities of Hamburg and Bremen survived as separate political entities. After several years of argument, Baden and Württemberg were united in one state. Others were Hesse, Schleswig-Holstein, and two entirely new creations, Lower Saxony and North Rhine-Westphalia. The Saar also became a separate state upon joining the Republic. In the Russian zone, five states were established in 1945, corresponding to former states or Prussian provinces: Mecklenburg, Brandenburg, Sachsen-Anhalt, Thuringia, and Saxony. These were dissolved a few years later, however, and the entire area was divided into fourteen administrative districts.

A number of the states created at the end of World War II were artificial units without historic precedent. Because of that, and because of considerable inequalities in size and population, suggestions are advanced from time to time to reorganize all of western Germany, perhaps into five states. Undoubtedly this and similar proposals will continue to be heard. As presently constituted the states frequently do not satisfy the citizens. To this day, they often find it difficult to regard the states as anything but administrative units created for the convenience of the occupying powers, although as time passes boundaries seem to become less controversial.

Here, as in so many other respects, the wishes of the Allies prevailed, but they had differing plans and aspirations. An analysis of the victors' attitudes toward Nazism illustrates this. The British saw in National Socialism a disease which would be eliminated with the eradication of the germ carrier, the Nazi party and its leadership. The French saw Hitler as the direct heir of Bismarck and therefore connected German unification with totalitarianism. Any punishment would be useless if not accompanied by the destruction of Prussia and of German unity. The Americans wavered between these two viewpoints. The Russians explained the success of Nazism as inherent in the structure of German society; they therefore emphasized the importance of social revolution rather than punishment of the individual evildoer.[5] Given such basically divergent philosophies, strong disagreements between the four powers in their day-to-day relationships had to be expected. The Potsdam Conference had produced an agreement among Americans, British, and Russians to treat Germany as a single economic unit during the occupation period. This proved impossible from the start. Although all the victors had agreed that Germany should be rebuilt on a democratic basis, there were strong differences of opinion as to what democracy really meant.

Perhaps a four-way split might eventually have developed. But Europe was exhausted, devastated, and in dire need of help that only the United States could provide. Under those circumstances, and with Britain, France, and their respective zones of occupation dependent on American aid, the three Western powers drew closer together. On January 1, 1947, the British and American zones were merged economically into Bizonia which, with the accession of the French zone a little later, became Trizonia. Following the call of United States Secretary of State George Marshall, the European countries met in Paris in the summer of 1947 to launch the Marshall Plan. The USSR and other Communist nations first attended, but then decided to denounce the conference as an imperialistic plot and to walk out. The remaining participants continued their labors. A massive aid program, largely underwritten by the United States, was worked out for Western Europe, including the economically unified Western occupation zones of Germany.

Disagreements between the Western powers and the Soviet Union multiplied. Their unanimity did not extend much beyond the dismemberment of Prussia. Such vital problems as denazification, democratization, and decentralization were discussed for weeks and months without ever reaching consensus. Almost inevitably this led to a situation where Trizonia and the Soviet zone went separate ways.

In 1946 and 1947, elections were held in the states of the western zones, and based on election results democratic governments were established. These governments were carefully controlled by the occupying powers. In 1948 the groundwork was laid for eventual fusion. The authority of the occupying powers was defined more clearly. The prime ministers of the *Länder* in the western zones made plans for a constituent assembly consisting of delegates from each of the elected state parliaments. This assembly convened in September of 1948. By May of the following year it had written what came to be known as the *Grundgesetz,* the Basic Law. This is still the valid constitution of the Federal Republic. The document was to be rewritten when Germany was reunited; in the meantime its authors claimed "to have acted also for those Germans to whom participation was denied,"[6] an obvious reference to those living in the Eastern zone.

In 1949, the Occupation Statute became effective and officially ended military occupation by the United States, Britain, and France, but it reserved to those countries many rights of intervention into the internal affairs of the newly created government of the German Federal Republic. Despite such obstacles, the Basic Law began to work. Theodor Heuss, an old-fashioned liberal of pre-Hitler days, became president, and Konrad Adenauer, who as mayor of Cologne had defied the Nazis to the last possible moment in 1933, was chosen as chancellor. Adenauer left no doubt from the beginning that he regarded the Occupation Statute as temporary. He immediately began working toward its modification and eventual elimination. This was accomplished by May 5,

1955, when all remaining restrictions were abolished, and the three Western powers solemnly acknowledged that the Occupation Statute was no longer in effect. The Federal Republic was now in full possession of its sovereignty, and with its admission to NATO, it became an integrated part of the Western defense system.

While these developments were going on, the Russians had not been idle. With the failure of numerous Four Power conferences to come to any agreement, and with Molotov's boycott of the Marshall Plan sessions in Paris, the barrier between East and West justified Churchill's naming it the "Iron Curtain." In June 1948 the Western powers and the Soviet Union announced separate currency reforms for their respective zones. When these measures were extended to West Berlin, the Russians decided to cut off road and rail travel into that part of the city from the west. The Western powers then supplied the West Berliners by air. The blockade continued until May 1949, when a Four Power agreement guaranteed land access to West Berlin, which has remained a Western outpost more than a hundred miles inside Soviet territory.

Just as the West German government gained more autonomy, so did its counterpart in the east. When the Bonn administration was first established, it was greeted with loud protests from the communist world. The communists accused the West of splitting Germany into two parts and warned of the danger of resurrecting a fascist and military regime in Germany. Allegedly, only the eastern sector was truly democratic and anti-Fascist, but something had to be done to offset Western efforts to restore at least partial German sovereignty. In October 1949 the German Democratic Republic was called into existence by the Soviets. Party struggle was conveniently avoided because under pressure from the communists and their allies a "United Front" was formed from all the previously existing parties. Wilhelm Pieck, a Communist of pre-Hitler days, became president. Otto Grotewohl, supposedly representing the Social Democrats, assumed the office of minister-president in the one-party regime. This regime was in time integrated into the Warsaw Pact, the Communist military alliance. Thus, the Iron Curtain not only separates one part of the world from the other but also divides Germany itself. Barely a decade after Hitler had begun adding new territories to his realm in the attempt to build a mighty empire, the "Third Reich," based on German supremacy, which was to last a thousand years, the country he had taken over had shrunk considerably. What was left was split in two by barriers far stronger than any that had separated Germans from Germans in the past.

3

Democratization— Constitutional Developments in Switzerland and Liechtenstein

Chapter 2 dealt with the question of how the five countries arrived at their present geographic boundaries. The next few chapters will deal with their political backgrounds and how they came to acquire their modern institutions. What has occurred could be called a *process of democratization,* for it may be argued that in at least four of these countries a high degree of political democracy has developed and has reached a remarkable degree of sophistication and stability. The only possible exception is Communist East Germany, the German Democratic Republic, where the term *democracy* is interpreted differently than in the West. There it has anti-Fascist and profound socialist connotations. Proclaiming the German Democratic Republic a "socialist state of workers and farmers," Article 1 of the 1974 version of the Constitution emphasizes that "the political organization of the working people in town and countryside [is] led by the working class and its Marxist-Leninist party."[1]

It can, therefore, be said that as the twentieth century draws to a close, every government asserts that it is acting in accordance with the best interests of the people, whom the rulers in every case claim to represent. This is important, for it means there is almost universal acceptance of the principle that governments have a re-

sponsibility to the people, an assumption which has only compara-
tively recently been recognized by governing circles themselves.

As for the term *democracy*, many different definitions have been
given. Translated literally from the Greek, it means rule by the
people. The United States Declaration of Independence lists certain inalienable rights with which man was endowed by his creator,
and then defines the purpose of government as securing these
rights for the governed. Abraham Lincoln, in his *Gettysburg
Address*, mentions "government of the people, by the people, for
the people." An American political scientist in our own era sums
up these various interpretations by stating that "Democracy is a
form of government in which the rulers are fully responsible to the
ruled in order to realize self-respect for everybody."[2] Whatever
the philosophic connotations of the term, there are certain practical implications. Emphasis is on the individual. He is no longer
regarded as an unimportant cog in a big machine, a minute part
of a whole, whose existence really does not matter and whose time,
energy, well-being, and, if necessary, his life may at any time be
sacrificed for ruler and country. The translation of the principle of
the value of the individual into practice may leave much to be desired under various governments, but the fact remains that whenever violations are alleged, vehement denials are usually forthcoming from the government involved. For instance, a Soviet
source has emphasized that the transition to communism means
the fullest development of personal freedom and the rights of
Soviet citizens. Socialism has granted and guaranteed the working
people the broadest rights and freedoms. Communism will bring
the working people further great rights and opportunities.[3]

Of course, some very serious questions can be raised regarding
the truth of this statement. Although the masses in the Soviet
Union probably enjoy more rights and opportunities than their
parents and grandparents did at the turn of the century, their
liberties and freedoms in such areas as speech and press, worship
and choice of occupation (taken for granted in Western democracies), are sadly lacking in Communist regimes. It is important to
note that Communist authorities would strongly object to these
reservations, and would go to any length to show them untrue and
invalid. In other words, even where individual freedoms do not

exist in practice, lip service is paid to them in principle. This is far removed from the days when governments saw the governed as subjects in the truest sense of the term.

The attitude of the Western democracies is perhaps best summarized by a statement made in 1928 by Oliver Wendell Holmes, associate justice of the United States Supreme Court: "I think it a less evil that some criminals escape than that the government should play an ignoble part." Involved here is the Anglo-American concept of being innocent until proven guilty. Although continental law shares neither this tradition nor the exact practice of such an assumption, the Germans in particular have for quite a while prided themselves with possessing a *Rechtsstaat* where everything was done strictly in accordance with the law, where legality and order prevailed, and where rules and regulations were clearly observed. The populace by and large recognized, accepted, and took pleasure in this situation, long before the people were able to play a significant part in the law-making process.

As we have seen, the Swiss were the first of the modern Germanic states to achieve independence. Self-government was known to a certain degree initially, and it was further developed by them in the centuries to come. Local democratic practices were extended when the federal system was established. Devices such as popular consultation through referendum at federal, cantonal, and local levels were adopted. The entire process took a long time to mature, as witness the fact that women were not allowed to vote in federal elections until 1971, although some cantons had enfranchised them a few years earlier. In itself this is indicative of the kind of unsystematic, spontaneous, and quite individual growth that characterizes Swiss history.

When Uri, Schwyz, and Unterwalden began their struggle against the Habsburgs, what was at stake was vastly different from what we would designate as freedom today. The principle of equality in participation in government, now extended to every adult man and woman regardless of wealth, class, or creed had not as yet achieved its modern recognition. What was of utmost significance to all *Eidgenossen* was the right to run their own affairs in their own way. This meant a variety of different systems, a characteristic still much apparent in our own day. Thus, in 1513 when the member communities, which by that time had reached thirteen, jointly issued a document, they emphasized their varying systems by referring to their authorities as

we, the Burgomaster, the Mayors, Bailiff, Councils, Burgesses, Peasants, and the entire Communities of Zürich, Bern. . . .[4]

Three major motifs stand out in this design. There were first the original three forest communities and some others which came close to being pure democracies. In late April or early May of each year, open-air meetings were held at which every citizen attended bearing arms. Those assembled voted, usually by a show of hands, for their highest official and judge, the *Landammann,* and for the military and finance chiefs, clerks, and other local officials. Important decisions were made in the same way. The cantons were frequently subdivided, and local communities had their own systems of self-government. Strangely enough, however, these democracies also contained villages, ruled by the democratic entities, whose inhabitants were subjects, although they often had the right to name their own officials and determine their own internal affairs.

The other two broad types of government concerned more urban communities. In Basel, Zürich, and Schaffhausen the guilds furnished the members of the representative bodies. Old established families possessed certain privileges. Whether these governments should be regarded as "democratic guild" systems, as one source calls them, or "commercial oligarchies," as they are called by another,[5] is probably a matter of preference and emphasis. In any event, the towns owned the surrounding countryside, but their rights of ownership were frequently based on tradition and in practice were severely restricted. This was so much the case that at one time at least, important decisions, including alliances and war, could be taken only with the consent of the countryside.

Finally, there were municipalities, such as Bern, Luzern, Freiburg, and Genf, governed by members of local aristocracies to the exclusion of the lower classes. Here too we find subject territories in the surrounding areas. Although the governments of these towns were much more restricted than elsewhere and confined only to members of certain families, the rulers were often better prepared for their tasks and therefore did a better job than was done in the more democratic urban communities.

This brief summary illustrates one of the two peculiarities of Switzerland's federal system: its vast and frequently radically different variety of cantonal governments. The second peculiarity is that whenever the Swiss were not busy fighting outsiders, they fought one another.

It is remarkable under those conditions that the federation survived, especially after the Reformation. Like so much of Europe, the Swiss cantons were torn asunder by religious conflicts. We are accustomed to think of Switzerland as one of the breeding grounds of the Reformation; after all, both Zwingli and Calvin are intimately connected with Switzerland. The uninitiated might even suspect a common religion to be a common tie uniting the otherwise quite different parts of the population of Switzerland. Nothing could be further from the truth. Of the five countries studied here, only Austria and Liechtenstein are overwhelmingly of the same, Roman Catholic faith. In Germany the division into Catholic and Protestant states proved yet another barrier to unity, but Switzerland was able to survive despite its deep-seated religious differences. There was initial division and bloody fighting, nor did the Thirty Years War pass it by. Even the last civil war in the middle of the nineteenth century was motivated largely, though not exclusively, by religious conflicts. Eventually coexistence and mutual tolerance were accepted among Swiss Catholics and Protestants.

Whereas the three original cantons, and others like Wallis and Italian-speaking Tessin, are largely Catholic; Bern, Waadt, and Neuenburg have predominantly Protestant populations. The little canton of Appenzell is divided into two half-cantons along religious lines. The Swiss population is about evenly divided between the two major religions, with Protestants in a slight majority but Catholics steadily gaining. Since Switzerland demonstrates a high degree of diversity, the religious factor seems merely to be an additional ingredient which, like all the others, can well be accommodated within the federation.

The attempt to unify the country systematically originated from foreign sources, from the forces unleashed by the French Revolution at the end of the eighteenth century. These new ideas spilled over into neighboring Switzerland where there were underprivileged inhabitants receptive to them. In the beginning these philosophies were spread by returning Swiss soldiers who had served in the French armies. However, such new ideas became dominant only when French armies actually appeared on Swiss soil. Then all vestiges of feudalism were abolished, and Napoleon set up the Helvetic Republic. It was based on a strong central government in which the cantons were reduced to departments or administrative units. The establishment of a "one and indivisible" republic appealed to some of the Swiss but was rejected by most. Although some of these innovations were important milestones on the road toward democracy and unity, the virtual abolition of the age-old authority of individual cantons was hardly palatable to the majority of the Swiss people. After struggling along for a few years, the Constitution of 1798 was in 1803 replaced by the Act of Mediation, a far more acceptable compromise which demonstrated some of Napoleon's more statesmanlike qualities. Federalism was again allowed, and a small Diet, the *Tagsatzung,* with unequal representation was put in charge of a common currency, war and peace, foreign relations, and intercantonal relationships. This representative body had no fixed meeting place: it assembled alternatively in the six major cantons. Internally the cantons regained much of their previous autonomy, and all powers not exercised by the federal government stayed with the cantons. Some redrawing of cantonal boundaries took place; six new member cantons were mapped out from territories within the *Eidgenossenschaft.* Although the Swiss were unhappy with the provision that allowed the French emperor to use Swiss military forces, the new arrangements were basically to the liking of the people, so much so that the Swiss did not actively join in the anti-Napoleonic campaign after his defeat at Leipzig. Allied troops were, however, permitted to pass through Switzerland on their way toward administering Napoleon's final defeat.

After that defeat, the numerous measures instituted by Napoleon came under close scrutiny. Those in Switzerland were no exception. Some of the French-speaking areas annexed by France were now restored to Switzerland, but the six recently created cantons were allowed to remain separate entities within the Federation, bringing the number of cantons to twenty-two, a figure that has remained unchanged.

No longer dependent on France, Switzerland once more became an independent sovereign nation, but it was different from the rest of Europe in two respects. First, Switzerland was a republic. While France had also toyed briefly with the idea of not having a monarch, its attempts in the 1790s were short-lived, falling victim to Napoleon's ambitions. After the emperor's downfall, the old royal house of Bourbon was returned to the throne. The same thing happened in many other countries where dynastic changes had been made during Napoleon's rule. But the Swiss people had been without a monarch for many centuries and had no intention of installing one now. No other European country was in the same position, and outside of Europe, only the recently independent United States of America preferred an elected president.

Even though Switzerland was unique in this respect on the continent, the situation was by no means clear-cut. For instance, one canton, Neuenburg, was actually governed by the king of Prussia. This points to another major peculiarity of Switzerland: its overall structure was loose indeed, allowing all component parts to handle their affairs individually and very much in their own way. All twenty-two cantons were absolutely equal without respect to size or other important factors. Inequality among towns or people was no longer legal, but no other freedoms, such as of movement or religion, were safeguarded on a national basis. There was not much of a national government to speak of in any case. In the individual cantons, conservative and antiliberal forces were usually in firm control.

However, the desires aroused by the French Revolution could be denied only temporarily. The two major popular aspirations of the nineteenth century, demands for a more democratic system of government and calls for national unity, inspired a two-pronged attack against the reactionary character of cantonal administrations and against the loosely constructed confederation. As usual, the immediate impetus came from France. "When France catches a cold, Europe sneezes," Metternich had said, and while the sneezing was not as loud in 1830 as it was in 1848, it affected Switzerland.

As a result of increasing popular pressure in the 1830s, more democratic provisions were incorporated into the governmental structures of about half the cantons, a process known as "regeneration." In 1832, seven cantons concluded the *Siebener Concordat* in an attempt to safeguard their liberal Constitutions. This provoked the remaining conservative cantons into forming the *Sarnerbund.* Discussions aimed at reforming the federal constitution met with little success. The rift that developed between the conservative and liberal cantons assumed religious characteristics as the more conservative Catholic cantons eventually concluded the *Sonderbund,* a separate league, which preferred detachment from the main body of Switzerland in order to resist anti-Catholic measures and reforms that they regarded as infringements on their cantonal rights. When a call to dissolve the *Sonderbund* was ignored, the majority reaction was the same as in another republic more than a dozen years later: the union must be preserved by force of arms. Unlike that of the United States, the Swiss civil war did not last long, though it too ended with the defeat of the rebels.

The upshot of all this was a Constitution in 1848 which once again invited comparison with that of the United States. While it recognized the local powers of the individual cantons, it also set up a strong national government with a bicameral legislature. One house was to be elected according to population, while the other contained representatives from each canton on an equal basis. Unlike the American example, however, the executive was to be chosen by the two chambers. It consisted of seven members, one of whom routinely became president for a year without any appreciable increase in powers. The Constitution confirmed the sovereignty of the cantons "as long as this sovereignty is not limited by the federal constitution," and guaranteed the cantonal exercise of those rights that had not been delegated to the federal authorities. Moreover, each canton was now committed to a democratic form of government.

In effect, this latter provision severely restricted the previous far-reaching powers of the various cantons. In this sense it represented a new departure for the localist-minded Swiss. It was, however, the beginning of a workable, viable federal state. Immediately prior to the writing of the new Constitution, the anomaly of a monarch among republics was eliminated when Neuenburg declared its separation from the Prussian crown, although it took a number of years before this decision was accepted by all concerned both inside and outside the canton.

At this point it should be emphasized that the Constitution of 1848 established the basis for the way Switzerland is governed to this day. One major revision in 1874 further increased the authority of the federal institutions while establishing the principle of the federal legislative referendum. The changes in 1874 were basically a reinforcement of the steps taken in 1848. During the century that has followed, the Swiss have amended their Constitution frequently, adding, for example, such items as the constitutional initiative in 1891 and the optional referendum on treaties in 1921, under which Switzerland became the only country to join the League of Nations on the basis of a popular referendum. In June of 1974, they even took the first steps toward establishing what may one day become a twenty-third canton, when seven Jura districts in Bern voted for separation from the mother canton. The amending process, as the writers of the United States Constitution so clearly realized, is an important safeguard for every constitution: no one can foresee the future, and provisions must be made for bringing about changes to fit new circumstances. However, the Swiss have seen to it that the basic principles established in the middle of the nineteenth century have survived for more than a hundred years.

The story of neighboring Liechtenstein is told more quickly, but in its microscopic form, some of the tendencies generally observable throughout Europe can be seen there, too. In the eighteenth century, the principle of absolute monarchy prevailed. When the princes of Liechtenstein purchased two tiny alpine territories to satisfy their own ambitions, what happened to the inhabitants was of little interest or consequence to their new rulers. Before the territorial acquisition by the house of Liechtenstein, the people in those territories had traditionally elected certain local officials. Such customs were now discontinued, partly because they did not fit into the prevailing concept that sovereignty belonged to the monarch, but also because some of these traditions were often outdated, obscure, and subject to abuse.

However, the repercussions of the French Revolution were felt in Liechtenstein too. When the tiny country became an equal, sovereign member of the German league in 1815, it was incumbent on the prince to issue a Constitution. This he did in 1818 by calling a *Landtag*, or Parliament. Since neither nobility nor towns existed, only the clergy and the well-to-do from the countryside were represented. The *Landtag* usually met once a year, attended divine service, and listened as the prince's deputy read the Constitution and announced the tax ratings necessary for the current year. There was a vote on this issue and then some other, though very limited, topics could be raised. A resolution had to have an absolute majority and needed the consent of the prince to become effective.

The impact of Liechtenstein's first Constitution was negligible, to put it mildly. In fact, after 1848, and in reaction to the demands made in that revolutionary year, the assembly was not called for over a decade, thus proving clearly that it was not indispensable. The principality was represented at Frankfurt when the future of Germany was being debated. Its own future seemed quite uncertain in the event that the German empire should become a reality. When the dream failed, repressions set in everywhere, and Liechtenstein troops even helped to defeat revolutionary forces in Basel.

A new monarch and his new philosophy brought about new developments. A constitutional monarchy was established in 1862. The *Landtag*, now given considerable power to participate in the affairs of the country, consisted of fifteen members, twelve of whom were elected by the male population in free, equal, and secret elections. The other three were appointed by the monarch. This system was a considerable improvement over the previous one and a further step towards democracy because it created a partnership in governance between prince and parliament. Of course, popular influence was still limited; in a number of instances the will of the prince prevailed over that of the representatives of the people. For example, when Liechtenstein put an armed contingent of eighty men at Austria's disposal for use on the Italian front in the war of 1866, protests occurred in the *Landtag*. The action was unanimously condemned and the prince received what amounted to a clear warning that his conduct of foreign policy would come under increasing scrutiny by Parliament.

By and large, however, there was little popular resentment of the existing situation. Few seemed to object that the prince still resided in Austria and that even his personal representative governed the principality from nearby Feldkirch, also in Austria. Early in the twentieth century, however, Liechtenstein nationalism began to develop. It became visible for the first time in 1911 when, in a treaty with Austria, Liechtenstein acquired the right to issue its own postage stamps, a step which led to one of its main sources of fame abroad.

Despite its declared neutrality in World War I, Liechtenstein's relationship with Austria was close enough for the Allies to include it in their blockade. The resulting discontent and hardships led to the formation of political parties for the first time. The collapse of Austria-Hungary brought disenchantment with the prevailing circumstances to a head. On November 7, 1918, the *Landtag* expressed its lack of confidence in the prince-appointed governor by a vote of twelve to three, with all the elected representatives supporting the resolution. As a consequence of these actions, the governor resigned. Legal experts have since expressed doubts about the legality and constitutionality of the *Landtag* vote and of the governor's resignation. The three appointed members of Parliament resigned in protest over these legal questions. A political crisis, possibly one that would have affected the monarchy, was averted when the prince recognized the dismissal of the governor by telegram, and soon afterwards appointed his nephew to that position. This move was supported by the *Landtag*, which expressed its confidence in the new governor. Throughout all this, calm prevailed in the country. Some of the events came to the attention of the public only when they read about the developments in their newspapers the following day.

Two major steps followed. One, already noted, was renunciation of ties with Austria and eventually a treaty with Switzerland. The second was domestic. On October 5, 1921, a new Constitution came into force which, with certain alterations, is still the governing document today. Liechtenstein was proclaimed a "constitutional hereditary monarchy on a democratic and parliamentary basis." The electorate (all adult male citizens) now chooses all fifteen members of the *Landtag*. For all practical purposes, the parliamentary majority names the chief of government, the prime minister, by suggesting his name to the prince, who makes the official appointment. The same procedure is followed with the rest of the ministers. Some slight changes in detail occurred in 1965 but in ways to make the process more democratic.

Laws must be passed by the *Landtag*, whose jurisdiction is very broad, but the monarch is by no means a figurehead. He takes a stand on matters and speaks out on issues, and there is no doubt that he plays a significant part in the governing process. A veto on parliamentary resolutions or bills and disagreement with the administration or Parliament cannot be ruled out. The current monarch, Franz Josef II, having lived in the country ever since coming to the throne in 1938, is popular and understands his people well. Consequently, serious differences of opinion are most likely to be settled in private conversation, long before they reach major proportions or have hardened to such an extent that loss of prestige is involved in retreat by either side. In this way, it is possible for Liechtenstein to continue as the last monarchy of the former Holy Roman Empire, and as a monarchy where the reigning prince has more power than his British, Scandinavian, or Benelux counterparts, without at the same time diminishing the democratic character of the country.

4

Constitutional Developments in Germany Before World War II

In the beginning of our discussion, we raised the question, Germany: What? and we have concluded that it is difficult to determine precisely what should or should not have been included within the borders of Germany at any given time in history. A similar problem presents itself when we attempt to trace the contours of German constitutional development. We are immediately confronted by the question, Germany: When?

Switzerland's early history is important because it was then that its present political institutions began. Germany, however, has changed, often and drastically in both physical and institutional aspects over the centuries. Much that has happened since medieval days is of interest only to the historian, and has little immediate bearing on an understanding of constitutional practices today. Seven hundred years after its establishment in the tenth century, the mighty Holy Roman Empire of the German nation had become, in the words of the great lawyer Pufendorf, "neither monarchy nor aristocracy" but instead "some irregular body comparable to a monster." The religious wars that ended in 1648 with the Peace of Westphalia left Europe utterly exhausted. Catholics and Protestants had been unable to defeat one another and had to learn to live side by side. Since the German emperor was the center of the Catholic forces, his inability to win a war after three decades of savage fighting showed that the mighty empire was actually not much more than an empty shell. Its various members had in practice achieved freedom of action. No effective political structure influenced, let alone determined, conduct among the individual states. The aforementioned aspirations of the Liechtenstein family to a seat on the Imperial Council of Princes were aspirations to honor and prestige, not to power. They got no additional power or influence in decision-making, because in reality the council was not an effective body.

When Napoleon finally ended the German Empire in the early nineteenth century, he was not so much delivering a death blow as burying a corpse. Large parts of the old empire were now placed into the Confederation of the Rhine. The structure of the confederation is of little more than historic interest, because it lasted less than a decade, partly because its constitutional provisions never really went into effect. Napoleon used it largely to assure himself of mastery over the continent. But Bonaparte's activities included two important and far-reaching achievements. The number of German principalities was greatly reduced, an action that was to aid the future unification of Germany. Also, the states of the *Rheinbund* adopted certain concepts of the French Revolution, such as equality before the law and the abolition of serfdom. Some of these ideas lingered even after the French emperor's defeat and banishment.

The spirit of the French Revolution in the German-speaking lands was not confined to the members of the *Rheinbund*. Prussia had suffered a number of humiliating military defeats because it had "fallen asleep on the laurels of Frederick the Great." Its leaders introduced several significant social and military reforms while Napoleon was still in command of French affairs. Some of Austria's modernizations, like the abolition of serfdom, the elimination of torture as a part of the judicial process and the emancipation of the Jews, date back to the reign of Joseph II just prior to the outbreak of the French Revolution.[1]

Since not all these reforms were caused by conquering revolutionary armies, it is understandable that a number of them were permanent. This is not to say that they were gladly embraced by the men who shaped the destiny of Europe after 1815. Indeed, the next few decades were characterized by antiliberal and antidemocratic repressions. These were insisted upon by Austrian Chancellor Metternich, who felt that the conception and fulfillment of dangerous ideas had brought about the bloodbath of the French Revolution and that a repetition of these events must be prevented at all costs. Maintenance of the map of Europe drawn up by the Congress of Vienna seemed an important means toward that end.

Metternich's influence was largely exercised through the newly created German confederation, the *Deutsche Bund,* again a loose organization of sovereign princes who ruled the various German states. Its purpose was to protect the territories mapped out by the Treaty of Vienna and to safeguard domestic peace within their borders. A *Bundestag,* or Federal Diet, was to sit in Frankfurt-on-Main on a permanent basis, and the individual states sent ambassadors who acted as their spokesmen. In the *Plenum,* or general assembly, each of the thirty-odd members had at least one vote, although the largest six states, including Prussia, Austria, and Bavaria, had four votes each, five others had three, and three others had two.[2] Decisions were made by two-thirds majorities. Since it was anticipated that this rather large body might become a little unwieldy for the handling of day-to-day problems, a smaller council with a total of seventeen members was created; the eleven larger states were given one vote apiece, whereas the smaller ones were grouped into six *Kurien,* in which several states together cast one vote.[3] The chairmanship of this assembly of states was held by Austria. Under Metternich's leadership, Austria used its influence to make all of Germany a hotbed of reaction. It opposed liberal, democratic, and nationalist movements as subversive ideologies that endangered the peace of the land. Students, youth groups, poets, journalists, or other intellectuals who were not willing to abide by the restrictive rules and regulations were dismissed from their jobs, imprisoned, or exiled.

An idea whose time has come cannot be stopped that easily. The idea that swept the Germanic world was the two-fold demand for constitutions and for union with other German states. Despite earlier promises, only a few constitutions had survived in German lands. Prussia, under Metternich's pressure, had rescinded its constitution, thus removing constitutional restrictions on the king's power. The French uprising of 1830 had relatively few repercussions in Germany, and government opposition to all revolutionary ideas and movements, notably those centered in the universities, remained in vogue. Not until 1848 was the full force of long suppressed popular sentiment finally felt.

The storm of revolution that started in France in February of that year and drove the citizen king, Louis Philippe, from power, spread across the Rhine. Thrones tottered. In many instances they survived as institutions only through abdication of the incumbent in favor of another member of his family when revolts and military action had made it impossible for the older ruler to continue. Demands for freedom of the press, liberal constitutions in those states that so far had rejected them, and an all-German Parliament were voiced with increasing vigor.

Under the impact of these events, the latter became a reality. Parliament's eventual failure to unify Germany on a democratic basis while containing both Prussia and Austria as components is perhaps less surprising than the fact that it was able to come into existence in the first place. Nevertheless, free elections on the basis of universal manhood suffrage were indeed held. Every fifty thousand voters were represented by one deputy. On May 18, 1848, the first German National Assembly, consisting of 585 members, met in the Paul's Church in Frankfurt.

This gathering has often been criticized for not consisting of a true cross-section of the population and for including far too many dreamers, out of contact with reality. While these charges have limited validity, it was not necessarily bad that the assembly's membership was made up of some of the most prominent people of its time or that it contained learned professors, philosophers, historians, poets, lawyers, and jurists, even if this meant that not too many merchants and industrialists were present. The U.S. Constitution makers meeting in Philadelphia some six decades earlier may have been less educated than their German counterparts; however, they were much more in touch with reality. What the men of Frankfurt needed to do was to draw on the spontaneous support they were receiving from royalty and commoners alike, and to act decisively. Instead they wasted time making magnificent speeches on principles and fundamental rights. It was not until late March of 1849 that a German Constitution was finally adopted, and the imperial crown was offered to the king of Prussia. By that time the revolution had spent itself. Reaction was again in control, at least in most states. The king of Prussia, who earlier had flirted with reform, had a change of heart. He refused to become the crowned head of a new German empire because the offer originated with butchers and bakers, with parliamentary and revolutionary forces, and not with the crowned heads of the confederation. With this rejection, the efforts of the Frankfurt Parliament, indeed the Parliament itself, came to an end without having established any of its principles.

The cause of democracy had suffered another setback. Had it been otherwise, the course of European history might well have been quite different. Hope for German unification could no longer rest on a democratic foundation, no matter how spontaneous the feeling in this direction might be. When unification did come in 1871, it was based on the consent of the ruling princes, and it was cemented by what Bismarck so appropriately called "blood and iron."

One lesson taken from the Frankfurt Parliament was particularly important, however: its call for a head for the empire had gone not to Vienna, but to Berlin. Even after that dismal failure, the king of Prussia had attempted to form a union with some other German states and to call a German Parliament at Erfurt. This plan also ended in disaster, this time because of strong negative reaction by Austria, which was backed by Russian arms. It seemed clear, nonetheless, that if German unification ever was to be achieved, it would be under the leadership of Prussia, not of Austria.

Indeed, the next few decades brought a showdown between those two great powers. Austria became increasingly concerned with the various nationality groups under its control, such as Poles, Italians, and Hungarians, who resented being governed from Vienna, while Prussia continued to work toward German unification. One major tool was the extension of the *Zollverein.* This customs union was first concluded in 1819 between Prussia and a small principality surrounded by Prussian territory. Gradually the treaty was extended to include all other Prussian enclaves and then to neighboring states. Eventually it was extended to almost all German states—excluding Austria. Free passage of goods and the elimination of economic barriers within the area was an important step toward eventual political unification (a fact well remembered by advocates of the European common market a century later).

In addition, the Prussian government was now headed by Bismarck, a cunning and determined diplomat, who had been called to the position of minister-president during a constitutional crisis. Prussia possessed a legislative bicameral body consisting of a House of Lords and one chamber chosen indirectly, which strongly favored the high taxpayers as opposed to workers, peasants, and small shopkeepers. But even this undemocratic assembly could not be controlled by the king when he tried to increase the armed forces. His budget was rejected by the lower house, and in despair he asked Otto von Bismarck to take charge. Bismarck decided to go ahead with the new army proposals despite lack of parliamentary approval. This was another milestone for the future development of German constitutional history. If the policy of defying parliament had ended in defeat for the king and his minister, as had happened in England in the seventeenth century, similar results might have been forthcoming; in England at the end of the episode parliament was definitely in the driver's seat, and its supremacy has remained virtually unchallenged ever since. This was not to happen in Prussia. Despite lack of public support, in the face of dislike and even hatred, Bismarck steadfastly pursued his policy. Under his guidance, three wars were eventually fought within six years, each of them with great success. Before the third conflict had ended, German unification had become a reality. Under these circumstances, few people remembered past constitutional questions. The new German empire was established through arms, not through the will of its inhabitants. The quality of this event left important traces in its Constitution.

The first of the three wars developed from a campaign authorized by the German confederation against Denmark over the disputed duchies of Schleswig and Holstein. The area was eventually incorporated into Germany, with Prussia occupying Schleswig in the north and Austria the southern province of Holstein. This arrangement could not possibly last. Whereas Berlin and Vienna had cooperated in 1864, they fought one another two years later. This conflict was precipitated by Bismarck in his desire to eliminate Austria as a factor in German politics. Within a few weeks, Austria was decisively defeated, and the German confederation was dissolved. In its place arose a north German confederation dominated by Prussia, whose territory was further enlarged by annexation of some smaller lands. The southern German states that had sided with Austria remained independent political units but were militarily allied to the north German confederation. Austria, however, was specifically excluded. Prussia's hegemony over the German states was clearly established, and Austria's long association with Germany as an integral part of it was ended. Henceforth Austria was able, though not always willing, to act independently and, except for the seven years of Hitler's regime, its domestic policy was no longer intertwined with that of Germany. In other words, Austria, which for so long had dominated German affairs, ceased that relationship in 1866.

In 1870, Bismarck turned against France, Germany's traditional enemy. In the resulting war not only the North German League but also the southern German states lined up on the side of Prussia. Because of nearly perfect planning, the campaign was an unending Prussian triumph. In early September, French Emperor Napoleon III was captured when the fortress of Sedan fell to German troops. Soon afterward, Paris came under siege and bombardment. The city eventually succumbed and surrendered when its inhabitants were driven to the verge of starvation. Ten days earlier, on January 18, 1871, the king of Prussia had been proclaimed hereditary German emperor at Versailles.

The setting for this event was the Hall of Mirrors, built by King Louis XIV to commemorate his triumphs, frequently obtained at German expense. Here, in the heart of France, the German empire was resurrected from the ashes to which it had been reduced by the first Napoleon. Unlike 1849, the imperial crown was not offered to the Prussian king by butchers or bakers.

This time it was offered by the German princes, who were present at the coronation and cheered it on. The resulting monarchy was therefore not oriented toward the people.

The new national entity was headed by the herditary emperor, who was also the king of Prussia. It is somewhat of a misnomer to speak of it as an empire in the first place, because it consisted of twenty-five states, all of which retained not only their individual princely rulers, but also full freedom of action in a number of local matters. The princes were represented in the upper house or *Bundesrat* on an unequal basis. Prussia held seventeen out of a total fifty-eight seats, and Bavaria had six. Six states had from two to four votes each; the rest had one seat apiece. The larger states cast their multiple votes as a block and on behalf of their respective governments. This assured the Prussian predominance. The president of this assembly was the imperial chancellor, equivalent to a prime minister, who was the handpicked choice of the emperor. Until 1890 Bismarck held this post.

Indeed, the entire Constitution was written by and tailormade to fit Bismarck, whose only requisite for holding office was staying in the good graces of the emperor. This factor was to take on increasing significance, for there existed also a parliamentary body, the *Reichstag*. Its membership was elected directly by universal manhood suffrage, and it thus provided the basis of what might have been a democratic governmental system on the English model. That it did not was due in part to the fact that the *Reichstag* was never able to control the administration and, if necessary, dismiss the chancellor should he lose the confidence of Parliament. It was only in October of 1918 that the government became responsible to the people's representatives. By then, it was too late; the war was lost and the empire could not be saved. Before that time, the chancellor governed as long as the emperor wanted him to do so.

In addition to being chancellor, Bismarck also held the Prussian posts of prime minister and foreign minister, and this made him very powerful indeed. He used his position to pursue a policy of peace and consolidation of what had been acquired in three wars. After he was dismissed by the grandson of the old emperor, his successors found it increasingly difficult, if not impossible, to go against the wishes of the *Kaiser,* whose powers and ambitions were consequently held less and less in check.

One cannot quarrel with the composition of the *Reichstag,* only with its lack of authority. The country was divided into 382 election districts (397 after Alsace-Lorraine was officially incorporated). Each of these districts elected one representative by an absolute majority. If this majority was not forthcoming, a runoff between the two top votegetters took place. All men above the age of twenty-five, with certain exceptions, were entitled to vote, and participation increased steadily from 50.7 percent of those eligible to 84.5 percent.

Of grave consequence, however, was the absence of election reforms until World War I was practically lost. Changes in population were never considered. While electoral districts in the beginning contained about twenty thousand voters each, the distribution of population forty years later brought about many inequalities. Since these were not corrected, usually because of rapid industrialization, the big towns and the workers and their party, the Social Democrats, were adversely affected.

Nevertheless, social welfare legislation and other measures of vital interest to the lower income groups were adopted. Because of the absence of democratic accountability and because of strong flirtations with militarism, there is a temptation to compare imperial Germany with modern South American dictatorships or with twentieth-century Fascist or Communist regimes. Such comparisons would be misleading, however, for unlike these present-day regimes, Germans under the empire adhered to their principle of *Rechtsstaat,* where justice was said to prevail and where legal provisions were enforced by well-trained, independent judges who, self-confident and aware of their own importance, felt strongly that their only commitment was to the law itself.

Since the princes had made the empire they, not the people, exercised sovereignty. The masses were seen and heard. Their representatives in the *Reichstag,* divided though they were on ideological and political grounds, debated and discussed, but their influence was held to a minimum. Perhaps the most striking example of this impotence occurred in 1917. After three years of a war for which the deputies in the beginning had overwhelmingly voted their support, a resolution was introduced in the *Reichstag* calling for immediate negotiations with the enemy in order to achieve a just peace without annexations. Even though this resolution was eventually adopted by the sizable majority of 212 to 126 (with 17 abstentions), the emperor and his government could and did ignore the measure completely.

The generals, who had strongly resisted all attempts to make the government more responsive to parliamentary demands, changed their tone abruptly as military defeat became inevitable in the fall of 1918. By that time nothing could prevent the collapse of the armies, the abdication of the emperor, who fled across the border into neutral Holland, or the fall of the empire. The role of the military leaders in advocating democratization of the government as well as immediate peace at all costs must be stressed, however. Later on, the legend was spread that the moves to end the war and change the administrative structure were caused by enemies at home who betrayed the heroic troops who were winning the war on the battlefields.

On November 9, 1918, as all the thrones within Germany tumbled and fell, the German Republic was proclaimed. Two days later the armistice was signed. There was confusion among the long-suffering, war-weary people. In the months that followed, the new government, in addition to facing all sorts of difficulties due to the lost war, was subjected to frequent political attacks from the extreme Left as well as the extreme Right. In this atmosphere the elections for a National Assembly were held on January 19, 1919. All citizens of both sexes who had reached the age of twenty were able to vote on an equal basis. Of the more than thirty-six million eligible voters, 83 percent participated, and, of these, three out of four gave their support to the Socialists, Centre party, and Democratic party, all of which were committed to the new democratic regime. For security reasons the assembly met in the central German city of Weimar rather than in strife-torn Berlin, and so these parties became known as the Weimar coalition, just as the resultant republic is usually called the Weimar Republic.

It will suffice here to make some general remarks about the

Weimar Republic. The Constitution, as written by the National Assembly, was a very democratic document. It assured freedom of speech, press, assembly, and religion to each individual; it provided for an elected assembly, the *Reichstag,* to which the government was responsible. This body could dismiss the chancellor by a vote of no confidence. The *Reichstag* itself could be dissolved by the directly elected president. His action in this regard required the countersignature of the chancellor or the responsible minister who, as just indicated, based his authority upon the support of the *Reichstag.* In this way, necessary safeguards seemed to be present.

The president also had certain powers to handle emergencies under Article 48. As it turned out, the first president, Social Democrat Friedrich Ebert, used this provision to save the republic from its internal enemies, whereas his successor, aged Field Marshal Paul von Hindenburg, employed it to undermine and eventually destroy the democratic system.

To blame Article 48, indeed, to blame the Constitution, for the eventual downfall of the Weimar Republic would be unfair. The late Clinton Rossiter accurately demolished such an argument when he wrote:

> Yet it would be a fatal error to ascribe the demolition of the German republic to this single defective institution of emergency government. What Montesquieu said of a lost battle and Holmes of the passage of a law—that if either of these "has ruined a state, there was a general cause at work that made the state ready to perish by a single battle or law"—can be said of republican Germany's Article 48. If constitutional dictatorship helped to destroy it, still there was a far deeper cause at work to make republican Germany ripe for destruction. Perhaps the men of Germany could not have worked *any* constitution, while the "men of Massachusetts" could have made a ringing success of the Weimar Constitution and its Article 48.[4]

There were indeed forces at work that in retrospect make the Weimar Republic's doom seem almost inevitable, although its end need not have been accompanied by blood, violence, and the destruction of the entire continent. From the beginning, the young democracy was burdened with having signed an extremely harsh and unpopular peace treaty and officially assuming responsibility for causing the war—although the new rulers had had no power and little influence over the events which had led to it. Because the Treaty of Versailles was accepted by the leaders of the republic, even if under heavy pressure and in the absence of any real alternative, it was easy to blame them later for everything that went wrong as a result.

The war had caused much suffering. When it finally ended, Germany was forced to cede territory to several of its neighbors, surrender vast quantities of raw materials, give up all its colonies, and pay huge sums of money in reparation. Consequently, its economy was in perilous condition. A disastrous inflation wiped out the savings of a large part of the population. No sooner had the country survived this crisis when the Great Depression caused unemployment and deep dissatisfaction. Under these circumstances, any government would have experienced serious difficulties. What made the situation in Germany even worse was that the republic was unable to appeal to the minds and emotions of the people. Many longed for the glorious days of the empire when the undefeated military paraded the streets in shining armor. Among the disaffected were the greatly reduced armed forces, many of the returning veterans, the government bureaucracy and civil service, the diplomats, and the university professors and school teachers. These groups at best paid lip service to the Weimar Republic without quite believing in it. In numerous cases they worked actively for the restoration of a rightist regime. At the other extreme there were numbers of workers, idealists, and revolutionaries who wanted a more drastic change in society and favored the solutions advocated by communism.

Support for the republican regime thus dwindled. In the two *Reichstag* elections of 1932, the antidemocratic Nazis, German Nationalists, and Communists together received about 58 percent of the vote cast and consequently a proportional number of seats in Parliament. This put the Weimar government into an impossible situation. There was no way in which the democratic forces could obtain the parliamentary majority necessary to govern. After rule by emergency legislation proved unsatisfactory, President Hindenburg, recently reelected by a popular majority, but aging and therefore easily influenced, abruptly dismissed the last democratically chosen chancellor and replaced him, first with Franz von Papen and later with General Kurt von Schleicher, neither of whom commanded the support of a workable majority in the *Reichstag* despite repeated general elections. Finally, on January 30, 1933, the president called on Adolf Hitler, as the leader of the largest single party in Parliament, and appointed him chancellor.

It is important to remember that Hitler assumed his office legally and that he even took the prescribed oath of allegiance to the Weimar Republic. As a matter of fact, the Weimar Constitution was never officially declared invalid. It was simply completely disregarded. In the beginning at least, Hitler's government consisted of only three Nazis: Hitler himself, Wilhelm Frick as minister of interior, and Hermann Göring. Göring did not hold a specific portfolio, but as minister of interior in Prussia, he assumed control of the Prussian police, just as Frick by virtue of his office controlled the police in the rest of the country. The other eight cabinet positions were held by conservatives. These men, while not known for their love for the Weimar regime, nevertheless added respectability and lent credence to the claim that the Hitlerites were outnumbered and boxed in. Hitler's request to hold new elections in early March was within the keeping of the Constitution, although attacks on opponents and increasing street gang violence obviously was not.

A week before the election the *Reichstag* building was set on fire, and the Nazis immediately blamed the Communists. The true origin of the fire is still a mystery, although there is strong reason to assume that it was started by the Nazis themselves in order to make political capital out of the resulting fear of violence. Because of the *Reichstag* fire Hitler persuaded Hindenburg to invoke Article 48, enabling the government to suspend individual liberties. This was applied against enemies of the new regime. All Communist candidates were arrested and their party headquarters raided and property confiscated. Votes could still be cast for them and 12.3 percent of the electorate did so. But the elected candidates could not take their seats, thus reducing the opposition by eighty-one votes in the newly elected *Reichstag*. Even so, the Nazis were not able to get more than 43.9 percent of the popular vote, that is, to take more than 288 out of 647 seats. They obtained a majority in the *Reichstag* only through the help of their right-wing Nationalist allies and because the total membership was in effect reduced to 566 by their virtual elimination of the Communists as a parliamentary force.

Later that month, Hitler asked the newly elected Parliament to pass an enabling law. This act empowered the government during the next four years to pass laws by decree, including those affecting the Constitution itself. It required a two-thirds majority of those present and voting. The eventual 441 affirmative votes were obtained through pressure, threats, and the argument that if Hitler were not given this authority, he would simply take it by force. The specious argument was advanced that it would therefore be far more sensible to give him legally what he asked for. Despite the obvious bad logic of this reasoning, only the Social Democrats voted against the measure. They paid for their courage with exile, imprisonment, torture, or death.

This was the end of parliamentary democracy, because the so-called constitutional safeguards, such as noninterference with presidential powers, or the four-year time limit, proved utterly meaningless. The stipulation that the position of the *Reichstag* would not be affected was, in the words of William Shirer, "surely the cruelest joke of all."[5] All vestiges of federalism were now swept away, for Hitler could not tolerate power centers in the states where these could act as barriers to his total control. As his rule of terror increased, the opponents of the regime were hunted down. The civil service, including the judiciary, was "purified." "Unreliables," including Jews, were eliminated from public life. On July 14, 1933, a decree was issued outlawing all political parties except Hitler's own National Socialists. The *Reichstag* was promptly dissolved. During the election campaign that followed, only Hitlerites were permitted to compete, so that the eventual, expected result was that the 661 seats were filled by 661 Nazis. Parliament had become less than useless. In the words of a joke that secretly made the rounds in Germany at that time, the *Reichstag* had become "the highest paid singing society in the world." Its members met once or twice a year, listened to a few speeches by top Nazis, and sang the national anthem, tasks for which they were paid a substantial salary.

In August 1934, President Hindenburg died at the age of eighty-six. His death removed the only remaining possible check on Hitler's otherwise limitless authority. The question of succession was soon settled when Hitler announced that the office of president was not to be filled "out of respect for the aged field marshal." He himself would assume the authority of that office while adopting the title *"Führer* and *Reich* Chancellor." The electorate dutifully ratified this action in a carefully controlled and supervised referendum. The armed forces now were required to take a personal oath of allegiance to Hitler. He had used an earlier, apparent attempt at revolt by some of his own closest comrades to demonstrate his mastery over any foe, real or imaginary, by bloodily eliminating, not only those involved in the rebellion, but also many others whose continued existence might prove troublesome. Nothing was allowed to stand in Hitler's way. This illustrated perfectly the theory advanced two centuries earlier by the French philosopher Baron de Montesquieu. In advocating political separation of power Montesquieu said that there would be an end of everything if the same person or the same body of people were to exercise at once all three powers, those of the legislature, the executive, and the judiciary.

Having achieved unlimited and unrestricted power within Germany, Hitler now looked beyond its borders for future satisfaction of his ambitions. An internally divided Austria became the first victim. With the common language as a pretext and even harping on his own so often underplayed Austrian birth, Hitler annexed Austria in March of 1938. He succeeded without bloodshed, thus "taking home the land which happens to be my own homeland too." His territorial appetite was, if anything, only enlarged, and after the successful conquest, first of part and later the whole of Czechoslovakia, he decided to march into Poland. The result was that Britain and France declared war. An unbelievable number of victories, achieved in lightning campaigns in Poland, Scandinavia, the Low Countries and France, and across the Balkans, seemed to confirm Hitler's claim to intuitive invincibility. This made practically impossible any serious attempt at revolt within Germany. However, the fortunes of war took a different turn. Eventually the Russian front bogged down in mud, ice, and snow, and in time

the Germans experienced something they had not known in years
—defeat. In the west, Allied bombing became increasingly heavy.
In 1944, the establishment of a second front swiftly brought the
war to the soil of Germany itself. The Russians did likewise in
the east. By May 1945, it was all over. Hitler's Third Reich, that
was to have lasted a thousand years, hardly survived its twelfth
birthday, although that dozen years was far too long for those who
suffered through them.

5

Constitutional Developments in Postwar Germany

In many respects, 1945 was both the end and the beginning of Germany. The country lay in ruins. Four enemy powers controlled its territory. Refugees from the east poured into the country in large numbers. Any semblance of German authority had vanished; the word of the Allied commanders was law. Only gradually were Germans encouraged to look after their own affairs. In the three Western zones, grassroots democracy was nurtured on the *Land* or state level, while in the Soviet zone "socialism" of the Russian variety was introduced. Economic conditions eventually led to consolidation of the three Western zones and a definite break with the Soviets, thus paving the ground for the development into the two Germanys. When Truman, Stalin, and Churchill (replaced by Attlee when the British election results were announced while the conference was in progress) met in Potsdam in July of 1945, they had envisaged treating all of Germany as a single economic unit during the occupation period. An Allied control council was set up, which consisted of the military governors of the occupying powers. This council's decisions required unanimity. Since such agreement became more and more of a rarity, the representative of each country acted very much on his own as time went on.

Potsdam had provided against the establishment of a central

government for Germany. This policy was strongly supported by the French, who otherwise had negative feelings regarding the entire Potsdam settlement because of their exclusion from it. Interestingly enough, as Professor Sontheimer points out, the establishment of a central authority would have been in the interest of the Soviet Union, that was well prepared to put Communists into leading positions throughout the country. As it was, each zone pretty much went its own way. By the time that the Western zones eventually combined, local peculiarities had been emphasized to such an extent that the states continued to remain important power centers, a situation scarcely altered when a national government was reestablished.

The division of Germany into eastern and western parts can be attributed to a number of factors. The differences between the administering Allies is certainly one of them. However, it is well to remember that in the beginning France was at least as opposed to Anglo-American aspirations as the USSR. Economic reasons forced France to cooperate with the United States and Britain to some extent. In addition, the "cold war" intensified. Indeed, mounting tension between East and West was forcefully imprinted on the German landscape. From the start, the Soviets had insisted on transforming their zone into a social-economic system not unlike their own. The Western powers encouraged local democracy, based on free elections, to develop step by step, and the Soviets at first did likewise in the hope of gaining popular favor. But their methods of handling people were not designed to produce popularity, even if Russian atrocities may at least in part be explained, though not excused, by the wish for revenge for the numerous acts of barbarism performed by the Germans on Russian soil during the war.

In October of 1946, free elections took place in all four zones of Berlin, a city which traditionally favored socialism. The Communists were expected to do well, the more so since in the Soviet sector Social Democrats and Communists had combined under Soviet pressure to form the Socialist Unity party (*Sozialistische Einheitspartei* or SED). However, in competition with the traditional Social Democratic party, the SED obtained only 20 percent of the vote; even in the Soviet sector, it received less than 30 percent. The Social Democrats were supported by 49 percent of the voters, the Christian Democrats by 22 percent, and the Liberals by 9 percent. These results clearly indicated that the people would not willingly choose communism. To achieve their end, therefore, the Soviets came to rely increasingly on force.

While economic necessity drove the Western zones toward closer cooperation, the cold war and Russian methods separated these more and more from the Eastern zone. The final break came in June 1948 when the three Western powers undertook a currency reform after the Russian representative walked out of the Allied Control Council in March. Although these financial measures were necessary to the Western zones, they were greeted with hostility in the East and culminated in the Soviet blockade of West Berlin. No rail or road traffic was permitted into West Berlin. The intention was to bring the city to its knees, thereby administering a humiliating cold war defeat to the Western powers. They replied to the challenge with an airlift. The beleaguered city was sustained until the following May when free access was once more assured through an American-Soviet agreement. This defeat clearly signalled a miscarriage of Soviet plans. The whole episode was yet another step toward East-West hostility and the formation of two German states.

During the first half of 1948, the three Western Allies, together with the three Benelux countries, met in conference in London where they reached a basic understanding regarding the political merger of the Western zones and the establishment of a West German government. This sentiment was officially communicated to a gathering of the prime ministers of the eleven *Länder* at Frankfurt on July 1. The gathering was also directed to convene an assembly within the next eight weeks to be charged with drafting a democratic constitution. At the same time, the Allies made it quite clear that they insisted on retaining a number of controls.

The instruction to make provisions for a West German constitution was not altogether favorably received. It was, after all, an order from foreign powers; it contained instructions for the formation of a democratic system under circumstances that were not in themselves democratic (since Allied controls were not to be eliminated for the time being); and it greatly compromised any future prospects for reunification of all four zones.

Nevertheless, the suggested assembly, officially known as the Parliamentary Council, met for the first time at Bonn on September 1, 1948. The previous month, experts had gathered at Herrenchiemsee in the Bavarian Alps and had produced a document to serve as the basis for the deliberations of the Parliamentary Council. The latter consisted of sixty-five members, chosen by the *Land* parliaments on the basis of one delegate for each 750,000 inhabitants. The Christian Democratic Union and its Bavarian sister party had twenty-seven representatives, the Social Democrats had the same number, and the remaining eleven delegates belonged to various splinter parties, including two Communists. Berlin was represented by five additional nonvoting deputies.

Deliberations lasted until May of 1949 when the draft document was accepted by fifty-three votes to twelve, with two Communists, two Center party members, two German party representatives and six Bavarian delegates from the Christian Social Union providing the opposition. Following official approval by the Allied military governors, the document was submitted to the *Land* parliaments for ratification, which was obtained in all but one of the state legislatures. The exception, Bavaria, agreed to accept the document if it passed elsewhere.

Several additional events of that fast-moving period should be noted. Before the Parliamentary Council adjourned, it was decided that the capital of the new state was to be Bonn, although the vote of thirty-three for Bonn and twenty-nine for Frankfurt was not exactly overwhelming. Soon afterward, the military governors, John McCloy of the United States, Sir Brian Robertson of Britain, and André François-Poncet of France, officially had their titles changed to high commissioners, thus connoting the change of status of Germany. And on August 14, the German people participated in contested national elections for the first time since the Hitler nightmare. The newly elected Parliament assembled in early September. Subsequently, Theodor Heuss became the first federal president, Konrad Adenauer the first federal chancellor.

A new Germany was born, even though it excluded the Russian zone of occupation.

As yet, however, this Germany was not sovereign in its own land. In April 1949, while future constitutional arrangements were still being debated at a foreign ministers' meeting in Washington, the three Western Allies affirmed their intention to retain supreme control over a number of German affairs. Demilitarization, reparations, foreign agreements including international treaties, and control of foreign trade were among the controlled matters. Despite German objections, this new Occupation Statute became effective in September of 1949.

There was anticipation that the Statute might seriously impair the new constitutional regime. That it did not was due to several factors: the commendable restraint shown by the Allies; the forthrightness and singlemindedness of purpose with which Konrad Adenauer fought step by step for the abolition of restrictions on his country's exercise of complete sovereignty; and the general cold war atmosphere which tempted the Western powers to regard West Germany less and less as a former enemy who had to be held in check and punished for former wrongdoing, and more as a future ally who could play an increasingly important part in the cold war struggle to contain communism and the Soviet Union. By 1952 the Occupation Statute had been revoked. In 1953 the high commissioners became ambassadors, a clear indication that the relationship between Germany and the United States, Britain, and France had returned to normal. Although the European Defense Community Treaty, which had provided for German participation in the West European defense system, came to naught because the French National Assembly refused to ratify it, a new agreement was soon substituted for it. By special protocol on May 5, 1955, West Germany officially became a member of the North Atlantic Treaty Organization, and there was no question that it did so as a sovereign, independent nation with full control over its own external and internal affairs. The period when others made decisions for Germans, who presumably could not be trusted, had lasted barely a decade.

Some of the detailed provisions of the new system of government will become clearer in succeeding chapters; on the whole, it may be observed that its authors were concerned to stress its temporary character and to avoid the mistakes of Weimar. We have seen that when the Parliamentary Council was instructed to draw up the document, a major German fear was that it would make the East-West division permanent and final. A partial remedy was supposedly to be found in the very title of the document. It was not called a constitution but, rather, *Grundgesetz*, Basic Law, a name still used officially today. Its preamble states that the German people in the various enumerated *Länder* were only providing for a transitional period. A claim was advanced that it also acted for those Germans to whom participation was as yet denied, a clear reference to those in the Eastern zone. Finally "the entire German people are called upon to achieve in free self-determination the unity and freedom of Germany." The sentiment of the preamble is expressed again in the concluding article, number 146, which states that "this Basic Law shall cease to be in force on the day on which a constitution adopted by a free decision of the German people comes into force."

That such a possibility seems more than ever remote today is beside the point. In 1949, and in the years immediately following, the prospect of unification was a real one for the Germans. It remained a theme harped upon almost continually by their politicians. Only with the advent of the Brandt government two decades later was a more realistic attitude forthcoming. When the two German governments began to negotiate with one another and when both were admitted as members to the United Nations in the fall of 1973, their existence as separate, independent, sovereign nations was clearly recognized as a fact of life.

The *Grundgesetz* has in the meantime assumed the role of a constitution for the Federal Republic of Germany. It was perhaps inevitable that federalism would be stressed to a greater extent than in the days of Weimar, just as in the United States where the states existed before the national government. Some of the *Länder*, especially Bavaria, insisted on local autonomy. Regional power centers separate from and in competition with the national government have proven to be a good defense against potential dictatorship. The president is now no longer directly elected by the people but owes his selection to a Federal Assembly. This circumstance gives him less independent authority and seems to deprive him of any possible future claim that his position entitles him to supersede the *Reichstag* and the legally appointed chancellor. Parliament today is only partially elected by proportional representation. The result is that splinter parties have found it increasingly difficult to gain seats in the legislature. The *Bundestag* cannot dismiss the chancellor by a mere vote of no confidence. They can do so only by specifically naming and electing a successor by majority vote. The right to dissolve Parliament is now severely restricted, and the condition for such a step carefully described. Although some provisions are made for emergency situations, Article 48 was not resurrected when the *Grundgesetz* was written. Article 18, however, stipulates that "whoever abuses freedom of expression of opinion . . . in order to combat the free democratic basic order, shall forfeit these basic rights." This seems to be a clear warning to any future *Führer* that he will be stopped long before he can become a serious danger.

Periodic crises—such as the *Spiegel* affair, when the Adenauer regime attempted to proceed against that often critical magazine, or the discovery of a Communist spy among the closest advisors of Willy Brandt, a discovery leading to the resignation of the chancellor—have pointed to the vulnerability of this as of every human institution. In the mid–1960s there seemed to be danger from increasing popular support for extreme right-wing parties, but the fears subsided as support for the quasi-Fascist National Democratic party waned. No NPD candidate has as yet been elected to the *Bundestag*. From a purely legal point of view, it is interesting that in 1972, political conditions were artificially created to fulfill the constitutionally specified conditions for dissolution of Parliament a year ahead of time. This entire episode points to a desirable flexibility of the Basic Laws. While no one can foretell the future, the very fact that the Bonn Government has already lasted twice as long as its Weimar predecessor gives rise to optimism.

While all this went on in the West, the East was not dormant. The Russians in the beginning were not opposed to uniform Allied actions throughout Germany, on the obvious assumption that communism would carry the day. The Soviets were particularly interested in reparations for the enormous damage done by the Nazis on Russian soil. When shipments of German materials to the Soviet Union were terminated in the Western zone, they were continued from the Soviet zone. Other differences, in addition to political ones, were brought about by the intensification of the cold war, but it was the East rather than the West that adhered longest to the concept of a unified Germany. Even the merging of the Communists with the Social Democrats into the Socialist Unity party was to be carried on throughout Germany. However, this union was strongly rejected by the leaders, as well as the rank and file, of the Social Democrats in the west. Kurt Schumacher, who had spent almost the entire Nazi period in concentration camps, had no intention of submitting to Red dictators after surviving the Brown ones by what was almost a miracle. The SED became exclusively an East German organization and because it was Communist-sponsored and Communist-controlled, it had little chance of success outside the Soviet orbit.

It is claimed that in the development of the two Germanys, the East usually allowed the West to make the first move. Such a situation was valuable for propaganda purposes. It is instructive then to note that the Constitution of the East German state of Thuringia, as early as December of 1946, mentions membership within the German Democratic Republic. This fact led to the observation that long before the Western zones discussed form and possibiliies of an all-German versus a West German state organization or its name, the Soviet zone was already acquainted with the designation "German Democratic Republic."[1]

When the rulers of the Eastern zone called for a German People's Congress in Berlin in December 1947, they began their appeal with an expression of regret that parties in all the German zones had failed to cooperate. Several months later, the Second Congress voted for an all-German plebiscite on the question of German unity. Since there was no doubt that the Communists would have used the obvious desire of the German people for unity to suit their own purposes, the Western Allies rejected the proposal.

Ever closer cooperation, first between the American and British, then between all three Western zones, and the complete breakdown of the Allied Control Commission culminated in the Soviet withdrawal in March 1948. The next steps were almost inevitable. Western currency reforms provoked the Soviets into reacting with the Berlin blockade. Germany was now divided economically (although it was all blamed on the "lords of Wall Street"). The Soviets followed with their own currency reforms and the West then included West Berlin in its own monetary orbit.

While the Parliamentary Council in Bonn was debating the future Basic Law, the German People's Council in the east declared itself the only legitimate representative body of the German people. It denounced the proceedings in Bonn as detrimental to German interests. After the adoption of the *Grundgesetz,* the presidium of the SED once more called for German unity. This appeal carried little conviction: only a few days later the German People's Council proclaimed "the basis of a new, independent, free all-German state." Provisional representative chambers were constructed and a joint session of the two houses immediately and unanimously elected Wilhelm Pieck, chairman of the Socialist Unity party and a leading Communist, as president of the German Democratic Republic. At the same time, the existence of a provisional government under Otto Grotewohl was confirmed.

The Soviets, like the Americans, British, and French, intended to transform their former enemies into friends. In May 1950, Stalin proposed to reduce still outstanding reparation payments by 50 percent. Later the same year, East Germany was admitted to COMECON, the Communist-sponsored Council of Mutual Economic Aid, Moscow's answer to the Marshall Plan. Soon afterward, the DDR and Poland agreed to recognize their border along the rivers Oder and Neisse as permanent. This step was greeted with protests, not only from Bonn, but also from Washington, London, and Paris. It was maintained that only a general peace treaty could finally determine German frontiers. In the years that followed, East Germany and the Soviet Union repeatedly asked for such a peace conference. The West, fearing a Communist maneuver, would not agree to the proposed preliminaries until Helsinki in 1975. The Helsinki Document, despite some publicly expressed Western reservations, seems to have brought about a general recognition of the existing European borders.

Meanwhile, as the parliamentary elections of October 1950 approached, the Socialist Unity party proposed to the other political parties in East Germany the formation of a unified list of candidates. It was alleged that the Bonn regime and its "capitalist warmongering masters" had hostile intentions against the socialist state, and those plans had to be answered through a show of unity and strength. Given the circumstances of Communist control, no one in the Soviet zone was in a position to reject the SED's demands, whatever their misgivings. Consequently, one list of candidates was presented to the people, who approved it by a vote of 99.7 percent.

In reality, though not in theory, the one-party state had come into existence. Economically, Soviet-style "socialism" was put into practice. It was therefore not surprising that waves of refugees left the East and made their way to the West under conditions that became increasingly dangerous as Eastern authorities did everything they could to stop that flow. When a rise of the production quotas and a reduction in wages was announced, general dissatisfaction with the regime resulted in spontaneous revolts on June 17, 1953. These were put down by Soviet forces, not without bloodshed. General concessions had to be made, for it became clear that despite official description of the revolt as the work of Western agent provocateurs, the people had to be treated carefully if a repetition of these events was to be avoided.

In August 1953 the Soviet Union declared that no further reparations were to be exacted after January 1, 1954. On that same day the USSR returned more than thirty East German engineering, chemical, and other concerns that had been exploited by the Russians for reparation purposes. In March 1954 the USSR proclaimed the German Democratic Republic to be in full control of its sovereignty, and this was confirmed by a "solemn" agreement between the two countries in September of the following year.

Since the mid–1950s two Germanys have existed, each under the powerful protection of one of the two superstates, the United States and the Soviet Union. On May 14, 1955, the DDR was admitted to membership in the Warsaw Pact, the Communist system of alliance. With the German Federal Republic inside the North Atlantic Treaty Organization, the two hostile camps that faced one another across Europe met along a border that ran right through the heart of Germany. East Germany made every effort to hermetically seal its frontiers with the West, eventually building the wall across Berlin in August 1961.

The two Germanys were not even on speaking terms. Both claimed to be the one and only representative of the true Germany. For a number of years, Bonn maintained the Hallstein doctrine. This doctrine declared that West Germany would have to break diplomatic relations with any country other than the Soviet Union that recognized the legality of the East German regime. Eventually this doctrine had to be abandoned in favor of a more realistic approach. Under Willy Brandt's leadership, the two Germanys achieved a high degree of normalization in their relationship, paving the way to admission of both countries to the United Nations but, more importantly perhaps, to personal contacts among individuals on both sides of the German Iron Curtain.

Although certain principles about East Germany's Constitution were pronounced from time to time, the current document was not adopted until 1968, and amended in 1974. It replaced a constitution that had been in effect since 1949. "The Constitution of the German Democratic Republic of October 7, 1949, has fulfilled its purpose," declared Walter Ulbricht.

> In conformity with the spirit and working of its mission, it guaranteed the freedom and the rights of citizens and helped to develop our social and economic life according to the principles of social justice. . . . It contributed to safeguarding peace and raising the international prestige of our state. . . .
>
> In the meantime social developments have reached a stage in which the advanced construction of socialist society has become the main task.[2]

This new task demanded a new constitutional foundation. The 1968 document was amended with a minimum amount of public notice and concern. The new wording of the preamble speaks of the "continuation of the revolutionary traditions of the German working class," giving the impression that the evolutionary processes made some changes necessary. Apparently these changes had to do with the new relationship of the two Germanys. Omitted were references to "international obligations of all Germans" (Article 6), to overcoming the division of Germany and to supporting "the step-by-step rapprochement of the two German states until the time of their unification on the basis of democracy and socialism" (Article 8). The DDR is today apparently firmly committed to the existence and coexistence of the two Germanys. Unification is no longer among its state goals.

6

Constitutional Developments in Austria

Until the Austro-Prussian War of 1866, Austria was part of what was then considered to be Germany. Not only was Austria a leader in the German League, it was also a leader in repressing democratic and nationalist ideas throughout Europe. The major reason for this was that Vienna's domain extended over many different peoples, including Czechs, Slovaks, Slovenes, Italians, and Poles, so that any claim to national self-determination represented a threat to the Austrian empire. How real the danger was became evident in 1848 when the emperor was forced to flee from Vienna, and uprisings took place in Italy and in Hungary. Eventually all insurrections were put down, although Russian troops had to be called in for help. Attempts were then made to return to prerevolutionary conditions. True, Metternich was no longer in power and Emperor Ferdinand abdicated in favor of his nephew, Franz Joseph. But Austria once more spearheaded antinationalist measures. She forced Prussia to agree to the humiliating convention at Olmütz in 1850, which rejected any partial unification of Germany under Prussian leadership and returned to the pre–1848 arrangement.

The dissatisfaction that caused the unrest of 1848 could not be suppressed permanently. Austria was the main opponent to Italian unity, and the successful Italian war of liberation in 1859 was the first important evidence of continued dissatisfaction. The Italians also fought the Austrians in 1866 when Prussia made a determined effort to push Austria out of Germany proper. Since Russia had not been helped by Vienna during the Crimean War despite Russian assistance against Austrian revolutionaries in 1848–1849, Russia saw no reason to help Austria in 1866. Thus, 1866 was a disaster for Austria. Even though the southern German states lined up with the Viennese government, they were not able to stem the Prussian tide.

This defeat convinced the emperor of his vulnerability and of the need for reform. His response took two forms. The first was an attempt to solve the nationality problem through the *Ausgleich,* a system that accorded the Hungarians equality with the German-speaking population. In addition to having a common monarch, Austria and Hungary now shared the same ministers of foreign affairs, finance, and war. Otherwise, the two parts of the Austro-Hungarian "dual monarchy" were autonomous entities. While this pleased the Hungarians, it meant nothing for the other peoples within the empire. Their dissatisfaction was, if anything, increased by a reform that so clearly favored the Hungarians.

The second set of reforms concerned the problem of legislative representation. Although the Constitution of December 1867 restricted the emperor's freedom of action, it still left him in a dominant position. Although everything he did required the countersignature of responsible ministers, the monarch could veto measures passed by Parliament, and could in many areas bypass the legislature. The legislature was also hampered by its diversity. So many ethnic groups were represented in Parliament that the oath of office was administered in eight different languages. This was one reason for the numerous conflicts that seriously impaired legislative effectiveness. The *Reichsrat* consisted of two chambers, the House of Lords, or *Herrenhaus,* and the House of Deputies, the *Haus der Abgeordneten.* The latter was at first elected by five different classes of voters, but after 1907 on the basis of equal, direct, and secret manhood suffrage. One interesting phenomenon may be noted in passing. Agreement between the two houses was necessary for a measure to be adopted. If after prolonged efforts, discord prevailed on such matters as how much money to appropriate for a certain item or how large the army should be, the smaller figure proposed by either branch of the legislature prevailed.

Defeat in World War I brought about the disintegration of the Austro-Hungarian empire. Czechs and Slovaks, Serbs and Slovenes formed their own independent states. A new Poland was mapped out of areas previously owned by Austria, Prussia, and Russia. Italy and Rumania enriched themselves at the expense of the dual monarchy. All that remained was a relatively small area of some thirty-two thousand square miles, landlocked within a winding thousand-mile border and inhabited by several million German-speaking people. As previously noted, any possibility of their union with Germany was prevented by Allied fear.

On October 21, 1918, the German-speaking deputies of the *Reichsrat* met as the "Provisional National Assembly" and assumed full authority over the newly created country of "German-Austria." A provisional constitution establishing a democratic republic was proclaimed on November 18. It has rightly been described as "a pure type of parliamentary democracy."[1] In the absence of either the office of president or the institution of referendum, parliamentary authority was supreme.

In 1919 the first parliamentary elections were held in February. The Constituent National Assembly met for the first time in March. Also in 1919, the imperial family was banished and its property confiscated. The abortive peace treaty was signed at St. Germain.[2] After further discussions of proposed constitutional arrangements, the new Constitution became effective on November 10, 1921, the same day the newly elected legislature, the *Nationalrat,* held its opening session.

Although the principles of the 1918 proposals were retained, the Constitution was no longer of a "pure" type. There remained a close relationship between the chancellor and his ministers and the *Nationalrat* to which they were responsible; however, a second chamber now represented the various provinces. Parliamentary democracy was thus tempered with federalism. In addition, the position of president, admittedly with few powers, was created, and arguments soon developed over it.

The prevailing situation caused considerable dissatisfaction, perhaps not so much because of constitutional details, but because the size of the country, its internal politics, and its economic weakness made Austria extremely vulnerable. In retrospect, Austria's parliamentary democracy seemed doomed from the start. In addition to the weaknesses already cited, bitter political tripartite division developed between the conservative, clerically oriented countryside, the Socialist-oriented workers in Vienna, and a vocal, well-organized right-wing pan-German movement.

Because members of the legislature were elected by proportional representation, this system came in for its share of criticism, as it did in Germany at that time. However, the divisions in Parliament were not caused by a particular election system so much as by the deep rifts that split the country. The Socialists obtained a sizable number of seats in every election between 1920 and 1933 but never enough to assure them of a parliamentary majority. They were successfully excluded from participation in the government by the Christian Socials who administered the country with the aid of the pan-Germans and other relatively small groups. Amid attacks from the Right, the Christian Socials intensified their anti-parliamentary attitude.

In 1929, the Constitution was revised. The purpose was primarily to strengthen the office of president by providing for his direct election, although such elections took place only after World War II. Even this attempt to set up a fairly strong man on a democratic basis within a parliamentary framework could not save the system. At a time when Hitler was coming to power in Germany with the avowed aim of destroying the Weimar Republic, Austrian democracy was eliminated by a chancellor, appointed on a parliamentary basis, whose party was still committed to maintaining parliamentary democracy. In the words of one observer,[3] Austria's problem was really that it was a democracy without trained and convinced supporters, perhaps without any supporters at all. As this lack of support became more and more evident, Chancellor Engelbert Dollfuss, on March 4, 1933, one day before the German elections and a week after the German *Reichstag* in Berlin went up in flames, used the absence of one deputy from the parliamentary session to abolish Parliament altogether.[4] The Socialists replied to this and other curtailments of constitutional rights with a short uprising in February 1934 which was bloodily suppressed. Now all political parties were dissolved, with the quasi-Fascist clerical regime showing no mercy to the Socialists but much leniency to the Right. This did not prevent the murder of Dollfuss by Nazi terrorists, although a Nazi takeover was avoided for the time being.

The new chancellor, Kurt Schuschnigg, continued both the one-party rule of his predecessor and the policy of Socialist suppression. For a while he was able to rely heavily on support from neighboring Fascist Italy, but when Mussolini needed Hitler's support more than he needed an independent Austria, the Germans gained the upper hand. With a powerful army assembled along the Austrian border and with local Nazis causing disturbances throughout Austria almost daily, Hitler forced Schuschnigg to agree to his demands. These included adding Nazis to the Austrian government. Schuschnigg found himself driven further and further into a corner. As a last, desperate measure, he announced, at very short notice, a referendum on the question whether or not Austria should remain independent. However, no valid register of electors existed because no elections had taken place since 1930, and Hitler could therefore piously claim that the whole process was a fraud. Schuschnigg's demonstrated anti-Socialist attitude kept him from getting the immediate support he needed to unify the country and meet Hitler's moves. There is little doubt that the vast majority of the population, Christian Socials as well as Social Democrats, would have voted for Austrian independence had they been allowed to do so. As it was, Hitler's threats made Schuschnigg withdraw the whole idea of a referendum, and on March 12, 1938, German troops marched into Austria. Schuschnigg gave orders that no resistance should be offered, since he did not want "even in this terrible situation to shed blood." Austria became part of Hitler's "greater Germany," losing all signs of a separate identity. Now it was the *Gau Ostmark,* the eastern border district of the Reich.

After Schuschnigg had been forced to name Nazis to his cabinet, these had faithfully obeyed orders received from Berlin and had prepared for, and eventually officially requested, the German invasion of Austria. The Austrian people remembered their original desire for *Anschluss,* and their recent abhorrence of Hitler and his well-reported atrocities did not keep them from according the German soldiers a tumultuous reception. A month later they voiced approval of Hitler's annexation in a plebiscite. Austrians were treated as fellow Germans; in fact the elimination of anti-Nazis, Jews, left-wingers, and other "enemies of the state" which had taken five years in Germany was carried out in Austria almost overnight. To this day the concentration camp at Mauthausen near the city of Linz bears witness to the frightful horrors that were perpetrated on Austrian soil. When war came, no differentiation was drawn between Germans and Austrians; they were conscripted to serve side by side in Hitler's armies.

Under these circumstances, the victorious Allies were confronted by the question whether to regard Austria as an enemy or as the first victim of Hitler's aggression. A case could be made for either attitude. When the foreign ministers of the United States, Britain, and the Soviet Union met at Moscow, their declaration of November 1, 1943, recognized both viewpoints. It stated that

> Austria, the first free country to fall victim to Hitlerite aggression, shall be liberated from German domination.

But after proclaiming that the annexation by Germany shall be null and void, the declaration added, significantly:

> Austria is reminded, however, that she has a responsibility which she cannot evade for participation in the war on the side of Hitlerite Germany, and that in the final settlement account will inevitably be taken of her contribution to her liberation.

As the war progressed Austrian casualties increased, and the country was subjected to heavy bombing. In the spring of 1945, Russian troops marched into Austria from the east and captured Vienna. American and some French contingents entered from Bavaria, and the British converged upon Austria from Italy. Like Germany, Austria was soon totally occupied.

Again like Germany, Austria was divided into four zones of occupation, with the capital city parceled out among Russians, Americans, British, and French. Unlike Germany, where no organized political life independent from the occupation forces was possible, the Austrians almost immediately continued where they left off. Of course, there was a question as to precisely where they had left off, given the fact that Austria remained independent for some half-dozen years after both its parliamentary government and the constitutional liberties of large parts of the population had been eliminated. The solution to this problem was the reconstruction of the Austrian republic under the Constitution of 1920, as amended in 1929, and a declaration that the annexation of 1938 was null and void.

Interestingly enough, the proclamation which expressed this sentiment was issued by a body called the "Provisional Austrian Government." In early April of 1945, while Hitler was still sitting in his Berlin shelter hoping for a miracle to turn the fortunes of war and issuing strict orders that any thought of negotiating with the enemy was high treason punishable by death, Karl Renner was already discussing the future of Austria with the Russians. Renner had played an important part in the establishment of the First Republic and had served as its chancellor from 1918 to 1920; he had led his country's delegation to the peace conference; and his last prominent post was that of president of the elected parliament which Dollfuss had sent into permanent recess in 1933. Renner was living in retirement in a little village when the Russians occupied it on April 1, 1945. Two days later, he decided to see whether it might be possible to stop some of the excesses committed by the Russian troops. Once contact was made, higher-ups joined in on the Russian side, and other Austrians came out of hiding. Soon Renner was able to name a government for Austria, consisting of nine Christian Socials who now called themselves members of the "Austrian People's party," ten Socialists, seven Communists, and three independent experts.

It was this provisional government that decided to go back to the 1920 Constitution and its principles. What was remarkable, especially in contrast to Germany, was that a national government could be established so soon, even before the war ended officially. One major problem Renner had to overcome was the impression that he was a Russian tool. His own background as a staunch anti-Communist Socialist who had often been denounced by the Communists was apparently not convincing enough for the Western Allies, who withheld recognition until October and accorded it only after painstaking negotiations, subject to the provision that the Renner government clear all its actions with the Allied occupation authorities.

Despite these and other difficulties, parliamentary elections took place in Austria in November of 1945. Of those eligible to vote, 93 percent participated. The People's party received almost 50 percent of the vote: 1,602,000 out of a total of 3,217,000. The Socialists came in second with 1,435,000 supporters, while the Communists gleaned a very disappointing 174,000 votes, or four seats in the legislature of 165 members, a sign of unpopularity which was quite a shock to the Russians. Their attitude then became less friendly, especially since election results necessitated the reduction of Communist members in the cabinet to one, and he resigned in November of 1947 over Austria's participation in the Marshall Plan. The coalition of three parties thus became an alliance of two, but in this form it was able to sustain itself until 1966.

Austrian difficulties under such conditions were numerous. Nevertheless, the government functioned as well as it could. Following the 1945 elections, a People's party leader, Leopold Figl, assumed the office of chancellor with a Socialist, Adolf Schärf, as vice-chancellor, while the houses of Parliament elevated the venerable Karl Renner to the position of federal president, an office he held until his death in 1950.

Almost immediately after the end of the war, negotiations began about the restoration of Austria's independence and sovereignty. Like so many other efforts during that period, it took a long, long time, largely because of Allied disagreements. But unlike the German situation, eventually there were results. On May 15, 1955, Austria signed the *Staatsvertrag* with the four powers, restoring Austria as a "sovereign, independent, and democratic state." On October 23, the last Allied soldier left Austrian soil, and on October 26, the day now celebrated each year as a national holiday, Parliament passed a law stipulating that Austria was to be forever a neutral country, a provision that was officially recognized by all the powers of the North Atlantic Treaty Organization and the

Warsaw Pact. Thus, with the understanding that it would stay out of the East-West conflict, Austria was once more, at long last, sovereign. But unlike earlier times, the sufferings of the past years seem to have strengthened Austria's will to be independent. Its people give every indication of their determination to make a success of parliamentary democracy in the future, as indeed they have done in the most recent past.

7

Political Parties:
An Overview

Thus far we have attempted to establish how the individual countries came to their present borders and how various constitutions reached their present forms. We will now be able to deal with current political situations, although past events may have to be cited again by way of illustration and example.

This is certainly true in the chapters where we propose to discuss political parties. Except for the German Unity party in the Communist-controlled German Democratic Republic, all political parties to be discussed have a fairly long history of political activity. Some, like the Social Democrats, have retained in essence the name under which they first became known a century ago. Others, such as the German Christian Democratic Union or the Austrian People's party, assumed a new name after World War II, although their ancestry can be directly traced to older political groupings. But in almost all cases, party programs and platforms have undergone alterations necessary because of changing times and different circumstances.

Various factors, some outside the scope of this discussion, contribute to the formation of public opinion. Family attitudes and discussions around the dinner table establish a certain framework. A child's neighborhood, his church and its values, his schooling, his friends and classmates—all these and many more leave their impression on the young mind. Obviously, growing up in a world of plenty brings with it an outlook quite unlike that acquired from living in poverty or near-starvation. Books, newspapers and magazines, radio, television, stage and screen also greatly influence the thinking of individuals, groups, and nations.

The viewpoints and attitudes thus acquired affect the individual's approach to all aspects of life. They are constantly formed, changed, abandoned, or confirmed. This is true of all human endeavor; it is thus undoubtedly true of politics.

The term *politics* has been defined in a variety of ways by a number of different writers. In very general terms, it refers to the relationship between those who govern and those who are governed; those who rule and those who are ruled. When a modern writer, Harold Lasswell, speaks of the problem of "who gets what, when, how," he is actually talking about politics, namely the determination of who decides how relatively scarce resources are to be allocated and how those who make these decisions get the authority to carry out their plans. During the nineteenth century, demands for constitutions and for limits to the powers of the autocratic monarchs were attempts to open up the political process, to make rulers more responsible and more receptive to the wishes of the ruled.

One important lesson was soon learned: no matter whether the struggle was political and concerned constitutional powers, or economic and dealt with higher wages and better working conditions, the individual had no chance as long as he faced the well-entrenched forces of power and wealth alone. As an individual he could be crushed and defeated. But when an entire work force went out on strike in a factory, or when a determined mass of people presented their political demands, as they did throughout Europe in 1848, it was difficult to thwart them. Thus it became imperative to the people to form a unified, consolidated group that would work together toward obtaining specific ends, in other words to establish an organization. The organizations in economic activities became labor unions. In the political sphere they developed into political parties.

Two hundred years ago the English statesman-philosopher Edmund Burke defined a political party as "a body of men uniting for promoting by their joint endeavors the national interest, upon some particular principle in which they are all agreed." An American observer might object to such a description. We are probably willing to concede that in a political party people are uniting to form an organization, and that the purpose is in some way to promote the national interest, although we oftentimes get the impression, especially at the height of an election campaign, that the national interest allegedly demands merely that Mr. X, candidate of party Y, be given the support of the voters and then all will be well. But the "particular principle in which they are all agreed" is a point that most Americans would question, for the American party system allows persons of all philosophies, conservative and liberal, to find a home in one and the same party, thus illustrating former Governor George Wallace's contention that there is not "a dime's worth of difference" between Republicans and Democrats. Some of the reasons for this are historic. Others have to do with the fact that American politics are very pragmatic and that both major parties have at one time or another been on various sides of the same issue.

The European situation is quite dissimilar. Even if differences between Christian-oriented and Socialist parties in a particular country are becoming somewhat blurred in the last part of the twentieth century, their history and the hard core of their adherents strongly emphasize certain basic distinctive principles and goals. Moreover, because under the rules of a parliamentary system the party in power has the votes to get its legislative proposals passed and party discipline usually forces the members to support the platform and the wishes of the leadership, it is assumed that at least a large part of the party's election program will be enacted into law. Therefore the program which is presented to the voters is far more meaningful than the American political catalog of promises no one really expects to see realized. Perhaps more importantly, representatives elected as members of a certain party are expected to show loyalty and support for the party's position. Unless one believes in the program, one had better not become a deputy on that particular ticket. In other words, there must indeed be agreement, not merely on getting members of that party elected to office, but also on the policy to be pursued after the election.

With this in mind, let us now take a closer look at the political parties of the five countries under discussion. Political systems are sometimes classified by how many parties play an important part in the political process. A rather splintered society may be reflected in the multiplicity of its political groups. Some of these parties must somehow get together to form a coalition to make a viable government possible. In other countries, there may be just two major parties, one governing and the other opposing, until a change in the mood of the electorate reverses the roles. Elsewhere, one party functions, usually because any opposition is prohibited by law.

These basic systems are frequently found with various modifications. In the Federal Republic of Germany as well as in Austria there are two main parties, but in addition there is a small one which is consistently able to elect a few deputies to Parliament. Interestingly enough, however, whereas in Germany the minor party has participated in the government most of the time, allying itself first with one major party and then with the other, the Austrians have thus far always excluded their minor party from governmental responsibility.

There is a direct relationship between the way a parliament is elected and the way the seats are allocated. We find two distinctly different election systems. One is the "winner take all" rule, according to which the country is divided into a given number of districts, each of which sends one member to the legislature. Whoever gets the most votes in an area is declared the winner, even if the victory is obtained by the smallest of margins. In the British General Election of October of 1974, the seat in one Scottish constituency went to the Scottish Nationalist candidate, who received 15,551 votes. The Conservatives obtained 15,529 votes, Labour 15,122, and Liberals 3,626. A plurality of 22 votes (31.2 percent) was sufficient to assure victory. This is a very simple system and the winner is easily determined. It is used in the United States, in Britain, and in a modified way in France.

But the system also leads to injustices. In the above example, 68.8 percent of the voters were unable to get their choice elected. In the same election, the Liberal party received 18.3 percent of the total vote cast in Britain; yet it managed to obtain only 13 out of 635 seats. Because of such situations, this method is not particularly popular on the European continent. Of the countries under discussion, only the Federal Republic of Germany employs this system. Even here, however, only one-half of the members of the *Bundestag* are chosen in single member districts, while in the last analysis it is the percentage of votes received by each party that determines the number of seats allocated to it.

The alternative to this winner-take-all system is that of proportional representation. Although there are numerous variations of this method, its main characteristic is that not one but a number of seats are at stake in a given area and these seats are given to the individual parties approximately in proportion to the total number of votes polled. Thus in the Austrian parliamentary elections of 1971, three parties obtained 50.0 percent, 43.1 percent, and 5.5 percent of the total vote respectively and were allocated 93, 80, and ten seats in the 183-member Parliament. The personal choice of representative is much more a matter for the party rather than for the voter to decide, but this system certainly makes for fairer party representation. However, it also encourages splinter groups and may result in a legislature split into so many different directions that it makes the formation of a government based on a parliamentary majority exceedingly difficult and at times perhaps even impossible. This is why proportional representation is often blamed for having contributed to, if not caused, the downfall of the Weimar Republic.

Switzerland, however, is a good example of proportional representation having the opposite effect. Three major parties, Catholics, Radicals, and Socialists, each can usually obtain the support of about one quarter of the voters. The People's party appeals to another one eighth, while the remainder of the population supports Liberals, Communists, Independents, and others. This situation could (and has) easily result in near-chaos elsewhere. In Switzerland, however, changes of more than two or three seats per party are unlikely in an election, so that a distribution of seats along certain patterns is almost taken for granted, and the party standing in Parliament remains fairly constant from election to election. Moreover, the government is based on a coalition which survives the election contests and represents the four major groups in approximately the ratio of their popular support. The net result is the kind of stability that one usually associates with Switzerland: its governmental structure and political system seem to have the strength of the Swiss currency and almost that of the Swiss Alps.

The Weimar Republic was based on the democratic philosophy that all popular views should be heard. This led to a multiparty system which displayed many undesirable characteristics. At one time, more than thirty different parties competed in national elections and a large number of them obtained seats in the *Reichstag*. The result was chaos, especially since the Communists on the one side and the Nazis and other extreme nationalist groups on the other could agree only on their hostility toward the democratic republic. Forming a government had always been far from easy because it had to be built on the cooperation of several parties; in the end it proved impossible when pro-Weimar forces could not muster a majority. The country went from emergency legislation under a democratic chancellor to the dictatorial measures of Adolf Hitler.

It was understandable, therefore, that observers viewed with apprehension the political situation in the Federal Republic after World War II. Would the chaos be repeated? In 1953, as many as nineteen different groups received votes in the election of the second *Bundestag*. However, ten of these received fewer than one hundred thousand votes; six got less than ten thousand votes and therefore need not be taken seriously. Five parties secured representation in Parliament, as compared with ten in the 1949 elections. Measurable support for minor parties was decreasing, and has decreased steadily ever since. In 1969, the much-feared success of the right-wing NPD, the National Democratic party, did not materialize and even the liberal Free Democrats seemed near demise, for they garnered only 5.8 percent of the vote, with at least 5 percent being necessary for continued representation. But support among the electorate for the Free Democrats increased to more than 8 percent in the parliamentary elections of 1972. The party has done quite well in contests for state legislatures since that time, so that announcements of the death of the FDP seem to be premature.

Yet the Free Democrats are the only third party represented in the *Bundestag* if we count the Christian "union" groups, the CDU and the CSU, as one parliamentary unit, which for all practical purposes they are. The confused conditions of the Weimar Republic have not been repeated so far. Until 1969 the trend was in the direction of a two-party system. Whether or not this tendency has been halted or merely temporarily postponed, only time can tell. In any event, the Federal Republic today has something that may be called a two-and-a-quarter party system. It is more like a two- rather than a multiparty system because the third party is so small. Also, with the exception of 1957–61 when the CDU had an absolute majority and did not need the FDP, and of 1966–69 when the two major parties formed the Grand Coalition, the FDP was a junior partner participant in every government. In eight parliaments, its strength varied between sixty-seven and thirty; yet most of the time this was just enough to make it a needed ally whose support in a coalition created a workable parliamentary majority.

When the Christian parties and the Socialists joined forces in 1966 to exclude the FDP, the latter felt betrayed. This resentment manifested itself in the Free Democrats' willingness to work with the Socialists in 1969. That year the precise character of the post-election coalition could not be predicted until the votes were counted and not even then, as Mr. Nixon's ill-advised congratulatory telegram to the CDU indicated. What was clear, however, was that unless the CDU and the SPD could work out an agreement, the FDP would have to be taken into the government by one of the two major parties. In this way, the Free Democrats resumed their role as minority partner, even though on this occasion they joined a newly discovered friend, the SPD.

The FDP image, during most of the period since the establishment of the Federal Republic, has been that of a small but essential ally of one or the other of the major parties. A vote for the FDP was in a sense a vote for the government coalition. For this reason it may be argued that even with a third party in Parliament, the voters have in essence the choice that is characteristic of a two-party system, namely to decide whether they want the existing government to continue or whether they want to throw it out in favor of a large, viable opposition party which can present alternative programs and principles.

The Austrian experience is also of the two-and-one-quarter variety, with one very important qualification. The Freedom party probably has more staying power and its future seems more certain. Even its lowest numerical showing has given it six seats in the national parliament and the *Freiheitliche Partei* has never fallen below that figure. In 1971, it took a little over twenty-four thousand votes to elect a deputy and the Freedom party had close to a quarter of a million supporters. Its existence has never really been threatened to the extent to which the FDP has had to fight for its political life in the German Federal Republic.

But in Austria, the FPO, by never having been associated with any of the major parties, offers the voters a definite third alternative. At least, this is the case in theory, for in practice no one expects the party to have enough strength to carry on a government by itself. However, unlike the West German Free Democrats, the *Freiheitlichen* have never as yet been a junior partner to anyone. Until 1966, the Grand Coalition of the two major Austrian parties governed jointly, which left the small third force out in the cold. When the alliance did break up, the People's party had an absolute majority in Parliament, so that it did not need to rely on anyone. The situation was different, however, when the absolute majority was lost four years later and the Socialists came up with the largest block of delegates in Parliament but without a majority. Talk of a coalition was again in the air. The FPO might well have entered the government under a Socialist chancellor, had it not vehemently forsworn such a possibility earlier. Consequently, the Socialists formed a minority government by themselves. The Freedom party, while not participating in the administration, did support the government on a number of issues. Both the reform of the election law that increased the number of deputies and the move to hold an early election in 1971 met with the approval of the *Freiheitlichen* because these measures were to their advantage, or at least seemed so at the time. During the 1971 campaign, a future SPO/FPO coalition was a distinct possibility. One diplomat went as far as to seek a parliamentary seat on the FPO list in the hope of becoming foreign minister. When the coalition did not materialize because of the Socialist sweep, he decided not to claim his seat but return to his embassy instead. Once more the pattern was repeated and the FPO remained outside of the government.

These circumstances might change one day. The FPO may well become attached to one of the major parties as a junior partner. The *Freiheitlichen* have in recent years acquired a much more moderate image and are therefore much more acceptable by the others as a potential coalition partner. The party is certainly not now the pan-German, nationalistic, anti-Jewish movement which it was accused of being in the past. It still has the reputation of harboring more former Nazis than the other parties, but it seems to support the concept of an independent, democratic Austria, perhaps more because it is a political fact of life than for philosophic reasons. While more right-wing than the other parties, it has moved considerably toward the center and is no longer too far out to make impossible any cooperation with others. In terms of statistics, we have the same two-major-parties-plus-one-small-party situation that characterizes West Germany, the difference being, however, that in the Federal Republic the minor party has, except for the two periods mentioned, continually been a junior partner in the government, while in Austria the *Freiheitlichen* have never yet had the opportunity of holding office in a national administration.

Liechtenstein, on the other hand, presents us with a classic example of a two-party system. The country is so small and homogeneous that even the slogan "For God, Prince and Fatherland" is shared by both parties. Their names, *Fortschrittliche Bürgerpartei* (Progressive People's party) and *Vaterländische Union* (Patriotic Union), indicate little philosophic difference. Even their nicknames, "Blacks" and "Reds," refer to early leanings toward connections with church and labor respectively. These distinctions have no practical meaning today when parentage, family background, and personalities, in addition to some pragmatic considerations, largely dominate party affiliations.

Under these circumstances, the arrival of a third party on the political scene seems somewhat unusual, especially when the third party did not basically disagree with the other two. It appealed mainly to disgruntled personalities, people who for personal reasons felt that neither of the existing parties could provide them with a political home. Its election successes were somewhat less than spectacular. Although receiving about 10 percent of the total vote in the elections of 1962 and 1966, the Christian Social party was unable to obtain a single seat in the *Landtag*. In 1970, it offered only two candidates to the electorate and polled a total of sixty-five votes, which confirmed its insignificance. Only once before since the end of World War II, in 1953, had a minor party appeared and it had not made much of an impact. Surely this proves the existence of a two-party system in the truest sense of the term. It provides us with an even more clear-cut model than does Britain, which is usually cited as the best-known example of a two-party system but where recently several minor parties received the support of one quarter of the electorate even if their representation in Parliament remained quite small. Despite their lack of success, quite a few political groupings usually vie for the voter's attention in Britain; in the general elections of October 1974, there was not a single constituency in which fewer than three candidates appeared on the ballot. In little Liechtenstein, relatively few attempts are made to go beyond the established two parties.

Since there are fifteen seats in the *Landtag*, a two-party system must arithmetically result in one party having an absolute majority. One might expect that in a parliamentary arrangement one party will govern and the other will oppose. This at any rate is the custom in Britain, in West Germany, and since 1966 in Austria. But in Liechtenstein, under the mounting threat of the Nazis in the 1930s the two parties chose to forget their differences and formed a coalition, even suspending the holding of elections until the war ended. When normal political contests could be resumed after Hitler's downfall, the coalition government was continued with the majority party providing the prime minister and the minority the vice-premier. This pattern prevails to this day. Yet the alliance of the two parties has not necessarily carried over into parliamentary life, where arguments between the parties and even between the *Regierungschef* and the minority party at times become quite heated. *Co-opposition,* the local term, neatly describes the present situation.

The final system to be examined is basically a one-party regime, but once again modifications are apparent. In Nazi Germany only one party was allowed to function. Similarly in the Soviet Union the Communist party alone "is the vanguard of the working people in their struggle to build communist society and is the leading core of all organizations of the working people, both government and nongovernment," according to Article 126 of the 1936 Soviet Constitution. Any opposition to the party would be regarded as detrimental to the interests of the people. The same philosophy prevails in practice in Communist-dominated East Germany, although in theory some other parties are permitted to exist as long as they abide by Communist orders.

It will be recalled that the Soviet Union, like the other occupying powers, licensed a few political parties in its zone in the mid-1940s. These parties were required to be "democratic" and "anti-Fascist" and by Soviet standards the Communist party met these qualifications. Obviously the USSR had high hopes for its protegés, but these hopes were not fulfilled. Few Germans were willing to support the Communists on election day. Immediately after the end of the war, the Socialists had joined the Communists in the Soviet zone in calling for socialization of certain basic industries and for a united front of the working classes. Strange as it may seem, the Social Democrats took the lead in both these moves. At first the concept of a united party was rejected by Communist leader Walter Ulbricht. But as the Communists in Eastern Europe proved unable to win election successes and as the Socialists gained the favor of many German voters in local elections as a democratic independent party, the East German Communists began to clamor for merger. This was strongly opposed by West German Socialists under Kurt Schumacher, but under pressure from Soviet authorities it became a reality in the Soviet zone. In this way the Socialist Unity party was born. Socialists and Communists were supposed to work together on the basis of complete parity, but it was not long before the Communists gained the upper hand.

It has been pointed out that this merger was partly forced and partly voluntary.[1] It was forced because the Soviets insisted on it without consulting the rank and file. When the enrolled members of the SPD were consulted in a referendum, the Soviets prohibited the vote in their part of Berlin. In the three Western zones, more than 70 percent of those eligible opted for close cooperation between the two parties but 82 percent voted against merger. But a case can also be made for the union having been concluded voluntarily, since, despite Schumacher's strong pleading against such a move, Otto Grotewohl and the majority of the Socialist leaders in the Eastern zone agreed to the merger. After both parties held party conferences in April of 1946, a joint meeting was arranged which named Wilhelm Pieck and Otto Grotewohl by acclamation the presidents of the *Sozialistische Einheitspartei.*

The original parity in the distribution of leadership positions was eventually discontinued, since it allegedly stressed old and outdated divisions and held back younger, capable elements. The Soviet Union made the party do its bidding. Consequently, the SED was organized along Soviet lines. Included in its structure was a Politburo and a Secretariat, whose head, as in the USSR, became East Germany's most powerful personality. Like the Communist party in the Soviet Union, the SED departed from the original concept of a mass party. Beginning in 1948, the *Einheitspartei* underwent a face-lifting operation. It proclaimed itself a "party of a new type," namely one that provides leadership. Like its mirror image in the Soviet Union, the party is now deliberately aiming at a small, elite membership and considers itself a cadre party which supplies the leadership and the leaders themselves for all walks of life.

To complicate matters further and to illustrate the extent to which this one-party system strays from the model, it must be recorded that in addition to the Socialist Unity party there are today four other parties in existence in the DDR that supposedly operate as individual entities and that are also represented in the *Volkskammer,* or People's Chamber, East Germany's unicameral Parliament. These include two older parties which were founded immediately after the war, the *Christlich Demokratische Union* (CDU) and the LDP, the *Liberaldemokratische Partei,* which are equivalent to the CDU and the Free Democrats in the Federal Republic. In addition, two more parties, the *Demokratische Bauernpartei* (DBD), which supposedly looks after the interests of the agricultural population, and the NDPD, the *Nationaldemo-kratische Partei,* were established in 1948 for the avowed purpose of taking care of various sections not attracted by the other political groups. These four plus the SED make up the five parties represented in the *Volkskammer* and provide a rather ironic contrast with West Germany, where under conditions of free competition only two major and one minor parties have in recent years found their way into the *Bundestag.*

That the greater variety of parties in the DDR should not be taken seriously as exponents of diversified viewpoints can be shown by the facts that the SED has by agreement more seats than any two of the other parties combined and that the number of seats each party occupies has not varied in the slightest as a result of recent elections. Indeed, elections have nothing to do with party representation in the *Volkskammer.* The chamber also contains additional representatives from the Free Labor Unions, the Women's Organization, and the Free German Youth, all of which are Communist dominated. A one-party state is clearly in operation, no matter how hard the East Germans try to create a different impression. The precise allocation of seats is determined by consent prior to polling day. All five parties are part of a United Front which is not engaged in political competition. It goes without saying that the leadership of the four smaller parties lacks any real independence of action but faithfully carries out the directions of the Communists, who in effect have full control over country, people, and government.

When elections did take place on a competitive basis in the Eastern zone in September of 1946, the SED received 57.1 percent of the vote. In view of the presence of Soviet armies and because of the pressure applied, it is remarkable that 21.1 percent of the population actually voted for the LDP and 18.8 percent for the CDU, and this in a part of Germany where socialism had always been quite strong. A month later, local elections brought the SED only 47.5 percent of the voters' support. It is understandable, then, why the Communists forced the non-Socialist parties into a United Front which assigned them a minor, subordinate part in the total structure. But this still does not quite explain why the pretence continues to this day. Why, with all existing parties committed to the broad Socialist goals of the regime, do they still exist as separate entities?

The answer is somewhat complex. All parties in the DDR are part of the United Front as far as the electorate is concerned and as such present no alternatives to the voters. Together they receive an overwhelming expression of confidence at every election. In all probability the individual parties will not be permitted to exist indefinitely. Their status seems relatively temporary, to last until such time as greater unity and the disappearance of all class differences makes them dispensable. In the meantime, these parties act not only as transmission agencies for those parts of the population with which the SED has relatively little contact; "they also add a certain amount of flexibility to the system by passing on to the government the thoughts and interests of particular circles of the population, the disregard of which could lead to difficulties and conflict."[2] Originally, each party was to attract certain sections of society. Since the SED could not be expected to appeal to ardent followers of the Christian churches, the CDU was retained. Similarly, the Peasant party, the DBD, was to look after the interests of the farmers. Professor Heidenheimer suggests that with small businesses and farms no longer in private hands, the elements which these parties were originally supposed to represent had no further part to play in society, and he also expresses the view that "presumably their utility lies in providing educational and feedback mechanism for those ex-bourgeois strata which the SED cannot reach."[3]

This lip service to a nonexistent multiparty system is a rather interesting phenomenon especially when, a quarter of a century after the war ended, reference was still being made in an East German publication to the apparent necessity of having the National Democratic party appealing to "former nominal members of the Nazi party, former officers and professional soldiers of the Hitler army who have drawn the correct lesson of the past."[4] Such an acknowledgement sounds strange, apparently not only to us, for another edition of the same book published five years later omits the passage and characterizes the NDPD thus:

Most of its members are craftsmen, retail traders and intellectual workers. This party has done much to make sure that the sections it represents make an active contribution to the country's policy of peace and socialism.[5]

It goes on to praise the Democratic Bloc, which is composed of the four parties plus trade union, women's, and youth organizations:

The cooperation has played a major role in the years of socialist construction. Its purpose is to take all important steps toward the building of a new society in common and to shoulder responsibility together as well.'. . . There is no opposition in the GDR because the fundamental interests of all classes and strata are the same. It is, indeed, inconceivable because it could only be directed against common interests.[6]

In other words, there may be a number of different parties, but they all have the same principles and purposes. They exist to lend support to the ruling groups, not to provide opposition or alternatives. It is for this reason that we have classified the German Democratic Republic as having a one-party system. If George Wallace were living in the DDR, his remark about "not a dime's worth of difference" between the parties would be amply justified —except he would be severely punished for saying so!

8

The Communist Parties

On looking more closely at the political parties of these five countries, we can frequently detect certain basic philosophic similarities which are not confined by boundaries. Although a political party with real hopes of governing must be pragmatic enough to be able to cater to the particular circumstances and peculiarities of its own people, it nevertheless may well display an affinity with the ideologies of parties in other countries. This is especially true of the Communist party, although now not as much as it was in Stalin's days. With the defection of Yugoslavia from the Russian orbit and with China developing its own peculiar brand, Communist party organizations throughout the world have developed unheard-of independence and even have begun, to a greater or lesser degree, to criticize the Soviet Union itself. Some of them did this quite vehemently after the Russian intervention in Czechoslovakia in 1968. Nevertheless, there is general agreement among Communists on such vital matters as opposition to capitalism of the American variety. Communists also believe in the nationalization of the basic means of production, in the welfare state, and in the right of the colonial peoples throughout Asia and Africa to be independent and free from "Western imperialism." In France and Italy, they have become very strong political forces which from time to time make determined bids for inclusion in the government. Their influence in most of the Germanic countries is negligible.

The only exception is of course the German Democratic Republic. The Communist party there operates under the aegis of the Soviet authorities, even though Red Army occupation ended some time ago. At the beginning of that occupation, the Russians tried to establish conditions which, they felt, would make it easy for the Communists to gain public favor. When this effort failed, the Socialist Unity party was created, in which any claimed parity between Communists and Social Democrats soon proved a sham. A resolution adopted by the First SED Party Congress on January 28, 1949, mentions the development of the *Einheitspartei* into a "party of a new type." Calling the merger of Communists and Socialists "the most important event in the recent history of the German Labor Movement," the resolution stated that former ideological differences between the two parties had largely disappeared and that instead numerous new forces had sprung up inside the new party which did not belong to either of the two old ones. As a result, the SED claimed to be developing into a Marxist-Leninist fighting party, the conscious and organized vanguard of the working classes, and the highest form of class organization of the proletariat. Furthermore, the party stressed that it was based on the principle of democratic centralism, strengthened through the struggle against opportunism, and filled with the spirit of internationalism.

This pronouncement emphasized the leadership concept of the party, a concept that is underlined time and again in various statements by party officials and party organs. Within the SED, the Communists prevail. Within the United Front, the SED has the upper hand. For practical purposes, the other parties are mere tools for the Communists. David Childs tellingly refers to the CDU in the DDR as "establishment Christians," the LDP as "Marxian Liberals," and the DBD as "Socialist farmers."[1] No matter how one slices it, it is red inside.

The obvious pressure the Soviets needed to exert to develop the Communists as the predominant power in East Germany makes it easy to understand that communism is rather weak in the rest of the German-speaking area. In the days of Weimar, the Communist party was a relatively important force, receiving between 9 and 17 percent of the popular vote in seven parliamentary elections between 1924 and 1933. After the Second World War, the Communists obtained the backing of their supporters who had somehow survived the Nazi regime while remaining faithful to the Communist creed. In addition, they recruited those who admired the Soviet Union or who were in other ways attracted to the extreme Marxist position.

In 1948–49 the Parliamentary Council of sixty-five members drew the blueprint for a new constitution in the Western zones.

Table 3. Communist Support in German Elections

Reichstag:	Year	Percent of vote	Number of seats	
	1920	2.0	4	
	1924 (May)	12.6	62	
	1924 (Dec.)	9.0	45	
	1928	10.6	54	
	1930	13.1	77	
	1932 (July)	14.6	89	
	1932 (Nov.)	16.9	100	
	1933	12.3	81	
Bundestag:				
	1949	5.7	15	*
	1953	2.2	0	*
	1957	0	0	no candidates
	1961	1.9	0	**
	1965	1.3	0	**
	1969	0.6	0	***
	1972	0.3	0	****
	1976	0.3	0	****

Votes Received by Ernst Thälmann, Communist, for President

March 1925	7.0%	1.8 million	
April 1925	6.4%	1.9 million	
March 1932	13.2%	5.0 million	
April 1932	10.2%	3.7 million	

In the *Bundestag* elections, the Communists attracted votes under these labels:
*Kommunistische Partei Deutschlands (Communist Part of Germany) KPD
**Deutsche Friedensunion (German Peace Union) DFU
***Aktion Demokratischer Freiheit (Action of Democratic Freedom) ADF
****Deutsche Kommunistische Partei (German Communist Party) DKP

This council, which reflected the party composition in the various *Land* Parliaments at the time, included two Communists who joined ten others in rejecting what became the Basic Law of the German Federal Republic. In the first parliamentary elections since the war, the Communists received 1.4 million votes out of 23.7 million for a total of 5.7 percent of the votes cast. On the basis of this strength, they were allocated 15 of the 402 seats in the *Bundestag*. The next election in 1953, however, found their support halved. They were now favored by a mere 610,000 people, or 2.2 percent of the participants. Under the so-called Five Percent Clause, this deprived them of any representation in Parliament. They have not been able to get representation since, although it is interesting to note that had the election formula of the Weimar Republic still been in effect, they would have been entitled to 11 deputies. But now the government utilized Article 21 of the Basic Law which states:

> Parties which, by reason of their aims or the behavior of their adherents, seek to impair or abolish the free democratic basic order or to endanger the existence of the Federal Republic of Germany, shall be unconstitutional.

The matter was taken to the Constitutional Court where it dragged on for several years. Finally, in August 1956, a verdict was handed down prohibiting the party.

It is debatable whether or not it was wise to prevent the party from functioning by obtaining a court order against it. Support for communism was obviously declining. Its strongest showing in 1949 was in the industrial Solingen-Remscheid district where it received 21 percent of the vote; in 1953 this was reduced to 12 percent. In *Land* elections it fell in Bremen from 11 percent in 1946 to 5 percent in 1955; in Hesse, from 10.7 percent in 1946 to 3.4 percent in 1954; in North Rhine-Westphalia, from 14 percent in 1947 to 3.8 percent in 1954. The question may therefore justifiably be raised whether it would not have been much better to see the party defeated by popular verdict in free elections rather than making martyrs of them through judicial action. Depriving the Communists of a place on the ballot enabled them to accuse Bonn of being antidemocratic.

Be that as it may, the KPD, the *Kommunistische Partei Deutschlands,* was driven out of existence for more than a decade. Attempts to attract votes under such labels as German Peace Union or Action of Democratic Freedom failed; electoral support was simply not forthcoming. Then in 1967 the ministers of the interior in the various *Länder* came to the conclusion that the founding of a new Communist party could not be opposed and it was duly resurrected under the name of *Deutsche Kommunistische Partei,* DKP. However, its showing has not improved. In the parliamentary elections of November 1972, the Communists received only 114,000 out of the almost 38 million votes cast. In 1976, their total share of the vote again amounted to a mere 0.3 percent. Thus regardless of the name it uses, the Communist party is not a viable force in West German politics. This is quite understandable when one considers that the building of the Iron Curtain by the DDR along its western border and the erection of the Berlin Wall separated many Germans from their immediate families. This consideration is quite apart from the tales of horror that are still told by some Germans of their encounters with incoming Russian troops toward the end of the war. The Communists in West Germany would be hard pressed to win any popularity contest.

The fate of the Communist party in Austria is also characterized by decline, although it made a determined campaign in the 1971 parliamentary elections and almost succeeded in being represented in the legislature. A few hundred more votes in Vienna and this would have been achieved. Any complete disregard of the Communists would therefore be unwise; however, success again eluded them in 1975. Even if Communists were to return to the *Nationalrat* their number would most likely be small.

But they did play a significant part in Austria immediately after the collapse of the Third Reich. In the spring of 1945 Karl Renner negotiated with the Russians regarding the establishment of a provisional government. Under these circumstances the role of the Communists was obviously important. Some of them had been living in exile in the Soviet Union and arrived in Austria as soon as it was safe to do so. They and the Russians had high hopes that they would take charge. One prominent figure, former Austrian journalist Ernst Fischer, immediately declared himself strongly in favor of an Austrian national identity, an idea which had become quite popular.

Fischer was named state secretary of education in the new government and another Communist, Franz Honner, took over the ministry of interior, an office of special importance in Europe because it is responsible for the police. There were ten Communists in this first provisional administration, along with thirteen members of the People's party, twelve Socialists, and four Independents. No one could foretell the support the Communists would receive at the polls, but 30 percent did not seem an unreasonable estimate. The results of the November elections therefore came as quite a shock to the Communists when they received only 174,000 votes out of 3,217,000 cast. Their 5.4 percent share netted them four seats in the 165-member Parliament.

This was the end of the ministerial career of Ernst Fischer. In the meantime, the new government under Chancellor Leopold Figl contained exactly one Communist, Dr. Karl Altmann, who held the not too crucial portfolio of minister of electrification and energy for two years until his lone dissenting vote on currency reform legislation led to his departure from the cabinet. Despite occasional camouflage under such labels as "Left Bloc" or "People's Opposition," Communist strength in the *Nationalrat* never amounted to much and eventually disappeared altogether, as shown by Table 4.

If the Austrian Communists today look at their party as a cadre party which supplies leadership rather than as a mass movement, this may well be a case of making a virtue out of necessity. For clearly they do not have a widespread appeal, and this lack of support applies not only to the conservative, Catholic countryside. Despite the deep-seated left-wing convictions of some working-class elements in the population, the Russian occupation of the eastern part of Austria is still vivid in people's memories. The booming economy supports the claim that postwar Austria has had fewer industrial unrests and strikes than any other part of the Capitalist world. Surely, these are circumstances which are not conducive to support for communism.

If there is one country that does not have to worry at all about communism, it is Liechtenstein. Indeed, there is no Left nor much

Table 4. Communist Support in Austrian Parliamentary Elections

Date	Total vote cast	Percent of total vote	Number of seats won
November 1945	174,000	5.4	4
October 1949	213,000*	5.1	5
February 1953	228,000**	5.3	4
May 1956	192,000	4.4	3
May 1959	143,000	3.3	0
November 1962	136,000	3.0	0
March 1966	19,000	0.4	0
March 1970	45,000	1.0	0
October 1971	62,000	1.4	0
October 1975	55,000	1.2	0

*The votes were cast for the *Linksblock* (Left Bloc)
**The votes were cast for the *Volksopposition* (People's Opposition)

of a Right either in that country. The term *Left* originated with the French Revolution, when most revolutionary and antimonarchist elements in the French Assembly sat to the left of the presiding officer. It is in the sense of being radical and revolutionary that the term is used today, while *Right* connotes the opposite, i.e., authoritarianism, distrust of popular control, and reaction, which may in itself be a radical departure from the existing norms. Of course, these terms are relative and must be viewed in their proper perspective as to time and country. In the original meaning of the words, Left and Right do not exist in Liechtenstein, although at the height of Hitler's power there was a small but quite vocal Nazi extremist minority who dutifully echoed all pan-German, anti-Jewish outcries from Berlin. All that is left of this today are the yellowing pages of the Nazi newspaper *Umbruch,* carefully preserved at the *Landesbibliothek* in Liechtenstein's capital city. How extreme this journal was can be seen from the fact that in 1943, when Hitler was still quite a menace across the border, the Liechtenstein government prohibited its further publication because of the insults it had heaped on the government of neighboring Switzerland.

All this is long forgotten. If Hitler's early successes created a small Nazi movement in Liechtenstein, there was no such incentive for communism. The country is homogeneous, so much so that its two parties are both oriented toward Christian values and social progress and most people feel quite at home in either political group. It was therefore quite annoying for politicians of both parties when the new party in the 1960s took the name Christian Social. Although the nicknames Black and Red allude to some rather "ancient" relationships to Austrian conservatives and Swiss socialists respectively, this is merely of historic interest. One prominent statesman told this writer that industrialism has been achieved without socialism ever appearing on Liechtenstein soil. Industrialization came late, and when it came it was not accompanied by the distress and misery usually associated with its early phases. Therefore there was no need for radical left-wing parties. Before the appearance of the Christian Socials a third party got on the ballot only once. In 1953 the *Unselbständig Erwerbende und Kleinbauern (Arbeiterpartei)* clearly aimed at the support of the employees, the small peasants and workers, though even here the appeal apparently was more along bourgeois rather than proletarian lines. In any case, its poor showing of 198 votes out of 2,892 cast must have been disheartening, for the party seems to have disappeared. Even a halfhearted reference to the class struggle is misdirected in Liechtenstein.

A similar statement cannot be made about Switzerland. Industrialization did bring about sharp conflicts, perhaps best illustrated in the General Strike of 1918. In other Western European countries, such as Britain and Germany, around the turn of the century, the working classes in increasing numbers found the more bourgeois parties less and less to their satisfaction and turned to class parties of their own. These groupings maintained a certain solidarity with their comrades abroad through the connection of the First and Second Internationals. World War I strained this relationship, for the workers generally put national loyalties before international class interest and willingly and often enthusiastically went to war at the command of their governments. Switzerland presented a somewhat different situation because its government pursued a policy of neutrality, but here too the workers' party, the Social Democrats, agreed to the *Burgfrieden,* an understanding to seek security within the national boundaries through cooperation with the administration and the other parties. Still there were exceptions, and Lenin, living in exile in Zürich at that time, was able to find support among his Swiss friends for the Zimmerwald program which called for an international civil war between the revolutionary proletariat on the one side and the bourgeoisie and monarchies who were waging war among themselves on the other.

However, it was the seizure of power in Russia by the radical Bolsheviks that led to a deep and permanent split within the working-class movement, for the founding of the communist-inspired Third International forced various factions of the proletariat in the individual countries to decide whether or not they wanted to join the group of extremists and revolutionaries. The Zimmerwald spirit became quite popular among the Socialist leaders of Switzerland, and they were ready to join the Third International and its Bolshevik adherents. But the rank and file opposed this by overwhelming majorities, and thus the scene was set for the development of two Swiss parties, the Social Democrats and the Communists.

Since the birth of its party in 1921 Swiss communism has been closely tied to the Soviet Union. This fact, together with a radical program in a basically conservative country, condemned it to almost certain smallness. In the 1970s this program speaks of "the complete political and economic liberation of the workers through the elimination of capitalism and the establishment first of socialism and then of communism," an endeavor which is guided by the "teachings of scientific socialism, the Marxism-Leninism."[2]

Adherents of this philosophy are fairly hard to find. Still, they do exist, especially in Zürich, urban Basel, and the non-German-speaking cantons. A handful of Communists sat regularly in the *Nationalrat,* the popularly elected Parliament, though they never did get a foothold in the *Ständerat.* The outbreak of the Second World War and the consequent declaration of neutrality by the Swiss government put the country into a precarious political situation. It was felt that it was too risky for the country's security to allow extreme elements the right to continue free participation in the political process. In 1940 the *Bundesrat* prohibited the radical

Right as well as the radical Left. The latter reappeared several years later after the emergency was over under its present name of *Partei der Arbeit* (Party of Labor or PdA).

Since that time, the party has played a small but consistent part. In eight *Nationalrat* elections since the end of World War II, its strength has varied from seven deputies in 1947 to three in 1959 with four or five on other occasions. Its relative popularity immediately after the end of the war can be traced back to the general esteem in which the Soviet Union found itself as a result

Table 5. Communist Legislative Strength in Switzerland (Since 1944, the name used is *Partei der Arbeit*)

Nationalrat Year	Number of seats won	Total number of seats
1922	2	198
1925	3	198
1928	2	198
1931	2	187
1935	2	187
1939	4*	187
1943		
1947	7	194
1951	5	196
1955	4	196
1959	3	196
1963	4	200
1967	5	200
1971	5	200
1975	4	200

Cantonal Strength of Partei der Arbeit in 1970:

Canton	Number of seats won	Total number of seats
Zürich	2	180
Basel-Town	8	130
Tessin	2	65
Waadt	16	197
Neuenburg	8	115
Genf	18	100

*Federation Socialiste Suisse

of its victory over Hitler's war machine. Not only did fifty thousand voters or 5.1 percent of the total population give their support to the Party of Labor in national elections; the left-wingers did remarkably well in cantonal contests where they managed to capture 36 out of 100 seats in Genf and 31 out of 130 in Basel-Town. Altogether, in five cantons and two half-cantons, where there were 876 seats to be filled, the *Partei der Arbeit* obtained 144 or 16.4 percent.[3] However, such triumphs were short-lived, especially after the Soviet suppression of the Hungarian revolt in the late 1950s. By 1970, the Laborites were represented in six cantonal parliaments where they occupied a modest 54 out of 787 seats, giving them 6.9 percent of the total. This figure seems much smaller when one considers that in all of Switzerland there are 2747 cantonal parliamentary seats. As to membership in the *Nationalrat* in Bern, the leftists between 1971 and 1975 found their representation confined exclusively to the French-speaking parts, with three of them coming from Genf and two from the Waadt. While five deputies may be a small number, it was important for them to retain this amount since it is the minimum necessary for a recognized *Fraktion* with membership on the several commissions. It was therefore quite a blow when, in 1975, the party lost one of its seats that had been occupied by a woman from Genf. But this loss was in part offset by the victory of an autonomous Socialist in Tessin. While it is unlikely that the *Partei der Arbeit* will gain a foothold in the Council of States, a few members of the Party of Labor will probably remain in the popularly elected Parliament for some time without in any way endangering the rule of the middle-of-the-road parties.

9

The Social Democratic Parties

Leaving the Communists in sole possession of "Left field," we turn now to the Social Democrats. Despite a common origin, the differences between the two worker-oriented parties are sharp and fundamental. The Communists still regard Karl Marx as their patron saint, but the Social Democrats have moved considerably away from that position. This became necessary in order to broaden their base among the electorate. The successes at the polls of Willy Brandt and Bruno Kreisky can at least in part be explained by their ability to depart from the threatening image so often associated in the past with the Socialists and with their seemingly never-ending aims at further nationalization and more state ownership.

The Social Democrats usually favor government control of certain basic industries such as coal, transportation, and electricity. They also advocate the welfare state, with government aid to the people when they are old, sick, and unemployed. But as the name implies, the Social Democrats come to power through democratic means, namely through winning parliamentary elections, and they leave office when the people defeat them at the polls. Any laws passed by them go through the usual parliamentary channels and are freely discussed, debated, and voted upon. If the government takes over industries in this way, the owners and shareholders are compensated, in much the same way that an American farmer is compensated when the state exercises eminent domain and takes part of his land for road construction or when a businessman is forced to sell his warehouse for urban renewal. Moreover, democratic socialism never intends to eliminate private enterprise altogether, and there remains ample opportunity for individual private initiative and business motivation. In contrast, communism has forced its ideas on the people under its control, little individual freedom is maintained, and politically no real choice is given to the masses, least of all the choice of alternative political and economic programs. With both Communists and Social Democrats vying for working-class support, their competition in democratic countries tends to be quite vicious and violent.

The genuinely democratic character of the Social Democrats is often misunderstood in the United States, because the term *socialism* means different things in Communist and Social Democratic vocabularies. Within the framework sketched above, socialism is an end in itself for the labor parties of Western Europe. But in Communist jargon, it is merely a stepping stone, coming after the revolution and the dictatorship of the proletariat and before the achievement of ultimate communism. To the Communists the principle of socialism, as mentioned in the current constitutions of both the USSR and the DDR, is "From each according to his abilities, to each according to his work," which the Soviet Constitution of 1936 significantly elaborated as, "He who does not work, neither shall he eat." This is certainly not the creed of James Callaghan in Britain, Bruno Kreisky in Austria, or Willy Brandt and Helmut Schmidt in the German Federal Republic.

As we have already observed, the establishment of the Third International after the Russian Revolution forced Socialist movements throughout the world to decide whether or not they wanted to be associated with the Bolsheviks. Those who rejected extreme methods and goals became the Social Democrats, who at first were still primarily working-class oriented but gradually came to appeal to other groups as well. Whereas the Communists see themselves more and more as an elite, a cadre, a group supplying the leadership for the toiling masses, the Social Democrats have always aimed at forming a mass party. Their most recent triumphs in the Austrian parliamentary elections in 1975, when they received 50.4 percent of the vote and the West German contest in 1976, which gave them the electoral support of 42.6 percent, can be attributed to their appeal to broad sections of the population rather than to one particular class.

The German Social Democrats trace their history back to the late 1840s, when the misery of the Industrial Revolution led to the first organized efforts of the working-class movement. Consisting in the beginning of two distinct parties, they united and formed the Socialist Labor party of Germany in 1875. Because of increasing popularity, they soon became a group to be reckoned with, so much so that Bismarck became afraid of their influence. Using as a pretext an attempt on the life of the emperor in 1878, he pushed legislation through the *Reichstag* dissolving the socialist groups and outlawing their activities. At the same time, in order to divert the workers, he started what was for that era an ambitious program of welfare reform which included old-age, sickness, and accident insurance.

Twelve years of being outlawed could not stop the continuous growth of the party of the workers. After the anti-Socialist legislation was repealed in 1890, the party officially named itself the Social Democratic party of Germany and adopted the so-called Erfurt Program. By 1912, there were 110 Socialists in the *Reichstag,* a figure that increased to 185 and 190 in the early days of Weimar. The decline to 100 in 1924 was undoubtedly due to the split with the Communists. But the Social Democrats played a vital part throughout the life of the Weimar Republic, whose first president they furnished and in a number of whose cabinets they participated. Philipp Scheidemann, Gustav Bauer and Hermann Müller were chancellors at one time or another between 1919 and 1930. At least one-fifth of the voters constantly supported them in parliamentary elections and even the pressure of the Nazis could not prevent 18.3 percent from doing so in the last free contest before the complete takeover by the Nazis in 1933.

We have already mentioned that ninety-four Socialists alone had the courage to oppose Hitler's Enabling Law despite the certainty of Hitler's wrath and bloody revenge. As late as March

23, 1933, almost two months after the Nazis came to power, the Social Democratic spokesman, Otto Wels, opposed the new government from the tribune of the *Reichstag* despite all the threatening and intimidating gestures of the Nazi storm troopers. "In this historic hour," he put his party squarely on record as believing in the "principles of humanity, justice, freedom and socialism." A number of Socialist deputies were already in prison, in hiding, or in exile, and Wels after his speech managed to leave the country just in time to avoid the concentration camps, torture, and death that awaited so many of his colleagues.

With such credentials of anti-Nazi activities and defiance of totalitarianism, though not always employed in the most sensible way, there was little doubt about the right of the Social Democrats to resume their political activities immediately following Hitler's defeat. Some of their leaders had managed to remain in contact with each other during the dictatorship. Several were involved in the abortive attempt on Hitler's life on July 20, 1944. Julius Leber, Wilhelm Leuschner, and others were put to death as a consequence.

After the end of the Third Reich, Kurt Schumacher provided the resurrected Social Democratic party with a fiery leader. While appealing primarily to the factory worker, the small wage earner, and the lower middle classes in town and country, the Socialists tried to continue where they had left off in 1933 through no fault of their own. They were handicapped in that their traditional strongholds were in the East, and thus in the Soviet zone of occupation where left-wing groups were being fused into the SED under Communist leadership. This Schumacher vehemently opposed and prevented in the West. But he fought not only communism; he turned just as strongly against the Western powers and denounced their policy of dismantling German industrial plants and the establishment of closer ties between their zones, because to him this meant creating more obstacles to the eventual reunification of all of Germany. His aims, despite demands for socialization, were quite nationalistic, and they failed to get the widespread support that was hoped for. Nor did they manage to quiet the persistent fears of radicalism and internationalism that Socialist parties seem to be heir to, even though there was no repetition of the vicious charges of treason that had been aimed at Socialists of the Weimar generation.

Schumacher lost an arm on the battlefields of World War I and a leg in a concentration camp. What was left was not much more than a walking corpse, kept alive, it seemed, only by an iron will and a deep-seated commitment to the cause of democratic socialism. When he died in 1952, he was succeeded by the jovial and ineffective Erich Ollenhauer as party leader. Although the election showings of the Socialists soon reached the 30 percent mark and, except for 1953, consistently increased, and although they were the predominant party in some of the states and many of the cities, their strength until 1972 was always second to that of the CDU/ CSU. Thus in 1957, while winning over an additional 3 percent of the population, they had to watch their more conservative rivals garnering 50.2 percent of the vote, the one and only time in German parliamentary history that a single party received an absolute majority.

One reason the Socialists were kept in second place, apparently on a permanent basis, was the overpowering personality of their great opponent Konrad Adenauer, who could not be vanquished by anything but old age. With his retirement, one major obstacle to the eventual success of the Socialists was removed. But this in itself was not enough. Two other factors first had to appear: Bad Godesberg and Willy Brandt.

In 1959, at a party congress in Bad Godesberg, the Social Democratic party ceased to be a class-oriented workers' party and became, in its own words, "a party of the people." It declared that democratic socialism in Europe was rooted in "Christian ethics, in humanism, and in classical philosophy," and did not claim to proclaim absolute truths because of its respect for the different human creeds "which neither a political party nor the state has a right to determine." The conference professed its faith in free competition and free initiative by entrepreneurs as important elements of its economic policy and came up with the slogan "Competition as much as possible, planning whenever necessary." These were significant moves away from any narrow basis of orientation. Henceforth the SPD aimed not merely at attracting working-class elements but the broad masses of people in all walks of life, thus paving the way for election successes made later.

Meanwhile, there was the question of leadership. As the 1961 elections approached, the Socialists looked for a new and more dynamic candidate for chancellor and found him in the person of Willy Brandt. His position as mayor of Berlin had given him wide and favorable publicity as being strongly anti-Communist, although his illegitimate birth and his having worn a Norwegian uniform when the Germans were at war with that country resulted in unfavorable comments from certain quarters. With Brandt as their leader, the Socialists gained in 1961 and again in 1965, but both times fell short of overtaking the Christian union parties.

While nothing succeeds like success, nothing fails like failure, and after two unsuccessful attempts, Willy Brandt's leadership seemed in danger. Fortunately for him, Chancellor Ludwig Erhard faced difficulties in his own CDU/SCU and with his small FDP coalition partners. After protracted negotiations Erhard resigned and the *Bundestag* elected Kurt Georg Kiesinger as chancellor. The new cabinet contained ten Christian Democrats and nine Social Democrats, including Willy Brandt as vice-chancellor and foreign minister.

Not since 1930 had Socialists participated in a German cabinet and the Grand Coalition gave them two things they needed, experience and respectability. In this way they were able to present an entirely different image to the voters when the next electoral contest was held in 1969. No longer outcasts but instead armed with the insight about the ways of government, they were able to top the 40 percent mark of popular support for the first time. Their 42.7 percent share of the vote gave them 224 seats as compared with 39.3 percent for 201 seats four years earlier. True, the CDU/CSU with 46.1 percent and 242 seats still presented the largest single block in the *Bundestag,* but they had lost voters, percentage points, and seats. After some uncertainty, the new government was formed by the SPD in cooperation with the FDP. At long last, a Social Democrat was chancellor, and in the following election in 1972, Willy Brandt widened the support of his coalition and the SPD became the largest single party in the *Bundestag.* It had 17 million votes, 45.8 percent of the total, and 230

Table 6. Social Democratic Strength in Germany

	Year	Seats won	Percent of vote
Imperial Reichstag:	1871	2	3.2
	1874	9	6.8
	1877	12	9.1
	1878	9	7.5
	1881	12	6.1
	1884	24	9.7
	1887	11	7.2
	1890	35	19.7
	1893	44	23.3
	1898	56	27.2
	1903	81	31.7
	1907	43	29.0
	1912	110	34.8
Reichstag: Weimar	1919	163*	37.9*
	1920	102*	21.6*
	1924 May	100	20.5
	1924 Dec.	131	26.0
	1928	153	29.8
	1930	143	24.5
	1932 July	133	21.6
	1932 Nov.	121	20.4
	1933	120	18.3
Bundestag: Bonn	1949	131	29.2
	1953	151	28.8
	1957	169	31.8
	1961	190	36.2
	1965	202	39.3
	1969	224	42.7
	1972	230	45.8
	1976	214	42.6

*Excluding Independent Socialists.

Source: *Deutsche Parlamentsdebatten*, vol. 1, 1871-1918, ed. Axel Kuhn, 1970; vol. II, 1919–1933, ed. Detlef Junker, 1971; vol. III, 1949–1970, ed. Eberhard Jackel, 1971. All published by Fischer Bucherei, Frankfurt am Main and Hamburg. Particulars about the 1972 and 1976 elections were obtained from various sources, including special releases by the German Information Center in New York.

seats. It was widely expected that Brandt would remain at the head of the administration for at least four more years. However in 1974, the year that brought the resignations under fire of an American president and a Japanese prime minister, the Germans had their own scandal when one of Chancellor Brandt's closest advisors was discovered to be an East German spy. Brandt felt it necessary to resign from the chancellorship, though he retained his seat in the *Bundestag* as well as the chairmanship of his party. The position of *Bundeskanzler* was filled by Helmut Schmidt, formerly minister of economics, who maintained the coalition with the Free Democrats. It was as the leading partner of the SPD/FDP administration that the Socialists entered the *Bundestag* elections of 1976. Although they lost some popular support, they were still strong enough to win a parliamentary majority together with their Free Democratic allies and to continue the existing SDF/FDP administration.

In the meantime, the Socialists in Austria had duplicated the triumphs of their West German brethren. Austrian socialists also could look back on a century of fighting for the rights of the working classes. But in addition to the usual problems of exploited laborers in the aftermath of the Industrial Revolution, the Austrian Socialists under the empire faced nationality questions as well. In a country consisting of many different language groups that faced one another with increasing hostility, the Socialists looked to autonomous ethnic areas within the empire, according to their program of Brno in 1899. Originally there had been a number of working-class organizations throughout the lands of the Habsburg monarchy, but in 1898 they combined to form the Social Democratic party, which advanced claims to such democratic goals as universal and equal suffrage. Even though the *Reichsrat* lacked power and the government was by no means responsible to Parliament, the Social Democrats made themselves felt. In 1897, they obtained fourteen seats. A decade later, with eighty-seven deputies, they had become the largest single group in a legislature that was splintered into almost thirty different factions. But they were considered radical and often dangerous and therefore were excluded from all pre-World War I governments.

Like most parties elsewhere, the Austrian Social Democrats supported the war effort to begin with, but had severe doubts as the fighting dragged on, seemingly without hope. They were among the participants in the October 1918 conference in which the representatives of the German-speaking areas of the old Parliament met and formed the Provisional National Assembly. Because representation was based on the undemocratic 1911 elections law, the Socialists had only 32 seats as compared with 70 for the Christian Socials and 101 for the German Nationalists. The elections of February of 1919 were far more representative and resulted in 72 seats for the Socialists, 69 for the Christian Socials, 26 for the various German nationalists and a scattered three seats for some other groupings. On the basis of these results, the first government was headed by Socialist Dr. Karl Renner and included his party colleagues Otto Bauer (foreign affairs), Julius Deutsch (army), and Ferdinand Hanusch (social affairs) in addition to Christian Socials and some civil servants. It was the task of this coalition government to pick up the pieces after a disastrous war and to attempt to put the decimated country back on its feet. Because German Austria was only a minute part of the former Austro-Hungarian empire, sentiment for union with the new German republic was widespread, and the Socialists were in the forefront of the fight for eventual *Anschluss*. They were to maintain this view for quite a few years. Not even with Hitler's rise to power in Berlin did the Socialists change their minds altogether, although they stated that they would postpone their efforts until democracy was restored in Germany. As we have seen, it took Hitler's occupation and six years of war to bring about a change of heart, not only among Socialists but among others as well.

In the days following the end of World War I, after the Allies had vetoed union with Germany, the Socialists played an important part in efforts to create an independent, viable Austria. Revolts threatened the young republic from all sides, but the Socialists managed to convince the working masses to seek their fortune under the flag of social democracy instead of communism. It was under their leadership that far-reaching social measures, such as the eight hour working day and unemployment benefits, were instituted.

But the differences between the Socialists and their coalition partners were so great that the fall of the government was really only a question of time. It came in June 1920, and for the next few months a *Proporzregierung* was in charge; an administration in which each party in Parliament was represented in the government according to the proportion of its parliamentary strength but without being in the least responsible for the activities of the other parties. It was this monstrosity which adopted the new Constitution and prepared for the October 1920 elections. With these elections, a new chapter in the history of the Austrian Socialists began, for they showed themselves to be in a strong position without ever being in a dominant one. From then on, they were permanently in opposition, for the Christian Socials held the reins of government with minor party backing. In 1920, the Social Democrats won 66 out of 174 seats, and when the total number was reduced to 165, they obtained 68 mandates in 1923, 71 in 1927, and 72 in 1930.

That the Socialists, despite their consistent strength, remained excluded from the government was bad enough. What greatly aggravated the situation was the unsurmountable differences that separated them from the Christian Socials. The Austrians appropriately refer to each party as *Lager,* or camp, and Austria's political parties in the First Republic did indeed resemble military camps confronting each other. Even geographically there was a big gulf, with Vienna predominantly Socialist and the rural areas largely Christian Social. The nicknames the Austrians gave to their parties tell us something about the political mentality. The Socialists were the "Reds," denoting their revolutionary heritage. In reality, like their German comrades they had broken with the radical ideas of Karl Marx and were devoted to the democratic welfare state. They put their ideals into practice in the Socialist-controlled capital city where their source of pride was the building of modern apartment complexes at rents low enough to bring them within reach of the working classes. The Christian Socials, on the other hand, took their nickname "Black" from the color of garments worn by priests. They were under the strong influence of the Catholic church, had many clergymen actively participating in their ranks, and were generally quite conservative and anti-Socialist in their outlook.

The political picture was even further clouded by two additional factors: one was the pan-German nationalist right-wing group which was very much opposed to the Republic as such and eventually went over to the Nazis; the second was that various political parties had military auxiliaries which fought each other in the streets. In those skirmishes the *Schutzbund,* the Socialist worker's organization, was increasingly at a disadvantage. Although acts of violence were committed by all sides, the courts usually were far harsher in their judgments when the defendants were Socialists, whereas the right-wing *Heimwehr* often had its excesses justified on the grounds of patriotism.

We have already referred to Chancellor Dollfuss and his suppression of parliamentary democracy. The Socialists took a grim view of this step and organized their *Schutzbund* for battle. Against the advice of their leadership, the Socialists in Vienna called for a general strike. The government answered by mobilizing the *Heimwehr,* and a brief but bloody civil war erupted, culminating with the bombardment of the workers' apartment buildings by the armed forces of the Republic. It was all over in a few hours. Dollfuss now saw an opportunity to establish his fascist-clerical regime. The Socialist party was prohibited from functioning, although four out of every ten Austrians remained associated with it. The alienation of the working classes obviously helped Hitler, who was to take full advantage of the dissension within Austrian society.

The anti-Fascist character of the Social Democrats was clear enough, so that there could be little doubt that they would get permission to function again after Hitler's defeat. Indeed, as we have seen, Dr. Renner's problem was to convince both the Western Allies and his own countrymen that his original negotiations with the Red Army had not made him a Russian tool. Gaining recognition among his fellow Austrians was made somewhat less difficult by the respect due to his advanced age and the part he had played earlier in the establishment of the First Republic. At that time, the Socialists had been ideologically split, and Renner had been associated with the right wing. Now the moderates seemed to predominate, among them Renner's friend Dr. Adolf Schärf. Most of the so-called Austro-Marxists, once represented by such leaders as Max Adler and Otto Bauer, were either dead or in exile; those who remained soon became identified with the Communist party. Class warfare, at one time the Socialist watchword, had been all but forgotten. The Socialists in Austria, as in West Germany, have changed their image from that of a class party to that of a mass party.

Only within this frame of reference can one understand the profound differences that have occurred. In the First Republic, the Socialists were kept in permanent opposition and isolation, but in the Second Republic they participated in twenty years of coalition government. When the Black-Red alliance broke up in 1966, it was followed by four years of one-party rule by the Austrian People's party, the new name adopted by the former Christian Socials. But in 1970 it was the Socialists' turn to establish a one-party government of their own, first on the basis of being the largest single party in the *Nationalrat* even if they lacked an absolute majority, and after 1971 with 93 seats out of a total of 183 and with the support of more than one-half of all the votes cast. This last event was to be repeated almost exactly in 1975.

There were good reasons why the pitched battles that had torn the First Republic asunder could be avoided in the second. Among them was the realization that the ultimate beneficiary of the Black-Red conflict had been Adolf Hitler. Now, both confidence in and loyalty to a previously practically unknown Austrian nation was growing, a feeling shared by the supporters of almost all political parties. Even more significantly, sentiments of mutual respect and understanding had developed among the leaders and followers of both major parties, in part because they had both suffered during the Nazi dictatorship, in part because their ideological differences had become quite blurred. In the days of the First Republic it could be said that the Blacks looked to the Bible and the Reds to the writings of Karl Marx for the answers to their problems. Now both moved away from these positions and toward each other. When the Black Chancellor Julius Raab declared that he would rather have the "Sozis" at the cabinet table than in the streets, he indicated that coalition governments were preferable to protest marches, strikes, and street fighting. At the same time he implied that it was indeed possible to come to an understanding with the Socialists, that cooperation with them was not beyond reach, and that their tactics were not necessarily obstructionist and unreasonable. Nationalization of the major industries had been carried out immediately after the war under the auspices of both parties, and both parties were committed to welfare programs involving higher pensions for the aged and free schooling for the young. The goals of price stability and full employment were not the monopoly of one party but rather aims to be actively pursued by every Austrian government regardless of persuasion or "color."

The Socialists thus moved into the framework of the broad Austrian consensus and apparently felt quite comfortable in it. Election issues were concerned with pragmatic solutions, image, and personalities, rather than with fundamental quasi-religious doctrines. When the Black-Red coalition broke up in 1966, the People's party had all the advantages. It received 48.3 percent of the vote as compared with 42.6 percent for the Socialists. As they obtained 85 out of the 165 seats in the *Nationalrat,* the Blacks were clearly the choice of the electorate to carry on the affairs of government. The Reds had projected an image of being less modern and less forward looking than their opponents, although they were also handicapped when Franz Olah, a prominent Socialist, set up his own political organization in a dispute with his party and collected some 150,000 votes. Moreover, the electorate apparently took a dim view of the SPO's failure to repudiate Communist support when it was offered.

The 1966 defeat taught the Socialists an important lesson. William T. Bluhm points out that in opposition, the Reds were prudent, responsible, and constructive, just as the Blacks showed restraint and responsibility on their part.[1] When important national projects, such as emergency flood relief, had to be enacted, the government and the opposition party cooperated fully. This certainly left a good impression on all sides and helped to lay to rest some of the anxiety about Socialist motives that was still occasionally felt, especially in rural church-oriented areas. The Socialists had buried their anticlerical attitude, just as the priests no longer equated socialism with the devil.

Moderation was particularly expressed by Bruno Kreisky, the confidence-inspiring new leader. That this was possible with a man of Jewish background who had been imprisoned by the Schuschnigg regime and who had spent the war years in neutral Sweden was in itself an indication of the new developments in

Austrian politics. Kreisky had worked in the foreign affairs ministry during the coalition government. When he assumed leadership of his party in 1967, he was determined to stress the Swedish brand of non-Marxist socialism. He repeatedly disavowed in public any plans for further nationalization in the near future, even when it meant contradicting his own vice-chancellor, trade union leader Rudolf Häuser, during the 1971 election campaign.

The departure from radicalism soon bore fruit. By 1970, the parliamentary elections gave the SPO 48.4 percent of the vote and a plurality of the seats. Although 81 deputies was not a majority in the 165-member assembly, Kreisky decided on a one-party government. As federal chancellor, he managed to deepen the good impression created earlier and inspire the confidence of even broader sections of the population. Moreover, the economic situation was such that at the time of the next election in 1971 few people felt it necessary to vote for a change; on the contrary, more than ever before voted Socialist in parliamentary elections. With the membership of the *Nationalrat* increased to 183, Kreisky's party received 93 seats. Over 50 percent of the voting population supported him. Since 92 percent of the eligible voters turned out on election day, the victory claim was not exaggerated. Above all, the victory was a personal one for the chancellor. As an article in a Salzburg newspaper put it the next day: "In brief, Kreisky has won. The rest is commentary."

The remarkable thing about the 1971 parliamentary elections was that the most notable gains were made in rural areas where the Socialists had been weak, thus again proving that the radical image of the Reds was waning. Their greatest increases came, in terms of percentages of the total vote, in provinces where they held minority positions, such as Vorarlberg, Tirol, and Lower Austria. Where they had been strong in 1970, they remained strong in 1971, and even where they lost some votes, they increased their percentages, for the OVP lost even more and any increase by third parties was negligible. And the Socialists were able to duplicate this quite remarkable victory with almost precisely the same figures in 1975.

But it would be incorrect to measure Socialist successes in

Table 7. Austrian Provincial Election Results, 1970 and 1971 (votes given in 1,000s)

Province	1971 Nationalrat Elections				1970 Nationalrat Elections			
	SPÖ	ÖVP	FPÖ	KPÖ	SPÖ	ÖVP	FPÖ	KPÖ
Burgenland	84	78	5	.8	84	83	5	.8
Kärten	162	99	28	5	164	110	30	4
Lower Austria	387	405	25	10	408	460	24	8
Upper Austria	339	315	45	6	336	332	48	4
Salzburg	101	94	25	2	98	100	30	1
Steieremark	352	320	35	12	354	337	37	9
Tirol	113	169	15	2	110	177	17	1
Vorarlberg	52	73	16	1	46	81	20	1
Vienna (Wein)	619	339	44	22	623	371	43	16

Austria merely in terms of parliamentary elections in the early 1970s. Austria is one of the few European countries where the president is elected directly by the people, although no direct election for president was ever held in the First Republic and the Second Republic began with Karl Renner being chosen for the highest office by a vote of both houses of Parliament in December of 1945.

At the same time Leopold Figl, a Black, became federal chancellor. This set the pattern for the next quarter of a century: a People's party chancellor and a Socialist president. Apparently such an arrangement was perceived as part of the *Proporz* politics. The voters constantly supported the Blacks as the majority party in the *Nationalrat* while electing Reds to the presidency. After Renner's death direct elections for president were held, and thus far a Socialist has been chosen every time. In 1951 it was the mayor of Vienna, Theodor Körner who died in 1957, at which time the popular choice fell on Vice-Chancellor Dr. Adolf Schärf. Reelected to a second term in 1963, Schärf died long before his six-year term was up and the 1965 elections gave the office to Franz Jonas, the mayor of Vienna. In retrospect, this victory was quite remarkable because there seemed to be an anti-Socialist trend in the country; less than a year later, the OVP won an overwhelming vote against the SPO in parliamentary elections. Yet in

Table 8. Socialist Support in Austrian Elections

Year	Percent of vote	No. of votes (in 1000s)	No. of seats won	Winning president
1919	40.7	1,212	69	
1920	36.0	1,073	66	
1923	39.6	1,312	68	
1927	42.3	1,540	71	
1930	41.1	1,517	72	
1945	44.6	1,435	76	
1949	38.7	1,624	67	
1951	52.1	2,174*		Dr. Theodor Körner
1953	42.1	1,819	73	
1956	43.0	1,873	74	
1957	51.1	2,258		Dr. Adolf Schärf
1959	44.8	1,954	78	
1962	44.0	1,961	76	
1963	57.7	2,473		Dr. Adolf Schärf
1965	50.7	2,324		Franz Jonas
1966	42.6	1,929	74	
1970	48.4	2,222	81	
1971	52.8	2,488		Franz Jonas
1971	50.0	2,280	93**	
1974	51.7	2,392		Rudolf Kirchschläger
1975	50.4	2,324	93	

*All presidential contests listed here were between two candidates only, except the first one where a run-off was necessary. This accounts for the higher percentage than in parliamentary elections where a number of parties usually compete.

**The number of *Nationalrat* seats in the Second Republic was 165, but was changed to 183 in 1973.

1965 not even the well-known former chancellor, Alfons Gorbach, could win the presidency for the People's party.

It was in the spring of 1971, after the Socialists had formed their minority government, that the next presidential elections were held. Jonas won again, this time over Kurt Waldheim. Now president and chancellor were of the same party for the first time. The Blacks tried to make this a campaign issue in the parliamentary contest in October of 1971 by pointing out that their opponents wanted all the power in the state for themselves. This did not dissuade the electorate from giving Kreisky an unprecedented majority. In 1974, President Jonas, like all his predecessors in the Second Republic, died in office, and in the elections that followed it was again the Socialist candidate, Rudolf Kirchschläger, who polled more votes, thus continuing the apparent tradition of having a Red president regardless what party had control over the legislature.

As in the other German-speaking countries, the Social Democrats in Switzerland can also look back on a long tradition of service to the working classes. But unlike their German and Austrian counterparts, the Socialists cannot claim to be among the oldest of the Swiss parties. Since Switzerland experienced a democratic form of government in advance of its neighbors, there was a need for political organizations dealing with federalism and the concept of liberty before industrialization made feasible the establishment of a worker's movement. There were some labor-oriented groups around the middle of the nineteenth century, especially in the cantons of Genf, Bern, and Zürich, but it has been pointed out that it is quite difficult to label them simply as "Socialist."[2] Erich Gruner quotes Henri Druey's definition of socialism, "complete elimination of poverty among the masses," as much too oversimplified a program to be useful.[3] Although a few followers of the ideas of Louis Blanc, Robert Owen, or Charles Fourier actually got elected to office, they did so mostly on a personal or local basis. Only shortly before the turn of the twentieth century do we find a Social Democratic party of Switzerland with enough support to elect a few deputies to the *Nationalrat*. Apparently there was some intention among the founders of that group to give it the character of a nondoctrinaire social democracy which could attract wide sections of the population. This did not materialize and the Socialists retained their revolutionary reputation, which in turn resulted in the moderates among them being replaced by more radical elements.

We have already mentioned the Socialists' attitude toward the war, the Zimmerwald Program and the splintering of the party that came about after the Bolshevik revolution in Russia forced Socialists everywhere to take a stand either for or against extreme communism. Those who did not want to embrace the Third International now had to establish a separate party with a social and yet democratic program, a mass party that would gain widespread support together with respectability. This was no easy task in a basically conservative country that had been spared the horrors of war. Although the Social Democrats at first stressed their anti-Capitalist attitude, they gradually turned toward the center. By 1959, when the German Socialists announced their pragmatic Godesberg Program, their Swiss comrades similarly spoke of full employment and protection of private property, of human dignity, and of tolerance.

Their reward was twofold: they gained popular support and they were admitted into the *Bundesrat,* the Swiss government. During the interwar period, their membership in the popularly elected legislature had always been well above 20 percent, which made them one of the three leading parties and at times even the largest. Because the prevailing system of proportional representation in a stable country results in few electoral changes, winning or losing a handful of seats is almost like a landslide in British parliamentary or American congressional elections. When in 1943 the Socialists increased their representation in the *Nationalrat* from 45 out of 187 seats to 56 out of 194, this constituted an all-time high, never achieved by them before or since, but also never reached by any other party in the last few decades.

That election result made the Socialists not only the largest single party (with six more seats than the Radicals); it also enabled them to place one of their colleagues, Burgomaster Ernst Nobs of Zürich, in the *Bundesrat,* the first time that a Socialist had won admission to the Swiss government. The Swiss system is based on a permanent governmental coalition in which the seven cabinet posts are apportioned in accordance with approximate party standings in the *Nationalrat.* The word *approximate* must be stressed, for traditions die hard in Switzerland. Even though Catholics, Radicals, and Socialists had obtained an almost equal number of seats soon after World War I and maintained this parity with individual gains or losses limited to a handful of seats at each election, it was only during the Second World War that the first Socialist joined three Radicals, two Catholics, and one Farmer on the Federal Council. Socialist participation was short-lived, however, for a decade later their nominee, Finance Minister Dr. Max Weber, resigned over the question of direct federal taxation, which the electorate later rejected in a referendum. The Socialists did not suggest anyone to take his place and remained without representation in the government for the next years. In 1959, however, Willy Spühler, an economist from Zürich, and Hans-Peter Tschudi a law professor from Basel, were chosen as Socialist members of the *Bundesrat*. Since that time the "magic formula" has been in effect. This allotted two cabinet posts each to the Radicals, Catholics, and Socialists, and one to the Farmers, thereby representing the major parties in the administration in a ratio that approximates their strength in Parliament.

Table 9. Socialist Strength in the Swiss Nationalrat

Year	Percent of vote	No. of votes (in 1000s)	No. of seats obtained	Total number of seats at stake
1919	23.5	175	41	189
1922	23.3	171	43	198
1925	25.8	192	49	198
1928	27.4	220	50	198
1931	28.7	248	49	187
1935	28.0	256	50	187
1939	25.9	160	45	187
1943	28.6	252	56	194
1947	26.2	252	48	194
1951	26.0	250	49	196
1955	27.0	264	53	196
1959	26.3	259	51	196
1963	26.6	256	53	200
1967	23.5	234	51	200
1971	22.9	452*	46	200
1975	25.4	490	55	200

*1971 was the first time that women participated in national elections throughout Switzerland.
Source: Most of these figures are taken from *European Political Facts 1918-1973*, by Chris Cook and John Paxton (New York: St. Martin's Press, 1975).

Today the Social Democrats see themselves as "fighting for a social order which frees every human being from economic exploitation." They "condemn and struggle against every dictatorship," and support the unification of Europe. In their effort to achieve reduction of working hours, governmental care for widows and orphans, insurance against sickness, accidents, unemployment, and old age, their cause has become "the cause of all mankind" and the Socialist party of Switzerland has developed into a "people's party."[4] With this kind of program, the party continues to attract at least one of every five voters, giving them an approximate percentage of seats in the *Nationalrat*. In the Council of States, the *Ständerat,* where each canton is represented by two members and which by the very nature of its election favors the more conservative parties, the Socialists in 1974 held four of the forty-four seats. They still occupied two ministerial posts. Pierre Graber in December of 1969 was chosen to replace Willy Spühler and was in charge of the Political Department. In 1970 he served as president of Switzerland. The second Socialist in the cabinet at that time was Professor Tschudi's replacement, Willi Ritschard. Elected in 1973, he was head of the Department of Transportation and Energy.

Thus, in Switzerland as in Austria and the German Federal Republic, the Socialists have over the years gained respectability, an achievement which has been the recurring theme throughout this chapter.

10

Christian-Oriented Parties

The Social Democrats were not the only party which in the course of time changed from being narrowly doctrinaire to becoming much more broadly based. A similar change can be observed in that party which, in many parts of the Western world, became their chief rivals: the Christian Democrats, or by whatever name they happen to be known. Just as the Socialists departed from their position in left field and moved toward the center, so did the strongly church-oriented parties come in from the right. Both of them have now grown closer together than ever before, which has enabled them to turn their one-time bitter hatred for each other into friendly competition and often cooperation in the same administration.

The phenomenon of Christian-oriented political parties is nothing new, but after World War II their popularity increased as they adopted a more progressive and democratic attitude. Moreover, their previously strong Catholic viewpoints were broadened to appeal to Protestants as well. The 1956 statute of the German CDU speaks of a "democratic formulation" of German public life on the "basis of personal freedom" and in the spirit of "Christian responsibility." Individual liberty within a democratic framework based on Christian ethics may well describe the foundations of these political groups.

The Germanic countries have a large Catholic population. Austria and Liechtenstein are predominantly Catholic; Switzerland's statistics show a slightly larger ratio of Protestants, but their majority has been steadily declining and has probably almost completely disappeared if the foreigners living in Switzerland are counted, for they are overwhelmingly Catholic. West Germany also has slightly fewer Catholics than Protestants. The picture in the German Democratic Republic is somewhat obscured by the state's marked lack of enthusiasm for organized religion. An East German publication reported that when a census was taken in December of 1964, 59 percent of the population regarded themselves as Protestants, 8 percent spoke of their adherence to Catholicism, while the remainder apparently preferred not to be classified according to religion.[1]

With the possible exception of the DDR, therefore, Catholicism is widespread among the German-speaking countries. Whether this means that those concerned are genuinely devout, merely church-going, or simply listing their parents' faith as one of their vital statistics as is expected in many parts of Europe, is important for our purpose only to the extent to which there is a religious philosophy that carries over into every day life and thus influences political thinking. Nominal Catholics today are less inclined to support a church-dominated political party than were their more pious fathers and grandfathers. Party politicians are well aware of this, and so we find that after World War II the Christian parties adopted social programs that were designed to keep their Catholic following and to attract Protestants as well. In addition they attempted to appeal also to those whose religious beliefs were of a somewhat weaker nature. In other words, like the Socialists, they made an effort at becoming a broadly-based mass party and they were quite successful in this endeavor.

This was particularly true of those parties who were vying with the Socialists for the support of the voters, i.e., where they were and still are one of the two alternatives for governing the country. In Liechtenstein both parties are essentially oriented with little ideological distinction. In Switzerland, the newly named Christian

Democratic People's party is one of the three major parties and occupies the right flank of the democratic spectrum without challenge and with a fairly constant conservative clientele. In the DDR, obviously, the only political forces tolerated are those cooperating with the Communist state. This leaves the Federal Republic and Austria as the chief areas of two-way combat between Christian and Socialist Democratic parties.

In both countries, the broadening of purpose was accompanied by a change in name. Like their Socialist rivals, the Christian-oriented political groups date back to the nineteenth century. Napoleon had deprived the church of its secular possessions and difficulties developed when the state tried to intervene in matters which the clergy regarded as being in their own province. In the late 1830s, Protestant Prussia imprisoned the archbishop of Cologne over disagreements involving mixed marriages. The jailing of their prelate provoked considerable resentment among the Catholics. Even if there was little Catholic unity on other matters, some kind of political activity seemed to be called for in order to prevent governmental intervention in matters deemed to be the sole responsibility of the church.

As long as Austria was part of the German League, the Catholics in Germany amounted to slightly more than half of the population. With Austria's exclusion, the figure fell from 52 percent to 37 percent. Certain Catholics felt themselves threatened and founded a political party, the *Zentrum,* to safeguard their interests. This group almost immediately embroiled itself with Bismarck in a cultural struggle, the so-called *Kulturkampf,* in which it successfully fought the chancellor's attempts to strip the Catholic church of much of its power and influence. At the height of this conflict in 1874, the Center party won ninety-one seats in the *Reichstag* and became one of the largest parties. Almost 28 percent of the voters had given it their support, a figure never again achieved by the *Zentrum.* It had the great advantage of being truly in the political center, not committed either to the Marxist left or the nationalist-militarist right, and therefore able to move in either direction as expediency dictated. Its influence throughout the remaining years of Imperial German history remained great. With its share of the popular vote varying between 27.8 percent and

16.4 percent, electoral mathematics allotted it a minimum of ninety-one seats at every election and thereby provided it with between 23 and 27 percent of the total seats.

Together with the Socialists and the Progressive People's party, the *Zentrum* had, in 1917, supported abortive efforts for a negotiated peace in the *Reichstag*. Following military defeat in 1918, the same three parties became the moving forces first in establishing and then in maintaining the Weimar Republic. After receiving the support of almost one-fifth of the voters in 1919, the *Zentrum*'s strength fell to 11 percent by 1933. Translated into parliamentary seats, this gave the Center party some sixty or seventy seats through the 1920s, a number that was increased to a certain extent by about twenty deputies from the Bavarian People's party, the *Bayerische Volkspartei,* another Catholic-oriented group which was a little more conservative and based on Bavaria, a state always proud of its localism.

It was one of the tragedies of the Weimar period that the *Zentrum,* like the democratic center in general, gradually lost a portion of its electorate to the extremes on both sides of the political spectrum. In 1925, the Center candidate Wilhelm Marx failed to win the presidential run-off election, although with the support of the Weimar coalition parties he received over 45 percent of the vote in a three-way contest. He lost partly because an old war hero was the substitute candidate of the national opposition and partly because the Communists ran their own candidate rather than supporting Marx against Hindenburg. Interestingly enough, the leadership of the Bavarian People's party saw fit to throw its weight behind the field marshal rather than backing the Catholic Centrist.

Throughout the Weimar period, the *Zentrum* was represented in all German cabinets until 1932 and furnished several chancellors, the last one being Heinrich Brüning, whose dismissal that year began a series of events which eventually led to Hitler's coming to power. Although the Center's services to the republic cannot be doubted, its part in the Nazi takeover is a little more dubious. Its leaders and their Bavarian colleagues would have been quite willing to join in a Hitler-led government if the Nazis had asked them to do so. Furthermore, in the last free *Reichstag* debate in

March of 1933, when the Socialists risked their lives by openly defying Hitler, the *Zentrum's* party chairman, Dr. Ludwig Kaas, spoke of a "national feeling of responsibility far beyond any party-political and other considerations" which motivated him and his supporters to agree to give Hitler the practically unlimited powers the Nazis demanded. Kaas went to Rome soon afterwards, where he was instrumental in arranging the Concordat between Hitler and the Vatican, one of the first international measures that gave the new leader a degree of the recognition and respectability he urgently needed.

But there were prominent *Zentrum* politicians who were less co-operative with the Nazis. Among them was the mayor of Cologne, Konrad Adenauer, who several weeks after the Nazi takeover ordered the swastika flags removed from a local bridge where they had been hoisted without his authorization. Since there could be little doubt about Adenauer's attitude toward the Nazis, his days in public life were obviously numbered, and during the next twelve years he suffered several police interrogations and imprisonments.

It was this background that pushed Adenauer back into a leadership position after the downfall of the Nazi regime at the end of World War II. At the age of seventy-three, in 1949, he became the first chancellor of the newly created democratic and parliamentary Federal Republic of Germany. In his relationship with the Allies, Adenauer fought for more independence and for the gradual restoration of German sovereignty; his foreign policy consisted first of all in putting his country in a position where it was able to have a foreign policy. On the domestic front his fore-most task was to rehabilitate a war-ravaged, devastated, and de-moralized people. Much of the credit for achieving what has admiringly been called an economic miracle was undoubtedly due to Adenauer's economics minister and eventual successor, Ludwig Erhard. Within the framework of the policy of reconstruction, the CDU had to be quite pragmatic in its program. It stood left of center, largely because the right had been preempted by the Nazis. Just as there was no Germany as such, so there was no centralized party to start with. Several groupings sprang up. In Berlin the first steps were taken by former anti-Nazi prisoners who included within their ranks not only one-time Center adherents but also

Christian labor unionists and Protestants of various political leanings. In Cologne there were remaining elements of the old *Zentrum*. This group was soon in touch with like-minded people in Westphalia. An all-German meeting was held at Bad Godesberg in December of 1945 and the name Christian Democratic Union of Germany was adopted.

In the decades that followed, the CDU and its Bavarian partner, the CSU, consistently attracted a far larger percentage of voters than the Catholic parties had ever done before. The success was due not so much to any conversion of so many more people to the ideals of the old Center block, but rather to a large number of those who had supported the conservative right in the past now turning to the CDU/CSU, frequently because they had nowhere else to go. This inevitably led to a more rightist direction of the Christian Democrats.

It seems to be a truism that, at least in modern times, every government has to be more pragmatic than idealistic. Philosophic discussions have, to some extent, to be left to the opposition, which is not charged with solving the problems of the moment. The unionist parties, the CDU and the CSU, furnished the chancellors of West Germany for twenty years. Under their leadership, states the party program of October 1972 of Wiesbaden, "we have successfully achieved social security, economic growth, progress and peace through a social economy, through a social partnership, and through the policy of European cooperation." Both Konrad Adenauer, who was chancellor from 1949 till 1963, and Ludwig Erhard, who held the office between 1963 and 1966, had to work with smaller parties, especially the Free Democrats. A third Christian Democrat, Kurt Georg Kiesinger, formed a "great coalition" with the Socialists in 1966. Following the 1969 elections, however, the Socialists allied themselves to the Free Democrats and in that way were able to dislodge the Christian Democrats from office, an action that was reinforced by the SPD/FDP election victory in 1972. Four years later, the CDU and the CSU increased their share of the popular vote as well as their representatives in the *Bundestag*. But with the Free Democrats adhering to their alliance with the Socialists, the Christian parties were not quite strong enough to wrest the government from their opponents.

Table 10. Strength of Christian Parties in Germany

Imperial Reichstag:	Year	Seats won Zentrum	Percent of vote Zentrum
	1871	63	18.6
	1874	91	27.8
	1877	93	14.8
	1878	94	23.1
	1881	100	23.2
	1884	99	22.6
	1887	98	22.1
	1890	106	18.6
	1893	96	19.0
	1898	102	18.9
	1903	100	19.7
	1907	105	19.4
	1912	91	16.4

Reichstag: Weimar	Year	Seats won Zentrum	Percent of vote Zentrum	Seats won Bavarian People's Party	Percent of vote Bavarian People's Party
	1919	91	19.7		
	1920	64	13.6	21	4.2
May	1924	65	13.4	16	3.2
December	1924	69	13.6	19	3.7
	1928	62	12.1	16	3.1
	1930	68	11.8	19	3.0
July	1932	75	12.5	22	3.2
November	1932	70	11.9	20	3.1
	1933	73	11.2	19	2.7

Bundestag: Bonn	Year	Seats won CDU	Percent of vote CDU	Seats won CSU	Percent of vote CSU
	1949	115*	25.2	24	5.8
	1953	191**	36.4	52	8.8
	1957	217	39.7	53	10.5
	1961	192	35.8	50	9.5
	1965	196	38.0	49	9.6
	1969	193***	36.6	49	9.5
	1972	176	35.2	48	9.6
	1976	190	38.0	53	10.6

The old *Zentrum* appeared on the ballot a few times with these results:
*Ten seats with 3.1% of the vote
**Three seats with 0.8% of the vote (in alliance with CDU)
***Sixteen thousand votes (0.0%) were insufficient to elect a deputy

One complicating factor for the CDU is that it depends to a large extent on its Bavarian sister party for support. In the past this has meant the necessity of doing business with Franz Josef

Strauss, a wily and ambitious politician from Bavaria. So far, the two Christian union parties have been united in a seemingly permanent alliance, but Strauss and his followers occasionally make it clear that their support is not automatic. A glance at Table 10 shows that the CSU regularly sends about fifty representatives into the *Bundestag*. Without them the CDU would not be able to compete with the Socialists. Although a SPD/CSU coalition is most unlikely, politics does make strange bedfellows, and even a veiled threat of such a possibility can help the CSU in getting the CDU to adopt certain programs close to the hearts of the Bavarians, in giving the CSU some choice ministries in a CDU-led government, and perhaps even in securing the top post for Strauss himself.

So far, at least, the mantle of chancellor-candidate has evaded Strauss. After losing the 1969 election, Kiesinger found that he was losing support within the CDU, and the party turned to Rainer Barzel, leader of the *Fraktion* in the *Bundestag* and a former minister, to challenge Willy Brandt for the chancellor position. But Barzel did not live up to the hopes his party had for him. On two occasions he failed to oust Willy Brandt: once when his party attempted a vote of no confidence in the *Bundestag* but could not muster the required strength, and the second time when the 1972 elections showed that the public preferred the SPD/FDP to continue in the government. Eventually, Barzel himself was replaced and the CDU, with the somewhat reluctant agreement of the CSU, decided in 1975 to groom Helmut Kohl, prime minister of the state of Rhineland-Palatinate for the chancellorship in the event of a Christian Democratic election victory in 1976.

Meanwhile, the CDU/CSU opposition concentrated on attacking the government on such issues as the *Ostpolitik,* Brandt's policy of seeking an accommodation with the Eastern countries, especially the DDR, Poland, and the Soviet Union, and economic matters, including the administration's handling of inflation and rising prices. The German political arena is really characterized by a duel between the SPD and the CDU, spearheaded by their leaders Helmut Schmidt and Helmut Kohl, and one may wonder to what extent the party differences are fundamental and ideological.

If it is true of the German Federal Republic that the party contests are more pragmatic than philosophic, it is even more the case in present-day Austria. But there it is perhaps even more surprising. After all, in Germany the Christian parties and the Socialists had both incurred the wrath of Bismarck, had cooperated in opposition to various measures of the empire and had represented the core of the regime preceding Hitler's assumption of power. When the Center and Socialist *Reichstag* deputies found themselves cellmates in Nazi concentration camps, they did not have to overcome their dislike for one another, as was the case with Austrian political leaders.

The years of the Austrian First Republic, between the end of World War I and Hitler's bloodless occupation, were characterized by deep-seated hostilities between the Reds and the Blacks. They had both started out as democratic parties and cooperated in a coalition government in the early days after the breakup of the Austro-Hungarian empire, but their cooperation did not last long. The Blacks preferred an alliance with smaller parties, especially those desiring unity with Germany, a wish which in itself was shared with the Social Democrats. The Blacks were officially known as Christian Socials. Their devotion to Christian ideals was clear and some of their leaders were practicing priests, such as Monsignor Ignaz Seipel, who for several years was chancellor of the Republic. To what extent the party was actually committed to democracy may be questioned. One bishop regarded the republic as the work of anti-Christ in alliance with Free Masonry.[2] Others strongly favored a return of the monarchy, an issue that caused strong disagreement between the two large parties. Even if a majority of the Blacks favored the republic at least in the beginning, they were less inclined to support the democratic system as time went by. The regime came to cooperate increasingly with the *Heimwehr,* a paramilitary organization with Fascist tendencies, whose ideas and activities were preferred by the government over those of the opposition *Schutzbund.*

As the economic situation deteriorated, so did the outlook for the survival of Austrian democracy. With the collapse of the Viennese banking institution, the *Creditanstalt,* in 1931, the worldwide depression began. Seipel died the following year and the next chancellor, Engelbert Dollfuss, killed Austrian democracy at precisely the same time that Hitler delivered the death blow to the Weimar Republic. The Blacks now introduced a government fashioned after the example of Mussolini, who for a while became the protector of Austria's independence. The confrontation with the Socialists in early 1934 transformed Austria into a one-party "Christian-German state on a corporate basis." His work for an independent Austria, even within a Fascist framework, though under clerical auspices, earned Dollfuss the enmity of Hitler and led to his assassination by Nazis under German orders. The new chancellor, Kurt von Schuschnigg, did nothing to establish rapport with the Socialists, who had been forced underground. He did struggle valiantly for the survival of an independent Austria, albeit within the outlines of a Black dictatorship, but eventually, with a heartbreaking "God protect Austria," Schuschnigg surrendered his country to Hitler because he did not want to see "German blood being spilt by Germans."

In the days that followed, Austria was incorporated completely into the German Reich. The laws that prevailed in Nazi Germany now were extended to Austria, including the prohibition of any and all political parties except the Nazi party. Not only was the Christian Social party thus prevented from functioning, its leaders were at the best retired into private life and at the worst taken to concentration camps.

This nightmare had important repercussions during the decade following the end of the war. The Blacks had learned to hate fascism. They became convinced that Austria had to survive as an independent, democratic country, a philosophy shared with the Socialists. Indeed, the two parties developed an appreciation and respect for one another that augured well for the future of the country.

Like the Social Democrats, the Blacks were reborn in April of 1945 while the war was still officially going on, but when all but the most fanatical of Nazis had become convinced that the end had come. The new name adopted was Austrian People's party, *Osterreichische Volkspartei,* OVP. Some of the founders had been closely identified with the quasi-Fascist regime of the thirties while others had opposed the dictatorial tendencies at that time. Both groups included former inmates of Nazi concentration camps, and some of them had met earlier under dangerous conditions to talk about what could be done. Their opposition to Hitler was never in doubt and they received Allied approval and license to function as a political party.

The OVP was, and still is, made up of three distinct component parts: associations of farmers, of workers and employees, and of businessmen, all of which profess a basically conservative and Catholic-oriented philosophy. While this may be reminiscent of the Christian Social past, there were some fundamental differences: a genuine feeling for democracy, abhorrence of fascism regardless of whether it was inspired by Hitler or by Mussolini, a belief that an independent Austrian nation was possible as well as desirable, and an understanding that the Socialists were not necessarily accomplices of the devil.

Since both major parties had given up some of their rigidity and become more flexible, and since they both had adopted a more tolerant and moderate view about one another, working together was no longer out of the question. Cooperation became a reality. Austrians grew accustomed to a situation where a system of proportionalism, *Proporz,* was highly developed: every government department had secretaries and under-secretaries of opposing parties who had to reach agreement if anything was to be done at all. During election campaigns they fought each other, but afterwards a new coalition was negotiated. Under these circumstances, party differences had to be largely pragmatic and not of such fundamental significance as to make working together impossible.

One of the founding members of the OVP was Leopold Figl, who, before the *Anschluss,* had been a leader of the Farmer's League and a member of the right-wing *Heimwehr.* But this had not hindered him from being a strong advocate of Austrian independence, an attitude that sent him to a number of Nazi prisons during a five-year period. After his release, he made contact with like-minded individuals; indeed it was in his home in Vienna that some fundamental decisions regarding the future People's party were made. He almost became a victim of the wholesale slaughter of all possible opponents of Hitler after the unsuccessful assassination attempt on Hitler's life in 1944, but the Russians reached

Vienna just in time and liberated him and some of his collaborators. Figl served in the first postwar government under Karl Renner, and when the 1945 elections gave the Blacks almost half of the popular vote and a clear majority of parliamentary seats, Figl became chancellor while Renner moved to the presidency. The Black vote fell to 44.0 percent in 1949 and to 41.3 percent in 1953. That year the Socialists outpolled the People's party by about thirty-seven thousand votes, although electoral arithmetic gave the OVP one more deputy than the SPO.

As a result of the disappointing showings of his party, Figl was forced to vacate the chancellor post. He did remain in the government as foreign minister. In that capacity he signed the State Treaty which terminated the military occupation of Austria in 1955. The new chancellor was Julius Raab, another founding member of the *Volkspartei,* who had been a member of the legislature until Dollfuss dissolved it and who had served in Schuschnigg's last cabinet. That the Nazis regarded him as unfit for military service is proof enough of his unreliability as far as the Third Reich was concerned. He remained in the top position for eight years until he was replaced by Dr. Alfons Gorbach in 1961. Though in ill health, Raab allowed his name to be entered for the presidency two years later. He was defeated, as was Gorbach when he ran against Franz Jonas in 1965.

While Gorbach was *Bundeskanzler,* a new type of leadership emerged as the older generation was gradually replaced. The chancellor, though a former concentration camp inmate, worked diligently for reconciliation with the onetime Nazis and became identified with a different type of reform groups of whom it was said that they preferred to do politics with a sliderule rather than with a wineglass in their hands.[3] It was under the fourth, and so far last, OVP chancellor, Josef Klaus, that fundamental changes occurred, partly because Klaus himself did not have concentration camp experience, and partly because after two years as head of a coalition government, he formed a one-party administration. Following a sweeping OVP victory in the 1966 elections, the Blacks could begin their periodic negotiations for *Proporz* with the Socialists from a position of great strength, so great in fact that their attitude proved irreconcilable with that of the other major party.

Table 11. Election Support for Christian-Oriented Parties in Austria

Year	Percent of vote	No. of votes (in 1000s)	No. of seats won	Losing Black presidential candidate
Christian-Social Party				
1919	36.0	1,068	63	
1920	41.8	1,246	82	
1923	45.0	1,491	82	
1927	41.4	1,757	73	
1930	35.6	1,314	66	
Austrian People's Party				
1945	49.8	1,602	85	
1949	44.0	1,847	77	
1951	47.9	2,006		Dr. Heinrich Gleissner
1953	41.3	1,782	74	
1956	46.0	2,000	82	
1957	48.9	2,160		Dr. Wolfgang Denk
1959	44.2	1,928	79	
1962	45.4	2,025	81	
1963	42.3	1,814		Dr. Julius Raab
1965	49.3	2,261		Dr. Alfons Gorbach
1966	48.3	2,191	85	
1970	44.7	2,051	79	
1971	47.2	2,225		Dr. Kurt Waldheim
1971	43.1	1,965	80	
1974	48.3	2,239		Alois Lugger
1975	43.0	1,980	80	

For the first time in twenty-one years, no agreement on coalition could be worked out and the OVP formed a one-party government.

Several factors are worth noting. First of all, despite its absolute majority in the *Nationalrat* the People's party attempted to retain the alliance with the Socialists. But even when negotiations failed, the two parties cooperated inside and outside of Parliament. Of course there were differences between them, but they were largely pragmatic and relatively minor, especially when compared with the deep rift that had been so apparent in the First Republic.

If no really earthshaking divergences were visible between the coalition that had governed the Second Republic until 1966 and the one-party regime that was in control for the next four years, neither could fundamental changes be detected when the Socialists formed their minority government in 1970 and their parliamentary majority administration following the 1971 elections. Governing by themselves was something new to them, an experience to which they had to grow accustomed. It was equally strange for the OVP to find itself in opposition. A crisis in leadership developed almost immediately and in June of 1971 Dr. Karl Schleinzer became his party's candidate for chancellor. He had been a member of the government before, holding the position of minister of defense from 1961 till 1964 and of minister of agriculture from 1964 until 1970, and was therefore quite well known in the country; however, he seemed to lack charisma and was no match for Kreisky, whose SPO won an overwhelming victory in 1971's parliamentary elections.

As the next elections approached in the fall of 1975, Schleinzer was again to be the standardbearer of his party. But on July 19 he was killed in a car accident. With elections scheduled for October 5, the party had to move fast. On July 31, a special party conference chose Dr. Josef Taus as its candidate for chancellor. Taus was mainly associated with the banking world, his governmental service having lasted only from 1966 to 1967. During the 1971 campaign, I was repeatedly told that Schleinzer, despite his years as minister, needed more exposure as party leader. In my conversations with Austrian politicians in August of 1975, members of all three parties agreed that the new face of Taus would work to the advantage of the OVP. As it happened, the OVP came in second best, just as it had in 1971, and it is idle speculation whether it would have done better had Schleinzer not been killed.

But it is in the presidential contests that the OVP has been singularly unsuccessful, at least so far. In 1951, their losing candidate was Heinrich Gleissner, who had been governor of Upper Austria before the Nazi takeover and again after the war. On that occasion, two ballots were necessary because the FDO's predecessor, the League of Independents, ran a surgeon from Tirol, Dr. Burghard Breitner, as their candidate. Breitner got enough votes to deny victory to either party on the first try. In 1957 Dr. Wolfgang Denk represented the OVP and the *Freiheitlichen* in an attempt to deny the presidency to Socialist Adolf Schärf. Two former chancellors, Dr. Julius Raab and Dr. Alfons Gorbach, were the next two unsuccessful contenders for the highest office, followed in 1971 by former foreign minister and at the time ambassador to the United Nations, Kurt Waldheim. In 1974 it was the turn of Innsbruck's Mayor Alois Lugger to be defeated, although he held his opponent to a 150,000 vote plurality. This was no mean achievement for a person whose previous appeal had been largely local. But in any event, the party which describes itself as being "of the progressive middle" and whose philosophy is based on a "Christian understanding of man and society without being bound to a particular religious group or clerical institution" is likely to continue as a major factor in Austrian politics.

In the principality of Liechtenstein party differences have completely disappeared. That they once existed can be deduced from the fact that both parties still retain their nicknames, Reds and Blacks. But these labels are of historic interest only. The party system developed in Liechtenstein later than in any of the other countries under discussion, at the end of World War I. Until that time, candidates were elected to Parliament on the basis of personalities rather than issues. In 1917 a lawyer, Dr. Wilhelm Beck, founded the *Volkspartei,* the People's party, later to be called *Vaterländische Union* or Patriotic Union, which expressed criticism of the close relationship that existed between Liechtenstein and Austria. Since it was important to publicize its views, the People's party did so in the *Oberrheinische Nachrichten,* a newspaper published in Switzerland. As one attitude was stated politically, the opposition to it had to be organized as well. Thus in 1918 the *Bürgerpartei,* the Citizen's party, was established which backed the government's close cooperation with the Habsburg monarchy and found its newspaper outlet in the *Liechtensteiner Volksblatt.*

Events played into the hands of the People's party. The Allied blockade of the Central Powers included Liechtenstein, despite the proclaimed neutrality of the principality. There was a threat of starvation, avoided only through Swiss assistance. Because so many of the administrators, civil servants, and judges were Austrian, the Allied action was understandable, as was Liechtenstein's unhappiness with Austria when the Danube monarchy disappeared in defeat. The People's party's opposition to Austria and its insistence that Liechtenstein should be governed by Liechtensteiners became quite popular. The breakup of the Austro-Hungarian empire affected Liechtenstein inasmuch as it too severed its connection with Vienna. After a few years of not being tied to any country, it entered into a customs union with Switzerland on January 1, 1924.

A few years earlier, on October 5, 1921, the new Constitution of Liechtenstein became effective, a document which to this day provides the framework for the governance of the principality. It placed the hereditary monarchy on a democratic and parliamentary basis, which in legislative terms meant a popularly elected Parliament. From 1922 till 1928 the People's party ruled under the leadership of Dr. Gustav Schädler. The party had originally advocated two prime objectives: in foreign policy separation from Austria, and on the domestic scene democratization of the institutions and their administration through native Liechtensteiner.[4] This was accomplished almost immediately after the war. These concepts could soon be accepted without reservations by the other party as well. In 1928 the governing People's party was defeated at the polls after a series of catastrophes, including disastrous floods and a savings bank crash, had hit the country. The Citizen's party took over and remained the majority party for the next forty-two years.

There are several indicators of the basic stability of the little nation. During these four decades only three chiefs of government have presided over its affairs: Dr. Joseph Hoop from 1928 to 1945, Dr. Alexander Frick from 1945 until 1962, and Dr. Gerard Batliner during the next eight years. When Austria was incorporated into the German Reich in 1938 and Hitler's empire became Liechtenstein's neighbor there was immediate danger that the *Führer's* ambition to unite all German-speaking peoples would include the tiny principality. Whether it was the failure of the internal *putsch*, the overwhelming vote of confidence in the prince, the effect that any such annexation might have on Swiss opinion, or simply Ribbentrop's view that the conquest of Liechtenstein was hardly worthwhile, the fact remains that Hitler never attacked. But the situation was serious enough for the parties to forget their differences. Instead of fighting one another in election contests, they formed an alliance and in 1939 conducted the *"stille Wahlen,"* silent elections, in which a joint list was presented to, and approved by, the voters. Political activities were not resumed until April of 1945.

Obviously such a course of action could not be undertaken unless there was widespread agreement between the two parties. Uncontested elections in Germany's Weimar Republic or in Austria's First Republic would have been inconceivable. In these instances, the bitterness among the parties and their mutual distrust were too much to overcome even in times of dire emergency. But close cooperation between formerly feuding political parties was possible in Britain during Churchill's wartime administration, and under similar circumstances, the Christian-oriented parties and the Socialists in present-day Austria and in the German Federal Republic might well agree to forgo a scheduled election if the situation were desperate enough. These parties' political divisions have become more apparent than real. Their common interests, which include deep concern for the survival of their countries as free, independent, and democratic nations within the present constitutional framework far outweigh any of their differences, which are more pragmatic than ideological.

Cooperation between the two major parties developed after World War II in Austria and Germany, but it was visible before the war in Liechtenstein. Twenty years earlier the Citizen's party's apparent kinship to Austria's Christian Socials earned them the nickname Blacks. The Austrian connection has long since disappeared and the attachment to the teachings of the Roman Catholic church is a characteristic that is shared by the other party. But it should be noted that the Blacks changed their party's name to *Fortschrittliche Bürgerpartei,* Progressive Citizen's party, just as in far away Canada the Conservatives began to call themselves Progressive Conservatives. Both parties have shown that the twentieth century has not passed them by, and that they do indeed contain strong progressive elements.

Liechtenstein's other party, the *Volkspartei,* also underwent changes in name as well as in substance. It is now known as *Vaterländische Union,* a difficult name to translate because it has connotations of *national, patriotic* and *native*. The party stresses patriotism and national identity, and obviously it wants to emphasize the part it played in the separation from Austria. Some of its original supporters were workers who, especially in the building season, found employment in Switzerland, particularly in Zürich, where they became familiar with the activities of labor unions. Thus the nickname Reds. But if this conjures up a Marxist, radical, anticlerical image, it is misleading. Although the Liechtensteiners proudly claim that, despite their size, they have the most industrialized country per capita in Europe, they also maintain that the change-over from agrarianism was accomplished without socialism. The nicknames Black and Red may at one time have had some political meaning; they do not today. The adherence of both parties to a basically progressive, Christian philosophy justifies their inclusion in this chapter on Christian-oriented political groupings.

Having become the majority party in 1928, the Blacks maintained this position until 1970, although their majority was small most of the time. Eleven elections were held between 1945 and 1978 for the fifteen seats in the *Landtag*. Only on one occasion did the Blacks manage to capture nine seats and thus obtain a three-seat margin over their rivals. At all other times, the majority party held eight seats and the minority seven. The Progressive Citizen's party had the advantage until 1970. That year the Patriotic Union was able to win thirty more popular votes than their opponents which, by the rules of proportional representation, gave them a one-seat majority in the legislature. Their candidate for chief of government, Dr. Alfred Hilbe, who until then had been deputy chief of government, now became his country's chief executive while the Blacks had to get accustomed to being in the minority. Although the presidency of the *Landtag* fell to the Reds, the Blacks were given two of the five ministries under the principle of coopposition, which in Liechtenstein means opposition in Parliament but cooperation in a coalition government. This pattern had been followed consistently since elections were resumed after World War II.

The governmental changes of 1970 were unexpected. It is a matter of political speculation whether the Blacks had become

Table 12. Election Results in Liechtenstein

Year	Number of seats gained by Volkspartei (now Vaterländische Union) nicknamed "Reds"	Number of seats gained by Bürgerpartei (now Fortschrittliche Bürgerpartei) nicknamed "Blacks"
1922	11	4
1926	9	6
1928	4	11
1932	2	13
1936	4	11
1939	7 unified list	8
1945	7	8
1949	7	8
1953	7	8
1957	7	8
1958	6	9
1962	7	8
1966	7	8
1970	8	7
1974	7	8
1978	8	7

a little too sure of themselves after four decades in office and had assumed victory as a matter of course, whether there was a genuine feeling in some quarters that it was indeed time for a change, or whether it was merely a fluke, because the majority of thirty was the smallest in quite some time. Although one of the leading politicians told me that there were fundamental ideological party differences, the election propaganda on both sides stressed personal qualifications and integrity of leadership rather than philosophic divergencies. This can hardly be otherwise in a homogenous and unified country. One is tempted to characterize Liechtenstein's party system as one where one party is called upon to govern and the other to oppose, at least in the legislature, and where the issues are pragmatic rather than fundamental.

It was therefore quite fascinating to see in the early 1960s the appearance of a third party, the Christian Socials, nicknamed the "Greens." The two major parties were annoyed, since both of them claimed to advocate Christian and social programs. Apparently the new party had hoped to attract people who were dissatisfied with the existing parties and who felt that they could not advance fast enough within the Black-Red constellation. In any event, the Greens consistently failed to obtain the 10 percent of the vote necessary for representation in Parliament. For this reason they have thus far not played a significant part in the political life of the country. Their influence, never great, seems to be diminishing even further; apparently they are experiencing financial difficulties. Their newspaper, the *Wochenspiegel,* is now independent of the party; and the Greens have recently been unable to fill slates of candidates in both election districts.

After the Red majority had given them the major offices in the government, elections were held four years later, in February of 1974. Again only a handful of votes separated the Patriotic Union from the Citizen's party, but this time the Blacks captured eight seats in the *Landtag* to their opponents' seven. The previous deputy chief of government, Dr. Walter Kieber, now became *Regierungschef* and his party received two further positions in the government while the Reds had to be satisfied with two ministerial posts, one of which was the post of deputy prime minister.

In February of 1978, new elections brought about another change in government. The electoral arithmetic on this occasion worked against the Blacks. In the *Unterland,* the election district with the smaller population, both parties gained three seats apiece, although the *Fortschrittliche Bürgerpartei* led their opponents by several hundred votes. But in the *Oberland,* with a total of nine seats at stake, the Reds were ahead, 14,058 votes to 14,040. This was enough to give the Reds five seats. Since each voter could vote for nine candidates in that district, exactly two more people voted for the Reds than for the Blacks. Added together, the Patriotic Union now had eight seats in the *Landtag,* and the Progressive Citizen's party had seven. As a result, the former *Regierungschef,* Dr. Walter Kieber, once again moved into the number two position, while the candidate of the new majority party, Hans Brunhart, became the new head of the administration.

In striking contrast to Liechtenstein's very similar parties, we can now examine another system where a party with a distinct

Christian ideology is supposedly different from the other political groupings, but in reality is completely absorbed by the all-embracing activities of a totalitarian state. In the Soviet zone, as in the other three zones of occupation, the Christian Democratic Union was licensed shortly after the end of World War II as one of the democratic and anti-Fascist groups around which the future political life of Germany could be built. In Berlin, the CDU was founded in June of 1945.

No sooner was this accomplished, than a "block of anti-Fascist democratic parties" was formed in July. This group was governed by an executive committee on which the CDU, as well as the Communists, Socialists, and Liberals, was represented by five members. Differences with the occupying authorities developed. Certain land reform measures in particular were fought by some CDU adherents, but their opposition was doomed to failure from the start. Dr. Andreas Hermes, a former *Zentrum* member, and Dr. Walther Schreiber, who had belonged to the German Democratic party, were now excluded from the leadership of the CDU. They were replaced by Jacob Kaiser and Ernst Lemmer, who also did not last very long. What all these men regarded as Christian-oriented, progressive, democratic policy was termed reactionary by the authorities in the Soviet zone. Religious instruction in public schools, as well as land reform, was among the thorny issues, and while the Christian Democrats were willing to cooperate, they were not prepared to go quite as far as the ruling Communists. Subsequently, some of the erstwhile CDU leaders fled to the West where in some instances they rose to high positions in the government of the Federal Republic.

Those who remained in East Germany, however, had to accept the principles of socialism in order to stay in the good graces of the rulers. Thus in 1952, Otto Nuschke declared his adherence to socialism and its indispensable economic conditions which would free man from the "continuous and agonizing struggle for his bare existence" and thus leave him time and leisure for family, community, and religion.

There was obviously great pressure to work actively for the Communist party. After the two socialist groups had merged, the SED became the favorite of the governing circles. However, the other parties, including the CDU, still had much public support. In 1946 elections were held in the five *Länder* into which the Soviet zone was divided at that time. The SED was the largest single votegetter in each state, with 47 percent of almost 10 million participants, but the CDU came up with a respectable 2,398,000 votes, or 24 percent of the total. Indeed in two states, Brandenburg and Sachsen-Anhalt, the CDU and the Liberals together outpolled the Socialist Unity party.

Something had to be done. Alleging a threat from "resurrected forces of imperialism and militarism" in West Germany, in the spring of 1950 all parties in the DDR were combined into a united bloc for the elections to be held later that year. (It is difficult to determine to what extent the motivation for this change originated from Stalin, from Ulbricht, and elsewhere.) A common list was worked out and presented to the voters who, with a participation of 98.5 percent, gave the list 99.7 percent support. Four hundred deputies of the *Volkskammer,* the People's Chamber, were elected. Of those, the SED was assigned 100 seats and the CDU and the Liberals 60 each. Nuschke became one of the five Deputy Prime Ministers and the CDU obtained four of twenty-one cabinet posts. This has remained the pattern. The seats have now been rearranged for a total of 434. The SED is assigned 110 of those and each of the four other parties, including the CDU, has 45. CDU politicians hold some leading positions in the state; in 1969 a CDU member, Gerald Götting, became presiding officer of the *Volkskammer*. Regarding the precise relationship between the Christian Democrats and the regime, we are informed that:

> The CDU believes in socialism because it sees realized in this social system the basic Christian aspiration for peace on earth and charity. The members of the CDU live up to their humanistic mission by taking an active part in the organization of a socialist system and by cooperating with Marxists in a comradely way.[5]

This is obviously an East German comment. But Western sources contend that, despite subordination of the CDU to the state, the party does make itself heard in the DDR. It is credited with having played a part in "achieving a certain *modus vivendi* between Christians and the regime," with having stopped the state's open warfare against the church, with having received concessions about freer travel for the aged and about some limited rights for religious conscientious objectors, and with having obtained negative responses in the *Volkskammer* regarding a proposed law on abortion.[6] If such is indeed the case, one can argue that the CDU has some modifying influence in the DDR, even if real independence of action is absent.

While the CDU in the German Democratic Republic is assured of a certain number of seats in Parliament and of a place in the government, it is severely restricted, to say the least, in being able to voice any opposition to the doctrines of the rulers of the state. A neat contrast to this is provided by the *Christlich-demokratische Volkspartei* or CVP, the Christian-Democratic People's party of Switzerland. It too is a permanent component of the government of the country and if it is not assured of the same number of seats in the legislature every time, it is at any rate practically certain that every election will net it about forty seats in the *Nationalrat,* for this has happened quite regularly over the last half-century. As a result, the CVP has for many years been able to claim two of the seven ministerial posts in a nation in which a coalition government is also a permanent fixture.

But whereas the DDR requires commitment to "socialism" Soviet style, the strength of the Swiss parties, including the CVP, derives from the support of the voters, received in free, open, and secret elections in which the various factions present their different programs to the people. Proportional representation and extraordinary stability, where voters follow more or less the same pattern, are largely responsible for the lack of change in party representation which did not alter greatly when the electorate doubled in 1971 with women's suffrage.

Unlike Austria or the German Federal Republic, no overall Christian party has developed in Switzerland, where half the population is Protestant. There is a small *Evangelische Volkspartei,* an Evangelical People's party (EVP), whose support is regional in Zürich and a few other cantons. In its program of 1961, it referred to guidelines of political activities which, according to sixteenth-century theologian Ulrich Zwingli, were to be found in Holy Scripture. The party is quite small, has only a few seats in Parliament, and has therefore allied itself with the Liberals in order to be able to be represented on legislative committees.

It is the Catholic party, however, which represents a major force in Swiss politics. Like the Evangelicals, it is quite conservative in nature. From 1957 onward, it was known as the Conservative Christian Social People's party, but thirteen years later it changed its name to *Christlich-demokratische Volkspartei*.

In an earlier chapter we referred to the *Sonderbund,* the attempted Catholic secession of 1847. When the rebellion was put down, the Catholic cantons developed what Erich Gruner called "lack of self-confidence," a symptom perhaps not unlike that experienced in the American South two decades later. In any case, a political organization was clearly called for to accommodate those who had backed the separation and who wanted an emphasis on Catholic values within a conservative framework. Opposition to the new constitution was only of short duration but, due to the Swiss character, it took quite a while until the various factions in the different cantons were able to unite. For half a century, separate groups sprang up and often disappeared again. Eventually in 1912 the Conservative People's party was formed, which was, as its name implied, quite conservative, antiliberal, and not particularly fond of the Constitution although it accepted it. This party embraced all of Switzerland. Its emphasis was on the rights of individual cantons as opposed to the national government, which is once more reminiscent of the American South.

As they established closer contact with the other parties and became partners in the coalition government, the Catholic Conservatives slowly gained respectability, lost their feeling of insecurity, and with it their antipathy toward the Bern regime. In 1891 Josef Zemp became the party's first member of the *Bundesrat,* the Swiss government. Since 1919 the Catholics have been represented by at least two members in the ministerial body of seven. No longer outsiders, they have become the backbone of the system, without whose support no government can be formed. In the early 1950s they even laid claim to three seats in the government. By that time, they saw their task not as opposing the Constitution but as defending it against forces that allegedly threatened established society in the rapidly advancing industrial world. It was only when

Table 13. Catholic-Conservative Representation in Switzerland

Year	Nationalrat (membership: 147-200)	Ständerat (membership: 44)	Bundesrat (membership: 7)
1896	30	15	1
1899	32	16	1
1902	34	16	1
1905	34	16	1
1908	34	16	1
1911	38	16	1
1914	38	16	1
1917	42	16	1
1919	41	17	2
1922	44	17	2
1925	42	18	2
1928	46	18	2
1931	44	18	2
1935	42	19	2
1939	43	18	2
1943	43	19	2
1947	44	18	2
1951	48	18	2
1955	47	17	3(since 1954)
1959	47	18	2
1963	48	18	2
1967	45	18	2
1971	44	17	2
1975	46	17	2

an accommodation between the Catholic Conservatives and the Socialists was achieved, when they were able to recognize each other as equals, that the present broadly based coalition became possible. Like the Socialists, the Catholics today have two members on the Federal Council. In 1975, these were Kurt Furgler, elected in 1971 and in charge of the justice and police department, and Hans Hürlimann, chosen two years later and heading the department of the interior.

The name changes that the CVP has undergone illustrate its internal struggles. In recent years it has definitely moved from right field into the center. Its adherents like to think of their party as being "of the dynamic middle," indicating that while they still defend the individual's rights above those of the state, they have come to acknowledge that at least some social responsibilities are the task of modern government. Still vitally concerned with the maintenance of Catholic values, they nevertheless realize that many of their followers are workers and employees who demand social legislation. If, as one CVP politician would have it, the party has truly become "the party of the little man," the concerns of the little man have to be expressed. This cannot be done through the proclamation of ancient, often outdated principles. The CVP has demonstrated its vitality and viability by merging Christian philosophy with present-day progressive ideas and policies, thus following the pattern of its sister parties in the German Federal Republic, Austria, and other Western European countries with large Catholic populations.

11

Other Parties

The five German-speaking countries present a variety of party systems, as we have repeatedly indicated. Switzerland's diversity of viewpoints and opinions is reflected in its multiparty system. Both the Federal Republic of Germany and Austria are modified two-party systems, in the sense that for all practical purposes the alternatives before the voters are governments dominated by the one big party or the other. However, in both countries one third party is large enough to act as balancer, as *Zünglein an der Wage*. The main difference between the two situations is that in Germany, with the two exceptions already noted, the smaller party consistently has been included in various administrations as junior partner, while in Austria the *Freiheitlichen* have never yet held office. Liechtenstein alone shows a model two-party system, for the third party there is insignificant. In the DDR a multiparty system exists on paper. In reality, one party dominates and the scope of activities of the other groupings is severely restricted and must conform to the directions of the Communist rulers.

Having dealt with the Communists as the most leftist and Marxist-oriented group, the Democratic Socialists, and the Catholic parties, we must now direct our attention to the remaining parties. Only one of these has attained major party status, the Radicals (or *Freisinnige*) in Switzerland. In the German Federal Republic, third parties have almost completely disappeared from Parliament. During the days of Weimar, the multiparty system was notorious. In 1925, in the first presidential election, seven candidates represented parties ranging from the extreme right to the extreme left. In parliamentary elections more than twenty different parties frequently entered separate lists. In 1932 there were as many as thirty-six. Even if we omit such minor groups as the "People's Rights party," the "Fighting Unit of Workers and Peasants," or the "Middle-class party,"[1] there were always about a half-dozen major political parties to be reckoned with. Their voting strength changed rather drastically in the fourteen years during which the democratic center suffered heavy losses at the expense of increasing support for the extremists. In the last election before Hitler's one-party state became fully operative, five parties each managed to receive at least 8 percent of the vote. In March of 1933, the Bavarian People's party came close to its average total of about 3 percent, while two other groupings which had been quite influential in the earlier days of Weimar, the *Deutsche Volkspartei* and the *Deutsche Demokratische Partei,* which had recently changed its name to *Deutsche Staatspartei,* were supported by barely 1 percent of the electorate.

For the next twelve years, only the Nazis were allowed to function politically. Nevertheless, some shadow of a Parliament was maintained, for the Weimar Constitution was never officially repealed and the one-party *Reichstag* was called together whenever Hitler felt it necessary to make some grandiose speech or pronouncement. In 1945, the task was to start German political life anew.

As they decided which parties to allow to operate, the Allies had one major consideration in mind: no adherents to Nazi doctrines could be tolerated. Whether the Communists could have met the required standards of democracy without Russian support may be questioned. The parties that did appear almost immediately after the end of the war were the Communists, Socialists, Christians, and Liberals who later became the Free Democrats. In the course of time, other parties followed. In the first *Bundestag* elections in 1949, these four original groupings accounted for 337 of

402 seats. The remainder was parceled out among an assortment of representatives from the Bavarian, Center, German, German Conservative/German Right, South Schleswig, and Economic Reconstruction parties, as well as three Independents. In 1953, not less than nineteen different parties competed in the parliamentary elections, but apart from the CDU/CSU, the SPD and the FDP, only fifteen members of the German party and three of the *Zentrum* were elected. None of these parties plays any significant part today, although some appear regularly on the ballot. Thus in the 1976 parliamentary elections, 14 minor parties (not counting FDP, KPD or NPD) participated and received between 21,000 and 217 votes, respectively.

Ever since 1961, the modified two-party system has given parliamentary seats only to the two major and one minor parties. This evolution has come about democratically. All parties are free to compete. The exception to this right relates to those parties that have an undemocratic character. In an earlier chapter, we have discussed Article 21 of the *Grundgesetz* and how it was applied against the Communists. The same provision was also used against the extreme Right. Since Nazism had brought Germany and the world to the edge of disaster, it was obvious that any thought of a rebirth of Hitlerism would immediately arouse deep anxiety both inside and outside of Germany. Five years after the end of the war, when Allied permission was no longer necessary for the establishment of political parties, a Socialist Reich party (SRP) came into existence. Although it pledged loyalty to the new republic and its constitutional system, the antidemocratic, totalitarian and anti-Jewish tendencies of the new group were not difficult to prove in court. Consequently, its activities were outlawed.

In the mid-1960s, another group developed the *Nationaldemokratische Partei* (NPD), which seemed to be destined for success. Although connections with Nazism were denied, the party appealed to old Hitler supporters by advocating many of the things the *Führer* had favored, such as anticommunism, anti-Semitism, leadership rather than parliamentarism, and a general attempt to return to the good old days of German supremacy. There was some discussion of invoking the provisions of Article 21, but the government eventually decided to refrain from legal action and to give the NPD enough rope in the hope that the party might hang itself. This it did, but only after a while. The party did rather well in elections to *Land* parliaments at first. Beginning in late 1966, the NPD gained between 6.9 percent and 9.8 percent of the vote in six different *Länder* within a period of eighteen months and obtained ten seats in the provincial legislature in Lower Saxony, twelve in Baden-Württemberg, and fifteen in Bavaria, in addition to fewer elsewhere. Although this was not a real threat to the democratic parties, anyone remembering the rapid rise of the Nazis in the 1920s had to be apprehensive. The crucial moment came at the time of the 1969 *Bundestag* elections. Would the party gain seats in the national legislature?

The problem centered around a provision in the election laws which gives any political group a number of parliamentary seats in proportion to the percentage of votes obtained, if it can capture at least 3 of the 248 seats by pluralities or if it can gather a minimum of 5 percent of the total vote. To have enough support to win in three districts was out of the question for the NPD. Gaining at least 5 percent of the electorate, however, was a distinct possibility, and the party's showing was watched with much fear in various quarters at home and abroad. As it turned out, the election law had provided a sufficient safeguard. The NPD obtained 1.4 million votes, which was enough to cause some uneasiness but not enough to be awarded seats in the *Bundestag,* since this amounted to only 4.3 percent. After that, they gradually lost their foothold in the state legislatures as well. By the end of 1975 they had all but disappeared. In the elections to the federal parliament in 1972 only 200,000 voters, or 0.6 percent, followed the appeal of the extremist party and this figure was further reduced to 123,000 (or 0.3 percent) in 1976. As trouble develops within its leadership, the NDP seems close to oblivion, although there does remain the danger that during severe economic crisis, the Germans may once again turn to another extreme group on the Right.

This leaves the Free Democrats, the FDP, as the only remaining third party of any importance. It was slower in developing than the CDU or the SPD, at least in its present form. Its ancestry is old and distinguished, going back to the Liberals of the last century.

It should be noted in passing that the term *liberal* has a connotation in Europe different from that prevailing in the United States. Here the term applies to someone favoring a certain amount of government intervention in order to help the poor, the underprivileged, the minority groups. A Kennedy, a Humphrey, a Stevenson would belong to this category, as opposed to a Nixon, a Ford, or a Goldwater, who seem to put their trust in the old Jeffersonian principle of that government is best that governs least, who feel that the forces of the marketplace will eventually rectify economic ills, and who are usually characterized as conservative.

Europe has a different tradition. One of the major forces still influencing European politics is the French Revolution. That event, which had repercussions throughout the continent, was particularly effective in establishing the principle of equality by sweeping away age-old prerogatives based on high birth, class, and wealth. Full adherence to that principle characterizes the Liberals, who also emphasize individual freedom. As a political party, the Liberals had existed in Germany before the foundation of the empire. In the 1860s they had opposed Bismarck's militarization, which built up Prussia's armed forces for the successful wars. After 1871, there was a split in the Liberal ranks. The National Liberals became more nationalistic and provided one of the basic pillars of Bismarck's political support. In 1910, the various other factions formed the Progressive People's party, with about 10 percent of the seats in the *Reichstag*. It was this party which, in 1917, supported the Socialists and the *Zentrum* in their unsuccessful attempt to end the war. After the fighting stopped, a reunion between the two liberal factions proved impossible. Although both supported the new republican regime, the right-wing German People's party did so only grudgingly. It relied for its support largely on big business and industry. In 1920, it attracted 14 percent of the electorate; in 1932 and 1933 it received barely 1 percent. It participated in a number of Weimar administrations, however, and had produced one of the few real statesmen of the period: Gustav Stresemann, an outstanding foreign minister.

The genuinely democratic elements coalesced first in the German Democratic party and then in 1930 in the German State party. It, too, was faced with a steady decline. Its seventy-five deputies in 1919 were reduced to five by March of 1933. At that time its spokesman, Reinhold Maier, who was later to become a prominent FDP politician, voiced support for Hitler's Enabling Law but not without first drawing attention to the importance of maintaining basic constitutional rights and freedoms.

After the end of the Third Reich, the Liberals sprang up in various forms and under different names in the several zones. They professed adherence to the democratic tradition, without what they regarded as the shackles of either Marxism or clericalism. As a result, they attracted a conglomeration of supporters, often quite independent in spirit, some of whom had actively fought Hitler and others who had paid more than just lip service to the Nazi regime. The party now stood for democracy; maximum freedom for the individual, especially in business affairs; German unification; and secularism. Its 1971 party program proclaimed that "Liberalism stands for human dignity through self-determination" and that it would "give preference to individuals over institutions." This "liberal, reasonable policy," said its new leader Hans-Dietrich Genscher three years later, enabled the FDP alone to lay claim to the political middle.

After World War II the party had one of its earliest beginnings in the Soviet zone, where the Liberal-Democratic party was founded in July of 1945 and in the first and most free election received almost a quarter of the total votes cast. In West Germany, the Liberals took off in a number of directions. There was a *Demokratische Volkspartei* in Württemberg-Baden in 1946 with Professor Theodor Heuss as chairman, and similar parties emerged in other states. Only in 1948 did the Free Democratic party establish some degree of unity among its followers in the three Western zones. In the first *Bundestag* elections in 1949 they obtained 11.9 percent of the vote. Since that time they have fluctuated between a high of 12.8 percent in 1961 and a low of 5.8 percent in 1969. While this showing is small when compared to the CDU/CSU and the SPD, it is nevertheless enough to enable the Free Democrats to remain the only minor party able to overcome the 5 percent hurdle and thus obtain seats in the *Bundestag*.

Table 14. Strength of the Liberals in Germany

Year	Number of seats obtained	Percent of vote obtained
Imperial Reichstag*		
1871	77	16.5
1874	53	10.0
1877	52	11.0
1878	39	10.5
1881	115	23.1
1884	74	19.3
1887	32	14.1
1890	76	18.0
1893	48	14.8
1898	49	11.1
1903	36	9.3
1907	49	10.9
1912	42	12.3
Reichstag (Weimar)**		
1919	75	18.6
1920	39	8.4
1924 May	28	5.7
1924 December	32	6.3
1928	25	4.9
1930	20	3.8
1932 July	4	1.0
1932 November	2	1.0
1933	5	0.9
Bundestag (Bonn)**		
1949	52	11.9
1953	48	9.5
1957	41	7.7
1961	67	12.8
1965	49	9.5
1969	30	5.8
1972	41	8.4
1976	39	7.9

*Deutsche Fortschrittspartei, Deutsch-Freisinnige Partei, Fortschrittliche Volkspartei
**Deutsche Demokratische Partei, Deutsche Staatspartei
***Freie Demokratische Partei

This rather unique position placed the FDP in a crucial position far outweighing its numerical strength. Except for 1957–1961 and 1966–1969, the FDP has been represented in every cabinet since

1949. Naturally, the party has undergone changes since it was first established. Its original emphasis on freedom and liberalism opened the door not only to such confirmed anti-Nazis as Dr. Thomas Dehler, Adenauer's first minister of justice, but also to others whose past was subject to considerable questioning. The party stood to the right of the CDU and seemed even more in favor of German unification than the others. Thus, it opposed many of Adenauer's attempts to bring about better relations with France out of fear that such measures would be detrimental to eventual unification. Moreover, they opposed the death penalty and strongly advocated amnesty for Nazi war criminals.

But in the course of time, a change came about. Some of the old leaders died and were replaced by a newer generation, such as Walter Scheel, former foreign minister and federal president since 1974, and Hans-Dietrich Genscher, who has held the portfolios of minister of the interior and of foreign affairs in the SPD/FDP coalition governments. The first federal president was Theodor Heuss, elected and reelected with CDU support. At that time, the Free Democrats were closely allied with the Christian parties, but they were unhappy when the Grand Coalition in 1966 left them outside of the government. Three years later, both major parties courted the Free Democrats, who then decided to cast their lot with the Socialists. Since that time they have been associated with the administrations of Willy Brandt and Helmut Schmidt. In 1969, the Socialist candidate, Gustav Heinemann, was chosen federal president with the help of the Free Democrats; in 1974 the tables were reversed and Walter Scheel received Socialist support in his successful campaign to succeed Heinemann.

The electors seemed to approve the new, leftist attachment of the FDP. In the elections of the *Bundestag* in 1972, more than 3 million voters, or 8.4 percent of the total, expressed their support for the Free Democrats as compared with a low of 1.9 million or 5.8 percent in 1969, which had been only just enough to overcome the 5 percent barrier. Later, as the FDP's ties with the Socialists seemed to become stronger, they met with a number of reverses in local elections, apparently shouldering their share of blame for the slackening off of economic conditions, inflation, and government scandals. But in the last of the 1975 *Landtag* elections, held in Bremen in October, the reverse was true. The FDP had fought the contest separate from the Socialists, though willing to enter a coalition with them after the election. The SPD received 48.8 percent of the vote as compared with 55.3 percent in 1971, while the Free Democrats increased their standing to 13.0 percent from the 7.1 percent four years earlier. In the 1976 parliamentary elections, the FDP held its own, while the SPD lost rather heavily.

All this poses some important questions for the FDP. One of them is whether they can overcome the 5 percent clause in the future. Another question is to what extent the party can project an independent image to the voters, despite the obvious fact that it can retain office only as the junior partner of one of the two main parties. Some far-reaching decisions will have to be made prior to each election since a poor showing at any time might be catastrophic for the FDP.

No such problem exists in the eastern part of Germany. With the Socialist Unity party in dominance, lip service is paid to the other parties that are allowed to exist, although their adherence to Communist principles is clearly indicated. It is said of the Liberal Democratic party that it "acknowledges the revolutionary and democratic traditions of the German bourgeoisie. It helps to implement their aims and humanist ideals on the basis of the socialist social system."[2] The middle-class tradesmen and entrepreneurs—obviously only of the "small and medium" variety since large-scale enterprises are state-owned, run, and controlled—are being brought into the system through this group. It likes to keep in touch with the West German Free Democratic politicians and expresses the conviction that the ideals its predecessors expounded in 1848 as well as at the time of the establishment of the Weimar Republic can be realized only through socialism. The Liberals are faithful adherents of the Democratic bloc. Like the Christian Democrats, they are allocated forty-five seats in the 434 member *Volkskammer* as their share in the one-list elections. They also have a number of representatives in leading positions: Hans-Joachim Heusinger is minister of justice and the president of their party, Dr. Manfred Gerlach, is vice-president of the *Staatsrat*.

Two other political parties exist officially, participate in the Democratic bloc, and are also allocated forty-five seats each in the

Parliament. Both of them came into existence relatively late, in the spring of 1948. Since agriculture is an important economic part of the DDR, it was felt that the farmers needed an organization of their own and the *Demokratische Bauernpartei Deutschlands,* the DBD or Democratic Farmers' party, was the result. Founded by a former Communist, Ernst Goldenbaum, the party played an important role in bringing about and in defending land reforms. It claims a revolutionary tradition in fighting against "feudal oppression and Capitalist subjugation" of the farmer and professes to be engaged in the construction of a "modern socialist agriculture."

There is also a National Democratic party, the NDPD. When one considers that a party with the same name and aiming at the same clientele in the West has aroused much fear because of its nationalist and neo-Nazi tendencies, one may wonder what such a party is doing in a Communist country. The answer is that the National Democrats were given the task of drawing into the system former, not too ardent members of the Nazi party and soldiers of Hitler's armed forces who are said to have seen the light and have resolutely broken with their Nazi past. This particularly includes officers who were taken prisoner by the Red Army during the war. Naturally, these people "have drawn the correct lessons from the past." The NDPD allegedly "exerted a great influence on the social strata united in its ranks, persuading them to take an active part in the developing of a policy of peace, democracy and socialism." Some rather prominent generals, including Field Marshall Paulus, who led the German troops at Stalingrad and was taken prisoner there, could be found in this group which, for a number of years, provided the DDR with its foreign minister in the person of Dr. Lothar Bolz. As the war recedes into the background and a new generation grows up which does not remember Hitler and his attempted conquests, the NDPD counts among its adherents small capitalists and those independents whose economic well-being is not totally controlled by the state. Its documents are full of the "German spirit," speak of the woman as the "guardian of life," and pay tribute to the "high spiritual and moral value of religion for our German people."

It should also be noted that in addition to the SED and the four "independent" parties other groups are represented in the *Volks-*

kammer although they are not political parties in any sense of the word. The Trade Unions have sixty seats; the Youth Organizations, thirty-five; the Federation of Women's Organizations, thirty; and cultural organizations, nineteen members, respectively. This is in accordance with the principle that as broad a basis as possible should be provided for in the elective chamber; that as many sections of the population as feasible should have spokesmen. Of course, in reality it does not matter very much since the Communists and their allies dominate the political life of the country. Article 3 of the Constitution states:

> In the National Front of the German Democratic Republic the political parties and mass organizations pool all forces of the people for joint action for the development of Socialist society. They thereby implement the mutual relationship of all citizens in socialist society on the principle that each bears responsibility for the whole.

With the Communists firmly in control, diversity is in effect one-party rule enforced from the top.

In an attempt to demonstrate diversity the DDR even goes to the trouble of incorporating nonparty groups. This brings to mind the unparliamentary regime that governed Austria in the four years before the *Anschluss*. After Austrian Chancellor Engelbert Dollfuss put an end to parliamentary democracy in 1933, he established a *Ständestaat* (loosely translated as "corporate state"). The term implied that the various estates and classes, the several occupational and cultural parts of society, all of which were supposedly working together harmoniously for the good of society, were represented in whatever body or bodies were designed to have an input in the decision-making process of the government.

The Austrian rulers, taking a leaf from Mussolini's book, wanted to eliminate any elected legislature, where the Socialists were bound to have a large influence, since at least four out of every ten voters would support them. At the same time, it was deemed important to give the appearance of having an institution in which public opinions could be expressed. Dollfuss, and later his successor Schuschnigg, set up a very elaborate system of groupings, such as farmers, state and private employees, youth, and cultural organizations. These were then combined into several larger assemblies, such as the *Bundeskulturrat* (Federal Cultural Council) and the *Bundeswirtschaftsrat* (Federal Economic Council). It was their task to give advice on proposed legislation, which the government might or might not accept. These component parts of society also sent representatives to another body, the *Bundestag*, which could accept or reject but neither debate nor initiate.

In addition to being organized on a corporate basis, Austria was also to be an authoritarian state despite a facade of public consultations. Activities of the various groups were severely restricted. They did not have the right to exercise power or initiative. The deputies were not freely elected, for if the workers had been given the chance to vote, they would frequently have chosen Socialists.

The *Ständestaat* never really became operative as planned, and Schuschnigg learned too late that Nazism and not socialism Vienna-style was the real enemy of a relatively free and independent Austria. Not all the groups were organized in the four years that followed Dollfuss' proclamation of the new Constitution on May 1, 1934. Having governed for a while on the basis of an economic enabling law which was a resurrected wartime measure, the chancellor then began to rule on the authority of transitory constitutional provisions.

It seems worthwhile to point out that nonpolitical organizations were given influential legislative functions, at least on paper, in parts of the German-speaking area quite a few years before the establishment of the DDR. Neither the corporate state in Austria nor the "Socialist" regime of the German Democratic Republic was particularly interested in receiving input from sources not clearly associated with, let alone critical of, the existing government.

There are several distinctions between the two systems, however, and one of them is the time factor. The DDR's one-party regime has endured for several decades and still seems to be going strong, whereas the Austrian *Ständestaat* was a short-lived institution in the mid–1930s. Today Austria has a government based on the freely expressed vote of the people. With relatively small fluctuations, the majority of the electorate supports either the Blacks or the Reds, just as they do in the Federal Republic. As in West Germany, only one third party is represented in Parliament, apparently on a permanent basis. With no 5 percent clause threatening its existence at every election, the *Freiheitliche Partei,* the FPO, is almost certain to endure for quite some time. The *Freiheitlichen* had seats in the Second Republic's *Nationalrat* almost from the start as the only third party thus represented, a fate shared with the Communists until 1959. But whereas the Free Democrats in West Germany can look back to a liberal and democratic heritage, the spiritual ancestors of Austria's *Freiheitlichen* were anything but liberal and democratic. For the non-Socialist and non-Catholic third force in the last few decades of the nineteenth century in Austria expounded philosophies that were antiticlerical, anti-Socialist, anti-Liberal, anti-Jewish, and very much pro-German. Georg von Schönerer and Vienna's mayor, Karl Lueger, were exponents of that attitude in the waning days of the Habsburg monarchy.

When the First Republic was established at the end of World War I, sentiment for *Anschluss* with Germany was widespread. The struggling Austrian Republic saw the vast majority of the electorate go either Black or Red, but a *Grossdeutsche Volkspartei* (Greater German People's party) and an agrarian party, *Landbund,* together held enough support in Parliament to represent the balance between the two major parties from 1920 until 1933. By siding with the Christian Socials and opposing the Socialists, they successfully kept the Reds out of the government. Their pro-German attitude in time became pro-Hitler, and their promotion of his goals culminated in Austria's incorporation into the Third Reich.

The Führer's rule and its results discredited any further pan-German movements. When the conquering Allies licensed political parties after the war, they gave the green light to the People's party, the Socialists, and the Communists. But any group that had been connected with the Nazis and with undermining the First Republic was viewed with suspicion and could not hope for Allied approval.

During the first few years, all three parties represented in Parliament participated in the government. When the Communists, the only opposition party, left the administration, not many people had seen in them a real alternative to the government's policies. Therefore there was need for expression of a nongovernmental viewpoint which, however, was not Communist, especially for the elections of 1949 when half a million previously disenfranchised Nazi supporters were allowed to vote. That year, the *Verband der Unabhängigen* (League of Independents or VdU) obtained a place on the ballot. With almost half a million votes and 11.7 percent of the total, they received sixteen seats in the *Nationalrat* and did almost as well four years later. Moreover, in 1951, in the first popular elections for president, an Independent candidate, Dr. Burghard Breitner, garnered about the same number of votes. This was sufficient to deny first-ballot victory to either major party and forced a run-off election.

Any political party composed largely of independents is actually a contradiction in terms and faces serious internal difficulties, because it is likely that the component parts have little in common. The Independents in Austria were no exception. The new Republic proved itself economically successful and politically viable, and the coalition was able to terminate the occupation by getting the occupying powers to withdraw in return for the promise of perpetual Austrian neutrality. Consequently, relatively few people felt compelled to cast their votes outside the Red/Black alliance, especially as the leaders of the VdU were soon engaged in bitter quarrels among themselves. By 1956, the party was dissolved and recreated under the name of *Freiheitliche Partei Osterreich,* although getting only 284,000 votes and six seats. In 1959, if obtained an additional 50,000 supporters and two more seats. It stayed above the 300,000 mark in 1962, but in the following four elections its support remained fairly constant at around a quarter of a million votes. This meant one figure representation in the *Nationalrat* from 1956 until 1970. In 1971 and in 1975 they received ten seats only because the total number of mandates had been increased from 165 to 183.

The image of the FPO in the mid–1970s is that of a third force tied neither to the Catholic nor to the Socialist doctrines. Their difficulty is that the philosophies which once dominated the Black and Red camps are no longer pronounced. Therefore, the necessity to have an alternative to the two major parties seemed essential to a relatively small number of people, 250,000 out of 4.5 million in 1971.

Since 1970 the FDO has been led by a former Nazi officer, Friedrich Peter, and has many former Nazi adherents amongst its

Table 15. Noncommunist Third Party Strength in Austria

Year	Grossdeutsche Partei, then Nationaler Witschaftsblock	Landbund	Heimatblock
1920	26		
1923	10	5	
1927	12	9	
1930	10	9	8

Year	Verband der Unabhängigen then Freiheitliche Partei	Percent of total vote	
1945	—	—	
1949	16	11.7	
1953	14	10.9	
1956	6	6.1	
1959	8	7.7	
1962	8	7.0	
1966	6	5.3	
1970	5	5.5	
1971	10	5.5	
1975	10	5.4	

followers. It accepts Austrian independence as a necessity, and its party program states loyalty to the Austrian democratic Republic while also acknowledging the cultural community of the German people. There is no *Anschluss* philosophy, and anti-Jewish sentiments are not openly manifested.

The *Freiheitlichen* would like to be part of an administration but have thus far been excluded from office. While the Grand Coalition lasted, the OVP and the SPO worked together and did not need the small FPO. In 1966, the Blacks had an absolute majority of seats in the *Nationalrat* and could get along without any support. When the SPO took over in 1970, it was the largest party in the legislature, but lacked a majority. A coalition with the FPO might have been a possibility, except that the *Freiheitlichen* had vowed during the campaign that they would not cooperate with the Socialists. The Kreisky minority government was the result. But although the FPO had only five seats, they did hold the balance of power. They chose to cooperate with the SPO when it came to reforming the election laws, which promised them greater parliamentary representation, and they voted for a measure that brought about the 1971 contest earlier than was constitutionally required. They had high hopes for a SPO/FPO coalition; indeed their main aim in 1971 was to prevent either party from gaining an absolute majority, and as the last votes were counted, they had reason to be optimistic. However, when the final calculations showed the Socialists in control of 93 of 183 seats, a one-party majority was assured and the FPO was once again out in the cold.

A future coalition with a major party cannot be ruled out, however. At present, such an alliance would most likely be with the Socialists, though conditions may change again in the future. By the mid–1970s the FPO had definitely moved toward the left, and for the moment the Socialists seemed to be enjoying more popular support than the People's party. The Reds would be in a better bargaining position and thus a more likely partner for the *Freiheitlichen* if the time should be ripe for a coalition in the near future. What makes this possibility all the more noteworthy is the nationalist image the FPO still possesses, and the fact that Socialist leader Bruno Kreisky is of Jewish background. The difficulty this presents to the Blues, as the FPO is sometimes called, is illustrated by an incident in the summer of 1973. A Viennese FPO leader spoke out against an alliance with the Socialists because he felt a "certain subconscious antipathy" toward Kreisky because of his "background." He denied any anti-Jewish implications and his party supported him in his denial, but his remarks created quite a furor. In the end Mr. Klement was motivated to resign "freely and voluntarily" from his party post, thus helping to maintain the respectability that the FPO is trying so hard to establish.

Switzerland has the only genuine multiparty system among the five countries. Some of the major Swiss parties (Communists, Socialists, and Christian parties) have already been discussed.

Several others need to be mentioned here; notably the Radicals, Liberals, Farmers, and Independents.

Although many of the deepest philosophical differences have long since disappeared, political parties in Switzerland must also be considered within the framework of their historic development. What complicates this picture is that some of the original parties have split and produced other groupings. On occasion, names have been changed and rendered differently in German as compared to French, which makes the translation into English all the more difficult. Sometimes a party is only of regional importance, and there are instances when a party is known by one name in one canton and by another name elsewhere.

The post-Napoleonic settlement of 1815 evoked a variety of responses in Switzerland. Liberal and progressive elements wanted a more decentralized governmental structure while conservative forces advocated a large degree of autonomy for the cantons and the provincial churches. The Civil War of 1847 brought these contrasting claims to a head. Victory came to those who desired logical development of the principles proclaimed by the French Revolution. The dilemma now facing the Swiss was in part due to new interpretations of their old ideals. They had long fought for freedom, but now freedom did not mean independence from foreign domination but individual freedom of thought and action. Similarly, equality no longer meant just equal rights for all cantons, large and small; instead it meant abolition of classes and of other differentiations among citizens. That these various interpretations led to claims and counterclaims, resistance, and even fighting is not too surprising.

The Constitutions of 1848 and of 1874 established a viable central government but at the same time maintained the cantons as important local units. Individual liberties were guaranteed, and there were provisions for secularism rather than religious dominance, especially in the schools. The Liberal-Radical elements were definitely in the saddle and the 1848 Constitution was their handiwork. Afterward a split occurred, and the Radicals advocated further reforms, which materialized in 1874 but which the Liberals opposed. From the end of the nineteenth century until

1917, the Radicals held comfortable majorities in every *National-rat* and this enabled them to claim six out of seven members in the Federal Council which governs Switzerland. The seventh seat, at one time in Liberal hands, went to the Catholic Conservative opposition in 1891 and remained until 1917 the only non-Radical representation in the *Bundesrat*.

In 1919, proportional representation was established. This was a fairer election system that allowed the party vote in an election to be more closely reflected in the number of seats obtained. This reform eliminated Radical predominance. But the party remains an important component of the Swiss political scene, and since the 1930s has consistently won around fifty seats in the *Nationalrat*. It is essentially a pragmatic, middle-of-the-road party and opposes the Catholic policy when that seems too conservative, just as it condemns Socialist programs when it considers them too far to the Left. It may be compared to West Germany's Free Democrats. Like them, the Radicals in Switzerland lay claim to a liberal tradition, and the term *Freisinnig,* which means something like free-minded or free-thinking and is often used in connection with this group, aptly describes the image it wishes to present. Now known as *Freisinnig-demokratische Partei* (FDP), it speaks of the individual as central to the value system and necessarily in possession of the largest possible degree of freedom, although it recognizes tolerance, consideration of others, responsibility, and equality and social justice as essential goals. Its representation in the government has gradually diminished, but since the modern history of Switzerland began in 1848, no government has been without Radical members. The "magic formula" of 1959 allocates them two seats, the same as the Catholics and the Socialists. FDP member Ernst Brugger was elected to the *Bundesrat* in 1970 and became minister of economics. He also served as president in 1974. The other Radical federal councillor in the mid–1970s was Georges-André Chevallaz, who was put in charge of the Finance and Customs Department.

The Liberal Democrats have now become a rather small and insignificant party whose membership in the *Nationalrat* seems permanently reduced to one-digit numbers. Their importance is strictly regional: only Basel-Town and the French-speaking cantons send Liberals into the lower house and the *Ständerat* includes two Liberals, one from Genf and one from Waadt. In order to make the most of their small number in the *Nationalrat,* they have teamed up with the Evangelicals and together they have nine representatives at present. Liberalism, democracy, and a maximum amount of individual freedom, limited by considerations for the common good of the community, are some of their ideals. But they remain a mere shadow of what they once were and have been excluded from the *Bundesrat* for a long time.

Of far greater significance is the *Schweizerische Volkspartei,* the SVP, which is of recent origin, since it dates back only to 1971. Before that time it was known as the Farmers, Artisans and Citizens party, and as the Democratic party in Glarus and Graubünden. Its opponents may charge it with being a conservative farmers' group or even a "bunch of archreactionary right-wingers," and by its own admission, it does not wish to appeal to "revolutionaries and Marxists." As its old name implied, it wants to represent farmers and artisans as well as the bourgeoisie. "Party of the middle and of reason" is one of the slogans it employs. With some twenty members in the *Nationalrat,* the SVP is the fourth largest group. Since 1929, it has claimed the seventh seat in the government. In 1965, its representative was Rudolf Gnägi, who was first put in charge of transport and energy, but who switched to military affairs two years later.

Two other fractions, on opposite ends of the political spectrum, must be mentioned. The *Landesring der Unabhängigen,* a group of independents, was founded in 1936 and advocated preparedness against foreign invasion, alertness to the destructiveness of Nazism, and the building of a strong economy through the breakup of monopolies and trusts. It favors cooperatives, appeals to the lower middle classes, and its dozen or so members of the *Nationalrat* come primarily from Zürich but also from Basel and some other areas.

Zürich is also the home of Dr. James Schwarzenbach, whose right-wing national action group opposed the increase in foreign laborers and their influence on the Swiss economy. This group unexpectedly elected eleven deputies in 1971 and has caused some anxiety among the more moderate population. Whether it will be

Table 16. Political Parties in the Swiss Nationalrat

Party	1971: No. of seats	1975: No. of seats	1971: Percent	1975: Percent
Catholics	44	46	20.6	20.6
Social Democrats	46	55	22.9	25.4
Freisinnige	49	47	21.7	22.2
Volkspartei	23	21	11.1	10.2
Liberals	6	6	2.2	2.3
Evangelicals	3	3	2.1	2.0
Landesring	13	11	7.6	6.2
Rep. & Nat. (Schwarzenbach)	11	6	7.2	5.5
Labor (Comm.)	5	4	2.6	2.2
Autonomous Soc. (extreme left)	0	1		1.3
Others	0	0	2.0	2.1
	200	200	100.0	100.0

permanent, or whether, like the Poujadists in France two decades earlier, it will almost immediately disappear again remains to be seen. A stringent antiforeign labor policy suffered a severe setback in October of 1974 when the proposal to deport half the foreigners within a three-year period was defeated in a referendum by a two to one margin. During the months that followed, the expanding economy was somewhat curtailed and fewer jobs were available. Many aliens became unemployed and consequently left the country. The problem seemed to be solving itself naturally and without any political measures being necessary, and this may well deprive the Action party of its main issue and constitute a major reason for its decline in the 1975 elections.

The political system of Switzerland is flexible enough to allow the immediate development of political parties that have a limited program but stand for a policy that has considerable appeal to some sections of the population and that is not voiced by anyone else. Although there is no absolute guarantee that reason will always prevail in the end, the traditional support that the major parties seem to enjoy on a permanent basis does set up a system of as sound safeguards as is possible in a democratic country.

12

Referendums and Upper Chambers

We now turn to the legislatures, where the philosophies expounded by political parties are put into practice. Before dealing with popularly elected parliaments, however, something must be said about two institutions that restrict these parliaments: the referendum and the second chambers. While the former is certainly more democratic than the latter, both can have restraining effects on the actions of the people's representatives.

The concept of direct democracy was familiar to the ancient Athenians. Their town meetings were held ten times a year and every male citizen above the age of twenty was entitled to participate. There were, however, many people in Athens who did not have citizens' rights and who were therefore automatically excluded. Nevertheless, within this restricted framework final authority rested with the Assembly of Citizens, even if, as George H. Sabine points out, the formation of policies and even a discussion of measures were not really a function of the assembly which was confined to electing magistrates, judges, and generals and often to ratifying decisions made by the council. Thus, Sabine calls direct democracy carried out by a town meeting "rather a political myth than a form of government."[1]

The practice of free, arms-bearing citizenry assembling in the open air under a huge tree where they reached vital decisions involving the common good was characteristic of the German tribes. With the coming of feudalism such customs gradually disappeared, surviving only in some rather isolated villages. Occasionally, they are still to be found in Switzerland today. In Appenzell, with a population of five thousand inhabitants, a town meeting is held every spring under a tree. Such a practice has become the exception; however, it is significant that it still survives.

What has survived on a far more prominent scale is the concept of direct decision-making by the people themselves. Like all modern states, Switzerland has adopted the principle of representative democracy. But unlike most other countries, popular consultation has become a refined democratic device in Switzerland. It takes two distinct forms, the initiative and the referendum.

These are easily distinguished. Initiatives give the people a chance to correct sins of omission while referendums deal with sins of commission perpetrated by Parliament and government, on which the voters pass final judgment.[2] Two kinds of referendum exist in Switzerland: the compulsory and the optional. The compulsory referendum deals primarily with changes in the Constitution. These must be approved by both a majority of the voters and a majority of the cantons. Most cantons provide for referendums for the passage of laws. The other type is called an optional (Fakultatives) referendum, and comes about when at least thirty thousand signatures are collected favoring a particular question to be submitted to the people. A simple majority of the electorate is required for passage. A referendum must also be held if eight cantons so request, but this provision has thus far never been put into practice. An idea of the frequency of referendums can be obtained when one knows that between 1848 and 1972, 1,157 federal laws and resolutions were passed in Bern that could be subjected to the referendum. Of those, 96 were obligatory. While the other 1,061 might have been submitted directly to the people, only 73 actually were. Of those, 28 were accepted and 45 rejected, and of the latter about half were submitted before 1900.[3]

In addition to the referendum, there is also the possibility of the initiative. The referendum we have just discussed deals with federal laws and resolutions which can be changed if the public so demands. The initiative is different, for it gives the people a chance not merely to voice objection to a law and thus prevent its execution, but to press for measures that otherwise might not have been started at all. The 1974 endeavor by the *Aktion* group to evict foreign laborers was given no chance of serious consideration by the legislature, but enough signatures were gathered for it to be submitted to the people. Had it passed, it would have become law; however, the voters in their wisdom rejected it. Its main function may well have been propaganda value: the small group obtained eleven seats in the parliamentary elections of 1971 because their point of view was prominently aired during the weeks preceding the initiative.

In September 1977, the Swiss voters decided by referendum that it would take one hundred thousand signatures to force an initiative. Before that, only fifty thousand were necessary, a figure which had remained unchanged since 1891. At that time, it was a large number in proportion to population, about 8 percent of the voters. With ten times as many voters today, the proportionately smaller percentage should be more easily obtainable. Be that as it may, the main point is that Swiss democracy does provide for the possibility of the initiative. Although the Swiss probably vote more often than most other people, certainly more than any other German-speaking country, it does not mean that they approve everything that is put before them. Between 1891 and 1972, sixty-one initiatives were held. Forty-five were unsuccessful and of the others, ten were subject to counterproposals at the same time. Only six were accepted outright, and these included the introduction of proportional representation and subjecting treaty ratification to the referendum.

Switzerland is not the only country under discussion that provides for direct consultation of the people. It is a convenient device in totalitarian countries where propaganda and results are carefully controlled. Thus it should come as no surprise that the referendum is an institution in the German Democratic Republic, where the *Volkskammer* is entitled to call for one whenever it is deemed necessary. The 1968 Constitution was put before the people in the final version and 94.49 percent of all eligible voters approved it. Two decades earlier, the SED had called for a referendum on the desirability of German unity to be held throughout the four zones of occupation. As there was no doubt about the outcome of such a vote and the propaganda value that would result from it for the Communists, the Western parties and authorities rejected the suggestion.

The Austrian Constitution also recognizes the value of direct democracy. It provides for the possibility of a referendum in case it is demanded by a majority of the *Nationalrat*. Such a referendum must be held if the constitution is rewritten in its entirety, and may be held in the event of partial alteration of the constitution. In November of 1978, the government felt that the best way of dealing with a highly controversial matter (the activation of the nuclear power plant at Zwentendorf, outside of Vienna) was by seeking public approval through a referendum. Chancellor Kreisky even threatened to resign in case of a negative vote. Although he was dissuaded from doing so when the electorate did say no, the matter was embarrassing and damaging to his image.

There have been some instances when the initiative has been used. The law provides that a certain number of signatures can bring about the submission of a proposed law to the legislature for its consideration. The reform of the radio and television industry, the reduction of the work week from forty-four to forty hours, and the abolition of the newly introduced additional senior year in high school (the ninth *Gymnasialklasse*) were all instances of the initiative being applied to bring pressure to bear on the legislature.

The German Federal Republic allows for a referendum only in the exceptional case of a reorganization of the federal territory, i.e., redrawing the border lines of the individual states. However, several of the *Länder* have provisions for such popular consultations which frequently also apply to the local communities.

In Liechtenstein, the referendum plays an important part in the legislative process. The size of the country is particularly suitable, for direct democracy becomes increasingly difficult in larger countries. In West Germany, as in the United States, occasional referendums are held on the state level. In Britain, the holding of a referendum on the common market issue in 1975 was as controversial as the question of entry was in itself. Liechtenstein's referendums have become quite famous in recent years, because as recently as

1973 its male population by a vote of 2,126 to 1,675 denied women the vote. Liechtenstein is thus the only country in all of Europe where the right to participate in elections is limited to men. There seems to be full agreement that it will be merely a matter of time before this is changed. In 1971, a similar referendum failed by eighty votes, however, so that the increase in the no-vote two years later must be regarded as a setback. Enfranchising women is consistently supported by government, Parliament, the local newspapers, and the royal family; apparently the only opposition comes from the majority of the participating voters.

Direct consultation of the people is, therefore, not always positive and constructive in itself, since without a referendum this measure would have become law in Liechtenstein long ago. Perhaps a certain conservatism, not to call it stubbornness, among the men of Liechtenstein has something to do with the rejection, for unlike the French who are inclined to vote yes in referendums, the Liechtensteiners seem to like to say no. For many years, the government has been trying to persuade the voters to agree to an increase in the membership of the *Landtag* from fifteen to twenty-one, only to see the suggestion defeated time and again, the last occasion being in 1972. In fifteen referendums between 1947 and 1968, eight were accepted and seven rejected. The attitude is therefore not always negative, but the voters apparently decide each issue separately.

One problem of democratization is whether the legislature should have one house or two. There is general agreement that one body should be elected by the people and therefore be able to claim to be representative of the electorate. When we have referred to the legislature or to parliament in recent chapters, it is this popularly elected chamber that was meant.

However, a case can be made for the existence of a second house, and this raises questions about whom it should represent, how its members should be chosen, and whether or not it should have the same powers as the other house. There are three basic reasons for having a second chamber: restraint, representation, and federalism.

Restraint means that there is some fear that the popularly elected house has too much power, and that legislation should be reviewed by another body that can put the brakes on if necessary. This idea of restraint is increasingly being discarded today. Countries like Sweden and New Zealand have in recent years switched to unicameral systems. However, in forty-nine out of the fifty states in the United States bicameral legislatures are still very alive, partly because of the tradition that emphasizes checks and balances and partly because of the example set by the two-house legislature on the federal level. The argument in favor of restraint is still valid, and it is certainly not anything new. Some of the ancients accomplished restraint by decreeing that the same political body had to pass each proposal twice, once when the members were drunk and the next time when they were sober. The reasoning was that in the first instance they had enthusiasm and in the second wisdom.

Restraint is probably not the major cause for the existence of the three bicameral systems (of sorts) that we find in the five German-speaking countries. Neither is representation, at least not today. Representation means that emphasis is placed on estates, groups in society, or economic interests. The British House of Lords, a relic of times gone by, is probably the best-known example. It once voiced the opinions of the nobility and the clergy, while the commoners met in the other house. The *Herrenhaus* of the Austro-Hungarian empire was organized on lines of nobility or high position in the state, but it vanished with the monarchy. One could also mention the system prevailing in the German Democratic Republic where, as we have already discussed, specific groups such as youth, women, and labor are entitled to special representation, but they are part of the *Volkskammer* and do not form a special branch of a two-house legislature.

This brings us to the third reason for bicameralism, which is probably the soundest and perhaps the only remaining defensible reason, if popular representation is a desirable principle today. While the people vote for what amounts to a house of representatives in direct elections, the states should also have their special body with input in the legislative process. A federal system is thus presupposed.

In our group of five countries, there are two unitary systems. Liechtenstein, even though historically divided into two parts that still constitute the two election districts, is not a federal country. Its unicameral legislature seems sufficient for its needs. The DDR is a little different, for it started out with a subdivision of five separate *Länder:* Brandenburg, Mecklenburg, Sachsen, Sachsen-Anhalt and Thüringen. The Constitution of 1949 provided for a legislative body inferior to the *Volkskammer,* which was called the *Länderkammer.* As the name implied, it represented the states: each *Land* had the right to send spokesmen to that body on the basis of one deputy for each half-million inhabitants, but with a minimum of one per *Land.* The Chamber of States was not powerful, since it could only introduce bills and delay them. Obviously the purpose of this body was not to hinder the People's Chamber but merely to express the federal character of the DDR. Whether federalism is actually possible in a one-party state is another question. The hold which the SED has over the DDR, and the fact that the other parties are independent in name only, prevented any true form of federalism from working right from the start.

In 1952, the five *Länder* were done away with. In their place appeared fourteen districts or *Bezirke.* It was felt that "the local organs of the executive must be reorganized in such a way that will give the state apparatus the possibility absolutely to fulfill the will of the workers as expressed in the laws of the German Democratic Republic and, founded on the initiative of the masses, to carry out a policy of the working people." This meant that the regime felt there was danger that the *Länder* might one day develop into effective checks of the national government and that such a possibility had to be nipped in the bud. The *Länderkammer* lingered for another six years, with delegates from the district assemblies making up its membership, until it was abolished altogether. Beginning with the 1968 Constitution, no provision has been made for bicameralism.

The other three countries profess federalism, and therefore bicameralism, but in varying degrees. In Austria the main parliamentary body is the *Nationalrat,* the popularly elected chamber whose composition determines the government and whose powers include those of passing legislation. By its side there also exists a *Bundesrat,* a Federal Council which supposedly represents the *Länder* into which the federation is divided. *Nationalrat* and

Bundesrat together form the *Bundesversammlung* or Federal Assembly, which declares war, witnesses the swearing-in of a president, and if necessary impeaches and removes a president. Apart from the presidential inauguration, which is ceremonial since the president is elected by the voters at large, the other tasks are unusual, and have not occurred in the history of the Second Republic. The Federal Assembly is thus not an important body.

Neither is the *Bundesrat*. Anton Pelinka and Manfried Welan, authors of one of the best commentaries on the Austrian Constitution, use such terms as "shadow existence," "constitutional stillbirth" and "being without either a direct or an indirect function" to describe the *Bundesrat*. In other countries there are often disputes between the popularly elected chamber and the upper house, but not in Austria. First of all, the suspensive veto, which may be overridden by the *Nationalrat*, and the right to introduce bills are only sparingly used by the *Bundesrat*. Second, when action is taken it is not so much on behalf of the individual provinces but by the parties, so that the Federal Council really acts as another battlefield for the party struggle, which goes on mainly in the *Nationalrat*. The *Länder* send an unequal number of deputies to the *Bundesrat*, chosen by the *Land* parliaments according to the parties represented there. Vienna sends twelve deputies, Salzburg three, and Tirol four, of whom three are Blacks and one is a Socialist, which approximately reflects the standings of the parties in the state Parliament. But all this is not important for, as Pelinka and Welan point out, the *Bundesrat* does not reflect the dichotomy between *Land* and federal authorities nor the division among the individual provinces, but only the interests which are articulated by the political parties.[4] The very seating arrangement is by parties and not by states, another indication that the parties are national rather than regional in character. Until fairly recently, the SPO was regarded as being chiefly Viennese. Kreisky is the first chairman who did not come from the Vienna group. The reason for this is that the Reds used to find most of their supporters in the capital, while the OVP was largely based on the rural countryside. The divisions of the latter are occupational, not regional, and comprise federations of workers and employees, of farmers, and of commerce. The deputies follow party lines rather than provincial interests, especially since Austria is now divided into two election districts whose delegates are chosen according to proportional representation. As far as the *Nationalrat* is concerned, additional votes for the party in one of the *Länder* may well elect a person whose home is in another. Members of the *Bundesrat* are frequently either older party faithfuls on the way to retirement, or aspiring politicians sent to the upper chamber by some provincial legislature to prepare themselves for election to the *Nationalrat,* which apparently a good many of them achieve.

If the *Bundesrat* in Austria could be given fairly quick treatment because of its relative insignificance, the body with the same name in the German Federal Republic deserves more attention because it is quite important. One reason is that federalism is taken more seriously in Germany than in Austria. It will be remembered that a national government was established in Austria before the war actually ended and that this government operated throughout the occupation. Despite division into four zones, one government prevailed, held elections, and was responsible for many of the day-to-day affairs of the state. As the occupying powers increasingly disagreed among themselves the Austrian government benefitted from that disagreement.

Germany, on the other hand, ceased to have a government when Hitler's appointed successor, Admiral Dönitz, surrendered unconditionally. Each occupying power slowly rebuilt the political structure on the *Land* level. History and geography had left their marks on the various parts of Germany far more profoundly than was the case in the German-speaking areas that remained as "Austria" after the dissolution of the empire. In addition to regional differences that exist, for example between the North Sea coast and the alpine southern regions, the *Länder* were often created for the convenience of the occupation authorities. While Bavaria, Schleswig-Holstein, and the city-states of Hamburg and Bremen are historic entities, North Rhine-Westphalia and the Rhineland-Palatinate are entirely new postwar creations. Prussia, which for the best part of a century had dominated Germany because of its size and political and military power, was simply erased from the map.

Just as there were states in North America before there was a

United States, so there were *Länder* in zones of occupation before the Federal Republic was created in 1949. The Basic Law states in its preamble that it was established by the German people in their respective *Länder*. Because the rebirth of a strong national government was to be avoided, considerable powers were retained in the individual states. Tradition was on the side of such a policy: during the peaceful days of the empire and under Weimar, the states handled many local matters by themselves. Hitler's "equalization" process was alien to strong regional interests and was discontinued immediately after Germany's collapse in 1945.

With state governments still important today, there is an obvious necessity for *Land* input in the national legislative process. The *Bundesrat* serves this purpose. A comparison with the United States Senate may be appropriate because here too the states are represented in the upper house of the legislature. However, there are some pronounced distinctions. For one thing, as in Austria, members of the *Bundesrat* are not elected by the people. In West Germany, unlike Austria, they are not chosen by the legislature but instead are named by the particular *Land* government of which they are members. Thus they represent the administration of a particular state, voice its views, and are made up of adherents of whatever political group happens to be in control of that state. As this control changes hands, the individual *Bundesrat* members change too.

Secondly, as in Austria, but again unlike the United States, there is unequal representation in the *Bundesrat*. The Basic Law provides for each *Land* to have at least three seats in the upper chamber. *Länder* with more than two million inhabitants are entitled to four, and states with more than six million people may send five representatives. Since 1957 four states have had five seats, three have had four, and three have had three each, for a total of forty-one. In addition, Berlin is entitled to four advisory members. The deputies from each *Land* vote as a bloc and one representative casts all the votes from his state. This is one more contrast to procedures in the United States Senate. But then it must be remembered that a U.S. senator is an elected deputy of the people of his state, while the members of the *Bundesrat* of the

Federal Republic express the opinions of the governments of their states.

This is clearly reflected in powers and functions. The U.S. Senate is at least the equal of the House of Representatives and even has authority over matters denied the House, such as ratification of treaties or confirmation of presidential appointments. The *Bundesrat,* however, is definitely inferior to the *Bundestag.* In a democracy the people are supposed to rule, and in practice this means that no legislative body can be superior to that elected by the people. Therefore, in a dispute over legislation the *Bundestag*'s views ultimately prevail. Furthermore, it is the *Bundestag* which elects the chancellor and which can, under specific circumstances, express its lack of confidence in him and cause his dismissal. All those functions are denied the *Bundesrat.*

West Germany's upper chamber is the direct heir of the *Bundesrat* of imperial fame and of the *Reichsrat* in the Weimar Republic which is not often mentioned when the institutions of the First Republic are discussed. That *Reichsrat* represented the *Länder* on an unequal basis, and with nonpolitical experts permanently speaking for the states regardless of changes in the political makeup of state governments. It facilitated state-federal relationships and scrutinized bills. It was a useful administrative device but hardly a political one. When Hitler dissolved it after the state governments had ceased to exist as independent units, his flagrant breach of the constitution caused minimum excitement.

Since the Bonn Republic emphasizes federalism, the new *Bundesrat* has a significant political part to play. All legislative proposals by the federal government must be sent to the Federal Council first so that input from the individual *Länder* will be forthcoming before the legislation is introduced in the *Bundestag.* After the latter has passed a measure the *Bundesrat* may object to certain provisions and ask for a joint committee to settle the differences. If this is not done the *Bundesrat* may, by a negative vote, prevent the measure from becoming law. This veto is not absolute for the *Bundestag* may override it. A majority vote in the *Bundestag* is sufficient to override if the *Bundesrat* objected by less than a two-thirds vote. But if two-thirds of the *Bundesrat* are opposed, it takes two-thirds of the membership of the *Bundestag* to over-come this veto. Occasionally some piece of legislation may even be introduced in the upper chamber by one of its members.

The *Bundesrat* can probably best be described as influential rather than powerful, for it gives the states a chance to have their views expressed and even insisted upon without at the same time being able to override the wishes of the federal electorate. The members of the *Bundesrat* represent the voters too, but on a local level, for the state governments are themselves dependent on a majority in the elected *Land* parliaments. Party affiliation plays a part here too, and there have been instances, especially in recent years, when the CDU/CSU-dominated state governments con-tinued to fight in the *Bundesrat* against such matters as *Ostpolitik* after having lost the battle with the SDP/FDP administration in the *Bundestag*. The federal government thus takes more than a passing interest whenever *Landtag* elections are held. A loss for the government parties may not only mean loss of prestige but also change of party composition in the *Bundesrat* and thus serious consequences for the national administration.

Since the importance of the individual parts of the federation is most pronounced in Switzerland, it is here that representation of provincial interests is most significant. But before discussing this, one semantic difficulty must be explained. Federal Council or *Bundesrat* is the name given to the second chamber in the German Federal Republic and in Austria. There is also a *Bundes-rat* in Switzerland, but here it is not the upper chamber but rather a council of seven members which governs the country. In other words, it is the executive, the government, the cabinet. What is called *Bundesrat* in Bonn and Vienna, in Bern becomes the *Stän-derat*, which is the Council of the Estates, or of the states. An official document of the Swiss Parliament even translates this term rather loosely as "senate." Council of States is probably the best functional, though not necessarily the best literary, rendition.

In any case, in this council we find the only upper chamber in a German-speaking country where the American principle of senatorial equality is maintained. Each canton, regardless of size, has two representatives in the *Ständerat,* and the half-cantons have one vote apiece. This adds up to a total membership of forty-four, a figure that will remain constant until the efforts to create a twenty-third canton, set in motion by a 1974 referendum in Bern, are successful.

It is indicative of the independence of the individual cantons that the selection process as well as the length of term of *Ständerat* members are left up to each state. Although the voters in most of the cantons make the selection directly, as of 1968 there were three instances where the Great Council, the local Parliament, made the selection and four cases where the choice remained in the hands of the *Landesgemeinde,* that gathering of citizens which meets as a group every year. Most cantons prefer four-year terms, though some prefer three years. Only a short time ago St. Gallen changed from one year to four.

The Constitution makes it clear that members of the *Ständerat* vote "without instruction," like American Senators but unlike *Bundesrat* delegates in West Germany. Legislation in Switzerland is truly a two-house procedure. The Federal Assembly, which is made up of the *Ständerat* and the *Nationalrat,* is required to participate in the law-making process. The two houses, except in some special circumstances, meet at the same time but separately, and there are regulations about how differences between the two chambers may be overcome. If such efforts should prove futile, the proposed measure fails to be enacted. Thus the two houses are virtually equal to one another.

Party composition in the two bodies demonstrates interesting divergencies. In the *Nationalrat* population is represented according to its size. Thus in the 1970s Bern and Zürich send more than thirty deputies each, four other cantons were allocated between eleven and fourteen apiece, while five of the cantons or half-cantons could claim no more than one. At the same time, each canton has two delegates in the *Ständerat,* even though Zürich had more than a million inhabitants, and Uri, thirty-three thousand. Because the rural areas tend to be more conservative than the big cities, we find that the Christian Democrats and *Freisinnige* enjoy an overwhelming numerical advantage over the Socialists in the *Ständerat;* in 1971–75 they had respectively seventeen, fifteen, and four seats in the upper chamber while in the *Nationalrat* each of the three parties had close to fifty deputies. The *Volkspartei,* with half the Socialists' strength in the lower house, had one more seat than the Social Democrats in the upper chamber. In effect, therefore, the Socialists are at a distinct disadvantage in the *Ständerat,* where they have 10 percent of the seats despite the fact that about one-quarter of the voters support them in popular elections. While the *Nationalrat* is elected by proportional representation where minority votes are taken into consideration, the *Ständerat* is chosen by a majority system, no matter what particular method each canton employs. Therefore, the "non-bourgeoisie groups" as those of the Left are often referred to in Switzerland, have an almost built-in lack of influence in that part of the legislature. But the problem is not quite as serious as it may appear. For one thing, there is elaborate machinery to iron out differences between the two chambers so that the Socialists, because of their strong position in the lower house, are assured of considerable input. Likewise, the Socialists hold two of the seven ministerial seats in the *Bundesrat,* the same number as the Conservatives and Radicals. Also, although there are considerable differences in political philosophy between the various parties, the very fact that they can cooperate in the executive means that cooperation should be possible in the legislature. Moreover, much local autonomy still rests with the cantons and their governments, assuring that the national administration is not all powerful. In the last analysis, actions by the federal authorities may be overturned by the people in a referendum.

However, there is no denying that the Council of States is more conservative than the National Council and therefore acts as a restraint. While created to express federalism, the principle of acting as a brake against rash legislation and innovation applies here as well. Members of the *Ständerat* tend to be older and have more political experience than members of the *Nationalrat.* Many have been civil servants in their cantons and there are quite a few lawyers among them, earning for the upper chamber the nickname "the legal conscience" of Switzerland. Because of size, its meetings are more intimate and the *Ständerat* is able to accomplish tasks more quickly than is the other chamber.

Facing the cantonal councillors in their chamber is a huge painting of a meeting of a *Landesgemeinde.* In the *Nationalrat,* on the other hand, the painting behind the presiding officer is a peaceful Swiss landscape, complete with mountains and lakes. Flanking the mural are two statues, one of the liberator William Tell and the other of Gertrude Stauffacher, another legendary figure of the liberation period. She symbolizes thought, just as Tell symbolizes action, even though (as the guidebook to the Swiss Parliament so fittingly points out) until recently Gertrude and some stenographers were the only women admitted on the floor of the chamber. This latter situation has changed somewhat, although women in the Swiss legislature are not numerous. In the 1971/75 period only one woman sat in the *Ständerat* and only a dozen in the *Nationalrat*. This is better than the situation in Liechtenstein, but certainly subject to improvement.

13

Popularly
Elected Legislatures

In all five countries popularly elected legislatures exist in some form or another. The extent of their power, however, differs considerably. In Switzerland legislative authority is equally shared between the two houses. No similar situation exists in any of the other four countries where the directly elected parliament is recognized as being closest to the people.

We can turn first to the exception, the German Democratic Republic. The *Volkskammer,* according to Article 48 of the Constitution of the DDR, is the "supreme organ of state power." It is also the "sole constituent and legislative organ" of the country, whose rights can be limited by no one. Its deputies are "elected by the people for four years in free, general, equal and secret ballot." In 1974 the term was changed to five years.

No matter what the time period, these elections do not amount to real choices in the Western sense. Rather, they are expressions of confidence in the administration and confirmation of decisions with which nobody can in actuality disagree. The Communist-led German Unity party plays the leading role in the *Volkskammer.* Four other parties and some organizations are also represented. But since everyone faithfully toes the party line, it would be false to speak of meaningful differences of opinion. The executive and the legislature are basically one and the same, according to the principle of "unity of decision making, execution, and control." The *Volkskammer* names the chairman and members of the Council of State, the Council of Ministers, the National Defense Council, and the Supreme Court, as well as the attorney general, all of whom can be recalled at any time. It makes laws, determines regulations, lays down rules and ratifies treaties. It can also hold plebiscites. On paper, therefore, the *Volkskammer* is indeed the most important and most powerful institution in the DDR. One could question whether there is enough time to fulfill all these functions, even if sessions were held on a year-round basis.

However, the *Volkskammer* does not have regular meeting times, but is called together for plenary sessions at the discretion of the leadership. Whenever the parliamentary body is not assembled, the *Staatsrat* is empowered to act on its behalf and the Council of Ministers can also issue decrees without having to bother the *Volkskammer*. In any case, it is within the leadership of the SED that decisions are made that are then rubber-stamped by whatever body is chosen to carry them out. All this may be "democratic centralism," but it is not democracy in the Western sense. The newspaper *Neues Deutschland* once referred to the one list system used in elections as "the expression of the unanimity of all patriotic forces, the way of peace, of happiness and well-being for the German people." Political differences and social divergencies are thus identified with the class struggle, and are eliminated once capitalism no longer exists. This theory may explain a system which must be understood in a framework of values quite distinct from the ones we take for granted in the Western democracies.

Geographically, the Iron Curtain cuts right across Germany. Because of the circumstances of 1945, East Germany developed its "Socialist" regime while West Germany followed the governmental example of those World War II Allies that occupied the Western zones. Weimar was Germany's only experience with democracy and a short one at that; in the absence of a German democratic tradition new institutions had to be created. In what was to become the German Federal Republic a parliamentary system was established, nurtured, and developed. Its main body, the *Bundestag,* was elected in free, secret elections for four-year periods. The election method presented quite a problem in itself. The choice was between single member districts and proportional representation. The latter was certainly more democratic, since minority votes in a number of localities could be added together so that few voters would be without someone to represent them. The Weimar system allocated one deputy to every 100,000 votes, resulting in a large conglomeration of small parties and a splintering of Parliament that eventually made governing impossible. On the other hand, electing representatives by majority vote tends to favor strong parties. The position of the Socialists in the Swiss *Ständerat* as compared with the *Nationalrat,* referred to earlier, is a good illustration.

Faced with this problem, the German Federal Republic devised a system which makes use of both concepts. The country is divided into 248 districts according to population, and each elects one deputy by a plurality, the seat going to the person who receives the largest amount of votes. However, in addition to being allocated a certain number of district seats, each *Land* is allowed an equal number of deputies, to be apportioned according to the principle of proportional representation. This final allotment will take into consideration the number of district seats won by a particular party. For example, Schleswig-Holstein has eleven districts, which means it winds up with twenty-two representatives. In the 1972 elections the CDU received 42 percent of the votes and captured two of the eleven district seats. It was allocated a further seven seats from the *Landliste,* which gave it a total of nine representatives. The SPD, which managed to get a plurality in nine districts, got another two seats because it captured 48.6 percent of the total vote, while the FDP with no districts to its credit received two seats on the *Landliste.*[1]

Until the late 1960s the CDU/CSU regularly won the most district seats, but in 1969 they were outnumbered by the Socialists 127 to 121, while in 1972 the figures rose to 152 to 96 in favor of the Socialists. The FDP has not been able to get any direct mandates since 1957 when they received one; their representation in the *Bundestag* is entirely due to receiving a percentage of the vote across the country. This percentage figure has to be at least 5 percent. With the bad experience of Weimar as a warning, present-day provisions stipulate that seats on the *Landliste* can go only to those parties who obtain at least 5 percent of the total vote, unless they happen to capture three constituencies by plurality vote. The latter has proved to be an impossibility for small parties and the 5 percent clause has kept extremists and small splinter groups out of Parliament. The formula certainly contributed toward the elimination of any multiparty system and helped the Federal Republic achieve a high degree of stability.

At the center of the political life of West Germany is the *Bundestag*, composed of 496 representatives and another twenty-two from West Berlin who, however, do not vote on crucial issues. The chancellor and his government must have the support of the *Bundestag* before they can assume office. Under specific circumstances the executive may be dismissed by the legislature. The government cannot function unless it has the support of Parliament, a vast improvement over the situation prevailing during the Weimar Republic. Moreover, it is in connection with the annual budget and proposed legislation which the chancellor feels necessary for effective government that the executive branch is dependent on the *Bundestag*.

It has been argued that in modern times the powers of parliaments have diminished the world over and that administrations, through party control and through the bureaucracy that supplies the expertise which no deputy can muster, actually control legislation. There is certainly some truth in this contention. The drafting of bills requires knowledge not inherent in parliamentarians, who have to rely on experts for their information. Even merely to suggest a piece of legislation is complicated, for it requires the expertise of bureaucrats to assess properly the implications of the measures under scrutiny. As to political leadership, the government led by a particular party creates an image which is crucial at the next general election. A political group achieves a majority in Parliament; it therefore assumes the responsibility of office or shares it with another party in case of a coalition. Individual members of the majority party are expected to back the government and it is the record of the administration which will reward or punish them the next time the voters go to the polls. This situation is blamed for what some people feel is a deterioration in the quality of the legislators; the best brains, who once gladly accepted the challenge of parliament where they could excel, now allegedly enter fields such as the sciences where individual initiative and know-how is still rewarded.

Such contentions tend to be exaggerated. Granted that much of the argument is accurate, a case can nevertheless still be made regarding the influence, if not the power, of the individual deputy. There is an elaborate committee system in democratic legislatures where a hard-working, well-prepared, and articulate member can indeed leave his mark on the course of legislation. His own personal qualities may well help to get the party elected, and this is certainly true of district elections where a party's majority in Parliament can be traced back to certain individuals having won in their own constituencies. These legislators in turn have a claim on the party they helped to elect.

Although party discipline exists in practice, and parties usually insist that their deputies support the party position in Parliament, many constitutions stress lawmakers' individual freedom of decision. Thus the *Grundgesetz* proclaims in Article 38 that deputies "shall be representative of the whole people, not bound by orders and instructions, and shall be subject only to their conscience." That under certain circumstances deputies can defy their party leadership and use their own judgment was clearly demonstrated during the first Brandt administration. As a result of the 1969 elections, the SPD/FDP together had a 254 to 242 seat advantage over the CDU/CSU. In reality, there were already at that time a few FDP members who did not support the coalition government. There were more defections so that within less than two years a deadlock was reached. The defectors, often genuinely in disagreement with the new *Ostpolitik*, felt that they had to vote their conscience, a freedom specifically guaranteed in the Basic Law. They influenced events to a far greater extent than their numbers warranted, and they brought about a situation where new elections were almost inevitable.

The skeleton of Weimar was once again in the closet when the Bonn regulations with regard to calling elections were written. In the days of Weimar, the president had the right to dissolve Parliament and call for new elections, but he could do so only once for the same reason. This safeguard was actually ineffective, because new grounds could always be found. The same constitution further stipulated that all actions of the president required the counter-signature of the chancellor, a provision intended as another safeguard. In reality it was not, for the last several chancellors were appointed without having the confidence of the *Reichstag* in the first place, and they governed and called for new elections without being supported by anyone except the president. While these provisions were not the only cause for the downfall of Weimar, they did nothing to strengthen the republic.

The framers of the *Grundgesetz* were well aware of these faults and attempted to remedy them. For one thing, the president is now elected indirectly and therefore cannot claim to be the only true representative of the people and consequently able to take measures that he regards as necessary under particular circumstances. Under the present setup, the president may dissolve Parliament prior to the expiration of its four-year term under only two conditions, both of which having to do with the position of the chancellor. If no chancellor candidate can muster the necessary absolute majority in the *Bundestag* on his appointment, the president has the option of either naming the person receiving the largest number of votes as chancellor or of dissolving the *Bundestag*. So far every chancellor could be sure of a majority though sometimes not of a large one; Adenauer was first selected by 202 votes out of 402. In any case, negotiations usually take place privately and behind the scenes, so that in the end the majority is forthcoming and the possibility of dissolving Parliament does not arise.

A second possibility has to do with the chancellor requesting the *Bundestag* to express its confidence in him and the legislature refusing to give him majority support. In that event the chancellor can advise the president to dissolve the *Bundestag*, provided no one else can command a majority. This method was used once, in 1972, when Brandt's supporters amounted to exactly one half of the membership of the *Bundestag*. The government was thus one vote short of the minimum needed to pass the budget. At the same time, the opposition's attempt to name its own chancellor failed.

All sides therefore agreed that new elections were the only way out of this stalemate. Brandt now asked for a vote of confidence in the *Bundestag* and when the vote was taken, he and his government colleagues abstained, so that he was sure to receive fewer than the necessary 249 votes. When he actually obtained 235, the stage was set for the dissolution of Parliament one year ahead of schedule. In the existence of the Federal Republic to that date, this was the only time that the *Bundestag* was dissolved to break a political deadlock. In order to do so, the *Grundgesetz* had to be somewhat twisted, or at least used in a way not intended by its authors, but the method used, as well as the process itself, had the full support of all parties, government as well as opposition.

One further point should be made regarding the activities of the individual members of the *Bundestag*. This has to do with the right of members of the legislature formally to raise certain points of inquiry with the government. It takes fifteen signatures to request an answer to a *Kleine Anfrage,* a "small inquiry," which is given in writing. Thirty legislators can demand a reply to a *Grosse Anfrage,* a "large inquiry," which takes place orally and may be followed by a debate. Less formal are the oral questions which every member of the *Bundestag* is entitled to address to the federal government, but even this proved somewhat stiff and so in 1965, an *aktuelle Stunde,* or "current hour," was instituted whereby for an hour various questions can be raised in off-the-cuff speeches not to exceed five minutes each. These are then answered by brief government statements. With this innovation, the more formal inquiries have somewhat subsided, especially since all sorts of urgent matters may be raised by the deputies. If the president of the *Bundestag* is convinced of the urgency of a particular matter, two hours notice is all that is required. Thus, the question hour which is such an important institution in Britain as a means of taking the administration to task and of keeping it under constant scrutiny, is beginning to play a similar part in the German Federal Republic. There is also general debate on whatever issue is before the house, where the individual member can shine. Taking all this into consideration, the deputy is not a rubber stamp unless he wants to be one.

If the elected representative is slightly less important in Austria, it is due in large part to the elective system. Austria adopted the practice of proportional representation without the single-member districts which the Federal Republic added. Under a revised set of rules, adopted in time for the 1971 elections, Austria is divided into nine election districts, each corresponding to one of the provinces, of which Vienna is one. Every election district is allocated a certain number of seats in the *Nationalrat* and this number is determined according to population. Provincial allocations fluctuate with shifts in population. Between 1971–1975, the western provinces gained people and the east lost them, and therefore Vienna and Lower Austria found their representation reduced by four at the time of the 1975 elections, whereas several areas in the west increased theirs accordingly.

Similar adjustments are made in West Germany. But in the Federal Republic a list of names is cited on the ballot under each party column and the voter is in effect told that if one seat is won by a party, the first name is elected, if two, the first two, and so on. Consequently, each party will put its most popular vote-getters like Adenauer, Brandt, or Scheel at the head of its ticket in the hope of achieving a coat-tail effect. A candidate on the list may also run in a district and if elected there, the rank order on the list naturally changes. However, in any event the voter will know the top candidates of each party.

But in Austria the ballot merely gives the name of the party which the electorate is encouraged to support. No names of individuals appear on the ballot for the *Nationalrat,* although the names of the candidates in each province are widely publicized during the campaign and so is their ranking as determined by the party leadership. This information is available but the voter must ascertain it for himself before the election; the ballot itself does not provide it. Write-ins are permitted, but in order to accomplish anything by it, the rather large number of some twenty thousand votes is required. Besides, the most popular write-in candidates are frequently politicians who head their tickets anyhow, such as Bruno Kreisky in 1971.

After the votes have been cast, quite a bit of seat-allocating takes place. Even if someone has won a seat he may refuse to serve. After it became clear that the Socialists had enough seats to establish a one-party administration in 1971, Willfred Gredler, who had hoped to become foreign minister in a SPO/FPO coalition, preferred to return to his post as Austrian ambassador in Bonn rather than become a member of the small *Freiheitliche* fraction in the *Nationalrat.*

There is also the question of precisely how the seats are allocated. In the province of Salzburg in 1971, the three parties received 101,000, 94,000, and 25,000 votes respectively. With nine seats allotted to the *Land,* a mathematical formula determined that 24,000 votes would elect a deputy. This gave the Socialists four representatives, the People's party three, and the FPO one. This left one seat to be filled, which was placed in a larger pool as were the remaining votes of each party. Two such pools existed, one for Vienna and two adjoining provinces in the East, the other for the rest of the country. The remaining votes in each group determined the allocation of the remaining seats. What individuals were chosen was a decision of the party leadership after they received the mandate, with no guarantee that the ninth Salzburg seat would go to someone from that province.

This detail helps to illustrate the point that a member of Parliament does not play an important part as an individual. What is important is that the party has elected a given number of deputies. No wonder that Chancellor Raab is said to have remarked that these deputies perform "merely gymnastic activities." Without his political party, the member would not be in the legislature. In return, he is expected to vote with his party. Although the Austrian Constitution, like the *Grundgesetz* in West Germany, specifically declares that representatives are not bound by any instructions in the exercise of their office, this is as unrealistic in Austria as it is in the Federal Republic, although there have been a few instances of independence.

Much of the work of a deputy is done in committee, and because the party organization is basically in charge of selecting the candidates, it can at least assure itself of having the necessary expertise in Parliament. One legislator told me that he felt he owed his selection as candidate and his being placed high enough on the list to assure his subsequent election to his specific training in a particular branch of economics which his party needed for a certain committee assignment. While this assures much more professional handling of questions in committee than is possible in the United States Congress, it also makes a deputy's independence practically impossible. Whether the representative who very often is the product of a labor, farmer, small business or similar organization affiliated with a political party wants to go against the leadership of his party is another question. Were he or she to do so, there would be pressure to resign. This might be resisted, but the deputy certainly would not be put up as a candidate at the next election, and by the very nature of the political game independent candidates cannot be elected. The alternative would be the formation of a new party. What Franz Olah, after his ouster from the Socialist party and his formation of the Democratic Progressive party, accomplished in the 1966 elections was to amass 150,000 votes, which contributed greatly to the Socialist defeat without at the same time gaining any seats for his splinter party.

A deputy's salary is low enough to keep away some of the more capable, independent-minded persons who can earn much more elsewhere, while it attracts the lower echelons of civil servants, union leaders, farmers, professionals, and businessmen who might not be able to receive the same pay scale plus pension in another occupation. Supporting their party becomes, in addition to everything else, an economic necessity. If a deputy decides to break with his party, he becomes ineffective in Parliament because he is then automatically excluded from the *Fraktion,* the club formed by his party, and this, Pelinka and Welan maintain, "deprives him of any possibility to participate in committees. Without his *Fraktion,* the deputy loses all significance as far as parliamentary activities are concerned. Only through membership in a *Fraktion* is he able to participate in parliamentary activities." It was this consideration that motivated the Liberal and Evangelical groups in Switzerland to combine, and that made it so important for the Swiss Communists to win at least five seats in the *Nationalrat,* that figure being the minimum necessary in Switzerland for a party to form a *Fraktion.* As to Austria, in more than 25 years Pelinka and Welan count only six deputies who broke with their parties and remained in Parliament as independents until the session ended.

One may wonder what effect this almost faceless list has on the electorate on polling day. There are numerous election rallies, speeches, and other attempts by the candidates to introduce themselves to the people. They may present their biography, listing education, number of children, and professional or other experiences which to an American observer seemed singularly uninteresting. In any event, the voters respond by going to the polls in amazingly large numbers. In October of 1975 90.28 percent of those eligible participated. The lowest turnout in the history of the Second Republic thus far had been reached! Although voting is compulsory in presidential elections, it is voluntary in the contest for Parliament in all but three of the provinces. However, some voters might be confused and go to the polls in order to be on the safe side. But perhaps a far more plausible reason for the heavy turnout is the argument that whereas the names of individual candidates may be of little significance, it is important to the people what party wins and who the next chancellor is going to be. While voting for candidates whom they may not know, the voters in fact decide who will lead the next administration and what fraction will dominate, and this is what really counts.

The relative insignificance of a legislator cannot be attributed to the small size of Austria. After all, Liechtenstein is much smaller, and there we find an entirely different situation. With a total population that is surpassed by many an American small town, obviously practically everybody knows everybody else. It is, therefore, virtually impossible for the members of the *Landtag* to be nameless puppets of their parties. Moreover, the election system itself is designed to stress personalities. The country is divided into two election districts, the *Oberland* and the *Unterland*. Because of their differences in population, they are allocated nine and six deputies respectively. Each party presents a special ballot on which its candidates are listed. Voting is compulsory. The voter may mark the names of candidates, strike them, or add others. Once the total number of valid ballots is established, it is divided by the number of seats assigned plus one. This figure determines how many votes are necessary to elect one deputy, and the frequency gives the preliminary seats each party has received. The rest are allocated through the principle of the largest remainder. The number of votes obtained determines rankings on the parties' rosters. Although voting is done through the list system, the electorate is also choosing among individuals, and the more votes a candidate can accumulate, the more likely is his election as a deputy.

In Liechtenstein, men vote in large numbers and their votes do makes a difference. When (in 1970) the Patriotic Union won the election for the first time since 1928, it did so by polling thirty more votes than the Progressive People's party. In 1978, eighteen more votes in one of the election districts meant victory for the Reds again in an election in which 95.7 percent of those eligible participated. Contests have always been close. With one exception during the past three decades, Parliament has been divided in the proportion of eight to seven. This emphasizes the importance of the individual voter.

The *Landtag* meets eight or ten times a year for sessions lasting one or two days. Fifteen deputies are always present because the candidates on the party list who were not elected function as substitutes when regular representatives are unable to attend. Substitutes enjoy the same rights of participation in debates, asking questions, and voting. Under this system the regular member may ask the substitute to attend if a subject on the agenda is of particular interest to the substitute, or within his special area of expertise. Such a procedure is not unknown elsewhere; it is also used in Norway. But what makes Liechtenstein so different is the absence of any real ideological party cleavage. Politics concern personalities rather than philosophies, and issues are personal and pragmatic.

This should not be interpreted as meaning that everything is peaceful and gentlemanly in parliamentary discussions. On the contrary, debates may get quite heated. Deputies can attack one another just as strongly as in those legislatures where party ideologies are far more pronounced. This is especially the case when it comes to such important matters as finance. There have been instances where one party has accused the other of not keeping its election promises, misusing voters' confidence in its activities, trying to undermine voters' support as expressed in the last election, and not giving the other side a chance. Tempers do flare up and accusations of "forgery" and "theft" are heard on occasion.

As the body representing the electorate, the *Landtag* exercises the usual legislative functions, such as passing on proposed laws, which its own members may introduce. A cabinet officer, frequently the head of government himself, attends *Landtag* sessions, participates in debates, defends government actions and proposals, and answers questions. Members of the administration are as a rule not members of the legislature.

Parliamentary authority is somewhat weakened by two factors. First, Liechtenstein has the rather strange phenomenon, in the twentieth century, of a hereditary monarch with substantial powers. The second limitation derives from the fact that the desires of the all-male electorate are not solely expressed by its representatives in the *Landtag* but may also be heard directly in a referendum. Whether in the *Landtag* or in referendums, Liechtenstein's male voters seem to prefer the old ways of doing things. They have refused to enfranchise women, just as they have so far stubbornly refused their leadership's advice to enlarge the *Landtag*.

Switzerland, while just as conservative as Liechtenstein, did finally enfranchise its women after several cantons had done so earlier. This points to an inherent weakness of the Swiss federal system. Each of the cantons is proud of its heritage as well as of its right to be independent and different. The *Nationalrat* is only one link in the governmental arrangements, and certainly not the strongest, because the *Ständerat,* the executive, and the bureaucracy also play leading parts. The independence of the cantons limits the power of these federal institutions. Article 3 of the Constitution states:

> The cantons are sovereign, as far as their sovereignty is not limited by the Federal Constitution, and they exercise as such all rights which have not been delegated to the federal authorities.

Even in the field of federal legislation, the *Nationalrat* is only a part of a bicameral body and not, as is so frequently the case in other countries, the predominant one. As pointed out earlier, the *Ständerat* does not play second fiddle in the *Bundesversammlung.*

While the *Ständerat* represents the cantons on an equal basis, the *Nationalrat* reflects the population by means that have changed in two important ways over the years: the election system has been altered and the size of the assembly has not remained constant. Since 1919 members have been chosen according to the principle of proportional representation. Each party compiles a list of candidates, solicits the support of the electorate, and wins seats in proportion to the percentage reached in each canton. The listing is up to the parties, but the voters can still make their individual influences felt. They can simply vote for the list as presented by their party, although it is significant that since proportional representation was first introduced the vote for unchanged lists has fallen from 85 percent to 53 percent. They may cross out certain candidates; write in other names twice (that is, vote cumulatively); or write in names of candidates from lists of other parties. Voters can also vote for a party list containing no names at all. About one-fifth of the electorate combine candidates of various parties; more than a quarter use the cumulative process. Since candidates showing the largest amount of support win, this process is quite influential.

The introduction of proportional representation met with considerable resistance at first, especially on the part of the Radicals, who had been the predominant political group and who now found their strength in the *Nationalrat* almost cut in half. On the other hand, the Socialists almost doubled their number of seats and within a few years surpassed the Radicals. This situation was reflected in the executive, the *Bundesrat,* with the Radicals again the big losers. Proportional representation has the distinct disadvantage of depriving one party of its right as well as its ability to govern by itself. Without a majority it must modify its program to accommodate other fractions whose support it needs. On the other hand, the system more truly reflects popular divisions and therefore enables Parliament to be a cross-section of the people.

The Constitution provides for a four-year term for the *Nationalrat*. Elections are held every four years on the last Sunday in October, and the session begins in December. Dissolution prior to the expiration of the term is virtually unknown. Although the law calls for one continuous session a year, Parliament usually meets for a few weeks beginning in early December, March, June and September and at other times for emergency purposes. When it does meet, as the official guidebook proudly points out, hard work prevails, emphasizing that the Swiss Parliament must be the only one in the world that starts work at 8:00 A.M.!

Until 1931, one representative was assigned to every twenty thousand people. This gradually increased the membership from 111 in 1848 to 196 in 1951. The ratio had to be increased somewhat as time went by in order to keep the size below the two hundred mark. As the population increase continued, this proved futile. Since 1963 the law provides for a total membership of two hundred.

In terms of actual legislation in the *Nationalrat* as well as in the *Ständerat,* a number of commissions are organized according to subject matter, such as foreign relations, the military, science, and research. The committees are almost identical in both houses, although a committee to scrutinize elections exists only in the *Nationalrat* because this is a federal matter, whereas the *Ständerat* elections are the concern of the individual cantons. Care is taken that extraparliamentary forces have a chance to voice their views prior to parliamentary discussion of legislation affecting them. Nonparliamentary groups of experts are instituted to enable special interests and scientific bodies to have an input on the drafting of a bill, unless they were instrumental in having the measure considered in the first place. Important as this procedure may be, it does not necessarily enhance the power, influence, and prestige of the Swiss legislature.

We may therefore conclude that in our own days popular representation has lost some of its earlier significance. Today, only in Switzerland, because of its smallness and local peculiarities, and in neighboring Liechtenstein are direct popular decisions made frequently, and referendums and similar devices employed with any degree of regularity. Even there, as in the other countries under discussion, much of the power of government is now shifting back to the executives, which have some sort of popular backing either through support in the legislature or through direct elections. This is not to imply by any means that parliaments and parliamentarians have become useless and obsolete. But it is true that the political heads, reinforced through a staff of experts and bureaucrats, exert real power in the decision-making process. It is to this branch of the government that we must now turn.

14

Heads of State

If the legislature passes the laws, there is another group of people who actually carry them out, who execute the existing rules and regulations, and who conduct the affairs of state. Legislatures in democratic countries have the task of overseeing how these affairs are managed, and of calling their executives to account. Indeed, administrations frequently owe their existence to the election successes of particular parties in parliament, whose favors they must constantly court and whose dissatisfaction may cause the fall of the current government.

Although this is the general model, there are a number of variations. None of our five countries is exactly like the others. Only in Switzerland is the entire political apparatus of the administration chosen by the legislature. In Austria and in the German Federal Republic, the chancellor is also picked by the legislature and he and his cabinet depend on the support of Parliament. However, the titular head of the government, the president, is independently elected and serves a precise term unrelated to that of Parliament or the chancellor. In Austria, the people vote directly for their president, while in West Germany the legislature and representatives from the *Land* parliaments together name the president. In both these cases, the powers of this nominal head of government are severely restricted. In Liechtenstein, the composition of the administration depends on parliamentary election results, but the highest position in the country is held by a direct descendant of the nobleman who once bought two tiny principalities and gave them his name. The position remains hereditary and is anything but a figurehead. Finally, in the German Democratic Republic, the entire *Volkskammer* takes on figurehead characteristics, and the real power, executive and legislative, is exercised by the dominant party, whose governing role cannot be challenged by anyone.

Every four years, when the Swiss *Nationalrat* assembles after an election, it chooses a seven-member cabinet charged with governing the country. The term of office is forty-eight months, with vacancies to be filled by special parliamentary action for the remainder of the unexpired period. The name of this cabinet is *Bundesrat,* or Federal Council. Each member of the *Bundesrat* has certain responsibilities. The portfolios include foreign affairs (called the Political Department), interior, justice and police, military, finance and customs, public economy, and transportation and energy. All are given equal importance. The Federal Assembly each year elects one of the *Bundesrat* members as president and one as vice-president. The vice-president usually becomes next year's president. No president may succeed himself immediately. The office thus rotates, with newcomers to the council usually having to wait till older sitting members were named again. There is no limit on how often one may serve, depending of course on how long one stays on the council. The forty-eight-month term is basically unimportant, because a Council member is usually automatically reelected if he wishes. Although he may not succeed himself immediately, a *Bundesrat* member may become president twice or even more, provided only that he stays in office long enough. During a visit to Bern a few years ago, my attention was drawn to a tall, well-dressed gentleman crossing a busy square by himself, as unassuming and unnoticed as anyone else, and who might easily have passed for a banker or businessman. "That was the president of Switzerland," I was told.

Since the introduction of proportional representation, standings of the parties in the *Nationalrat* have remained remarkably stable.

Since 1959, the *Bundesrat* has consisted of two Christian Democrats, two Social Democrats, two Radicals, and one member of the
SVP, the old Farmers' party, in seemingly permanent coalition.
In fact, party composition has been more constant than the names
of the parties. Individual *Bundesrat* members change infrequently,
at irregular intervals, and certainly not as the result of political
upheaval or unfavorable election returns. Once a member of the
Bundesrat, one is assured of reelection as long as one wishes. No
federal councillor has ever been legally forced to resign, although
a few have been pressured into doing so.

Since the *Bundesrat* is a federal institution, great care is taken
to keep the federal partnership of the twenty-two cantons in mind
to the fullest extent. A number of carefully developed rules about
the selection of the seven members prevails. The Constitution
provides that no more than one councillor may come from any one
canton. This does not mean that a member must necessarily live
in a canton different from the others, but rather that his citizenship
and his family's origin is identified with a particular area which no
other *Bundesrat* member claims as his own.

The rules observed today are far more elaborate, however.
Zürich, Bern, and the French-speaking Waadt are usually represented as the largest areas. Not more than a total of five *Bundesrat*
members may come from the German-speaking cantons. These
regulations are faithfully observed and a careful balance is maintained, into which the party "magic formula" ratio of 2:2:2:1 is
painstakingly placed. One drawback of this scheme is that, with
some of the larger cantons assured of membership, smaller ones
find themselves at a disadvantage. Thus far, six cantons have never
yet been able to elect a *Bundesrat* member of their own. But by
far the greatest fault of the system is that it is so restricted that it
does not necessarily allow the selection of the best qualified
people. What happens if there are two potential councillors from
the same canton, or if the most desirable candidate originates from
non-German-speaking areas which have already reached their full
quota, or if none of the most prominent aspirants can claim Bern
or Zürich as his ancestral home? If one adds territorial restrictions,
party composition, and the fact that a sitting member can usually

count on reelection if he so desires, it is not hard to realize that these rules and regulations can keep out people who might be far superior to those actually elected.

The *Bundesrat* governs Switzerland for a four-year period. One might object to the use of the term *govern*; certainly of all the five countries under discussion, the national government at Bern is the least powerful in relationship to its component parts. Matters such as foreign policy and trade with foreign countries, currency and customs, railways and post, and telegraph and telephone have to be handled by the federal authorities. Relatively little else is. Only since 1912 has there been an all-Swiss civil code; only since 1942 has a uniform criminal code been applied throughout the country. Educational matters or professional licenses for lawyers are left to the individual cantons. As a rule, when the Swiss talks of his government, he means first the authorities of his town and village, then those of the canton, and only after that does he think of the national government in Bern. This may all sound natural to an American, but it must be remembered that Switzerland with its twenty-some cantons covers an area only about one-third that of the state of New York.

The peculiarism of the Swiss is well known and the people often indulge in making derogatory remarks about citizens of other cantons. Although this provincialism may be regarded as a fault, it certainly does provide for checks and balances which would effectively prevent a dictatorship. An army general is appointed only when mobilization is ordered and then only by a vote of the two parliamentary chambers. Democracy in the smallest village, as much direct decision-making by the people as possible, powers given to the federal government only if they cannot be exercised by anyone else—this machinery may appear cumbersome enough to keep the Swiss from ever becoming a major power. But then this is beyond Swiss ambitions anyway. They are quite content to enjoy their democracy, their high standard of living, and their conditions of peace.

The Swiss president cannot be separated from the rest of the *Bundesrat*, for he temporarily presides over that body, as indeed he nominally presides over the nation, but he retains his portfolio and remains responsible for the activities of his department. After a year, he quietly steps down and continues his other departmental duties. In the German Federal Republic and in Austria, in contrast, the presidency is the last step in a distinguished career, from which incumbents are expected to retire amidst highly laudatory speeches and press reports. Being in charge of a cabinet office and administering it while holding the presidency would be unthinkable in either Bonn or Vienna.

The mode of presidential election varies with each of these two countries and to understand it, we must consider their historic backgrounds. In Germany's Weimar Republic, the president was elected directly by the people. True, the first incumbent, Friedrich Ebert, was the choice of the National Assembly in the trying days immediately after the Armistice. In addition to the serious problems facing the country from abroad, there was severe unrest on the domestic front and Parliament extended the president's term of office to July of 1925. But before he had a chance to seek reelection, this time by the people, Ebert died.

His successor was Field Marshal Paul von Hindenburg, the candidate of the right-wing parties. In the run-off election Hindenburg's name was substituted for that of the mayor of Duisburg, Dr. Karl Jarres. Although Jarres had led the pack in the first contest and received 38.8 percent of the votes, he could not expect to outpoll the candidate of the now combined Weimar parties, the Center, Social Democrats and Liberals. Therefore Hindenburg's name was substituted and this move proved to be successful. The old soldier, however, did not behave like a frustrated supporter of imperial Germany but, on the contrary, stayed within the boundaries of the Constitution which he had sworn to uphold. This gained him the support of his former opponents when the next presidential election came in 1932. After his reelection, however, Hindenburg regarded himself as the sole representative of all the people and took measures which were not only antidemocratic and contrary to the wishes of the elected *Reichstag* but which eventually led to a far worse dictatorship, that of Adolf Hitler.

These events were vivid in the minds of those who wanted to establish a new and better democracy after the Second World War. They wished to ensure that the president could not repeat the actions of the pre-Nazi era. To accomplish this, several changes were made. The election of the president was taken out of the hands of the people and placed before a federal convention, the *Bundesversammlung,* a kind of electoral college consisting of the members of the *Bundestag* and "an equal number of members elected by the *Länder* according to the principle of proportional representation."[1] This group convenes for no other purpose than the election of the federal president. Votes are by secret ballot and without debate. On the first two ballots an absolute majority is required for a decision, but after that the candidate with the largest number of votes is elected. Because West Berlin votes at this convention, the total membership in recent years has been over one thousand.

Today the president serves for a five-year period and is eligible for consecutive reelection only once. This compares with seven-year terms under Weimar, where reelection was possible. The Constitution of the First Republic did not specifically limit the number of terms, which was a possible danger point, but in practice the problem never arose: Ebert died before the scheduled popular elections could take place in 1925, and Hindenburg's death occurred during the third year of his second term. Hitler carefully refrained from filling the position afterwards.

Shortly after the Second Republic adopted the Basic Law, on September 12, 1949, the federal convention elected Theodor Heuss, the candidate receiving FDP and CDU support. His principal opponent was Socialist Kurt Schumacher. Heuss was a journalist and writer, a university professor, and a *Reichstag* deputy for the German Democratic party (called the *Staatspartei* after 1930). He had fought against the rise of Hitler and although he eventually voted for the Enabling Law, he did so out of loyalty to his party colleagues, whom he had warned earlier of the dangers of such a step. His elimination from journalism by the Nazis testifies to his hostility to the regime. He spent the next twelve years in private life writing books. After the war, he became one of the founding members of the Free Democratic party, and was active in Württemberg politics and then in those of the new republic. Never afraid to remind his countrymen of the crimes committed in their name, he also fought for German rehabilitation. "The world would be poorer without the German spirit," he once said, "just as we were poorer when we were without the world's."

Modest and unassuming, he became a model first president. Re-elected in 1954 to a second term, Heuss contributed by his own example toward putting German democracy on a firm basis. "Democracy is power for a limited time," he declared when leaving office, an admonition that could well be directed toward Adenauer.

Indeed it was the chancellor himself who for a brief moment had notions of moving on toward the presidency as his age and his own version of indispensability became quite controversial. Eventually, however, the presidency went to Heinrich Lübke, Adenauer's minister of agriculture, in a contest between candidates of the three parties that was won by the CDU. Lübke had been a *Zentrum* deputy in the Prussian Parliament before Hitler came to power, had been active in the agrarian movement, and went to jail several times during the Nazi regime. It was said of him that he had "few admirers, many friends, and no enemies."[2] He was re-elected in 1964 with the support of the Socialists. They favored him because he was an advocate of the Grand Coalition uniting the CDU and the SPD in the same cabinet. It has been suggested that Lübke at times stepped out of his role as nonpartisan figurehead whose constitutional functions were severely limited; that his refusal to sign a document appointing a particular judge, his advocacy of the coalition, and his activities in getting his choices named to high positions were at the least improper and at the worst illegal.

In any event, when his term expired in 1969, the CDU/SPD coalition had become reality. But this did not prevent a spirited contest for the presidency. The CDU nominee was Gerhard Schröder, former minister for foreign affairs and now minister of defense. The Social Democrats named Gustav Heinemann, a one-time member of the CDU and minister of the interior in Adenauer's first government. In 1952 he left the Christian Democrats, established a splinter party favoring neutralism which he dissolved again in 1957, and joined the SPD, which he represented in the *Bundestag*. The same coalition government with Schröder as defense minister had Heinemann as minister of justice.

When the *Bundesversammlung* met in 1969 the FDP announced support for the Socialist candidate, thus foreshadowing SPD/FDP cooperation. Apart from those two and the CDU, the only other party represented in the Federal Assembly was the semi-Facist NPD which had shown some strength in previous *Landtag* elections. This right-wing splinter party supported Schröder. The vote was close, with only a few ballots separating the two candidates. Because of several abstentions, nobody received an absolute majority on the first two ballots. On the third, when only a plurality was needed, Heinemann was the winner by five votes.

The first Social Democratic president since Ebert was a deeply religious, thoroughly honest, and undeceptive man who left the office with more prestige than he found when he entered it. He undoubtedly could have been reelected in 1974, like his two predecessors. But at the age of seventy-five, Heinemann decided it was time for him to return to private life. The SPD/FDP coalition that governed the country was experiencing waves of unpopularity as expressed in local election returns and the administration had just been rocked by a spy scandal that involved the highest government circles. But the Socialists and Liberals were able to unite behind FDP leader Walter Scheel, foreign minister in the coalition government. At the age of fifty-five, Scheel became the youngest president. He had made a name for himself as coarchitect of the *Ostpolitik* and as a party leader.

The powers of the president are constitutionally defined and limited. With the skeleton of the Hindenburg presidency always present in the closet, there is little the president can do on his own initiative, other than set an example by truly being his country's first citizen. The election process makes him beholden to the *Bundestag* as well as to the state legislatures, although his five-year term means that he will still be in office after those who voted for him have had to face their constituents in another election. His role is like that of a constitutional monarch who serves for a limited time only. While in office, he represents the nation internationally, pays state visits and receives foreign dignitaries, and exercises the power of pardon. All his decrees must be countersigned by the chancellor or the appropriate minister in order to be valid. He does have some discretion in the choice of chancellor, but the degree of his influence depends on the strength of the political parties and their ability to negotiate. He must first find a candidate who can obtain the support of the *Bundestag*. If he locates such a person, the president officially nominates him, the *Bundestag* votes him into office, and the president formally appoints him. This ends the president's activities in this connection. If an absolute majority in the *Bundestag* is not forthcoming for the person proposed by the president and if the *Bundestag* by itself cannot agree on someone who can command such a majority, then there is another parliamentary vote after two weeks. If again nobody has majority support, the president has a choice. He must either appoint the candidate receiving the highest number of votes in Parliament or dissolve the *Bundestag* and order new elections.

This circumstance is one of the two reasons that *Bundestag* can be dissolved. The other being when Parliament refuses the chancellor the vote of confidence he may request, in which case the president once more "may, on the suggestion of the chancellor" dissolve the *Bundestag*. Would the chancellor specifically ask for such a vote if he knew he could not win it? Could the president refuse the chancellor's request for dissolution? He clearly cannot proclaim dissolution unless the chancellor suggests it. The law specifically states that dissolution cannot take place if the *Bundestag* by a majority vote supports another chancellor, whom the president then must appoint. The only time the dissolution provision was used was in 1972, when a deadlock was reached and new elections were agreed upon by all parties. In all the instances mentioned the president's freedom to act independently is virtually nonexistent. He may propose but the *Bundestag* must agree; he may undertake but only when the chancellor or his ministers "suggest."

Bonn also carefully provided for emergency legislation differently than Weimar's notorious Article 48. The present Article 81 makes it possible for the *Bundestag* to be bypassed in emergency situations when Parliament refuses to cooperate, but this may be done only on the suggestion of the federal government and only for one six-month period which may not reoccur under the same chancellor. Moreover, when the president follows the government's advice and declares such a state of legislative emergency, he may do so only with the consent of the *Bundesrat*, the representatives of the governments of the individual states. This is quite different from the measures to be taken "when public safety and order are seriously disturbed and imperiled" described under Article 48 of Weimar.

The kind of benign father figure which Germany found in war hero Hindenburg in the 1920s was even more necessary in Austria after the collapse of the empire. Whoever it was had to replace Emperor Franz Joseph, who had come to the throne in 1848. Reigning until 1916, he had become, for generations, an institution. When he eventually died, during World War I, the demise of the Austro-Hungarian empire was soon to follow.

It is interesting to note that the question of a replacement for the hereditary monarch was solved by both the Austrian republics in a way opposite from that of Germany. An indirectly elected president eventually gave way to a popularly elected one. The Germans, as we have just seen, did it the other way around. Democracy was to be the guiding principle in the early days of Austria's First Republic. This meant predominance of the popularly elected *Nationalrat*. The far less prominent *Bundesrat* aided the *Nationalrat* in electing the federal president, whose functions were and remained those of a figurehead, even when the Austrian democracy came under attack. Until the first presidential elections were held in 1920, the presiding officer of the assembly, Karl Seitz, acted as chief of state. When the vote was taken for a permanent president, there was much disagreement. It took several ballots before a compromise could be reached in the person of Dr. Michael Hainisch. In 1928 the Federal Assembly had to choose a successor, and on a partisan vote the candidate of the Christian Socials, the presiding officer of the *Nationalrat*, Wilhelm Miklas, was elected.

There had been much dissatisfaction with a political structure that left Parliament as the focus of political events. After a not too successful attempt at reform in 1925, important innovations were made in 1929. The president was to be more powerful: he could now dissolve Parliament, proclaim a state of emergency, and name and dismiss members of the government. In order to make him truly a counter force to the legislature, he was to be elected directly by the people. Early elections were scheduled and a date, October 18, 1931, was selected. However, the elections never took place. There were economic reasons for this but, probably more importantly, political power plays. Eventually Miklas' term was extended, but only by a sixteen-vote margin. The constitutional reforms had been intended to strengthen the presidency, but Miklas found that his prestige had been weakened since his reelection had not been accomplished by the people themselves. Instead of having the strong president that the reformers of 1929 had wanted, this position was increasingly assumed by the chancellor. The president could not prevent the elimination of Parliament as a viable force in 1933–34, any more than he was able to stop the events of 1938, although he apparently did make some gallant but unsuccessful last-minute attempts to avert Austria's surrender to Hitler.

After the war, the Austrian situation again differed from that of Germany. It took five years for a national administration to be reestablished in Germany. In Austria, on the other hand, a provisional government was established even before the war had ended. Because it was possible to treat Austria not only as Hitler's ally and accomplice but also as a Nazi victim, more favorable Allied consideration could be expected. The constitutional question then arose whether to begin anew with a different governmental structure. If the old one was to be retained, at what point was the history of the First Republic to be taken up again?

The provisional government issued a decree on May 1, 1945, by which the Constitution of 1929 was reactivated. Parliamentary life was to continue where it had been interrupted on March 5, 1933. This implied adherence to the principle of a strong president elected directly by the people. However, the first presidential elections in December 1945 were conducted under the old system by the Federal Assembly. The post went to seventy-five-year-old Dr. Karl Renner, head of the provisional government and repeated Socialist candidate for president, in recognition of his services. Many saw in him the father figure they apparently required. After his death in December of 1950, direct elections at long last took place. It took two ballots for another Socialist patriarch, Vienna's mayor, General Theodor Körner, to emerge victorious. He became actively involved in the formation of governments, refused to accept the resignation of an administration in 1952, and insisted in 1953 that the Grand Coalition be continued.

Körner died early in 1957, before his term expired. As a possible successor, the OVP nominated the political unknown Dr. Wolfgang Denk, who also received the support of the FPO. He was opposed by Socialist vice-chancellor Dr. Adolf Schärf, who gained almost one hundred thousand more votes than his rival. This was not much of a majority, but enough to win. Six years later, the slim 51 percent vote was transformed by Schärf into a strong 58 percent showing, even though his opponent was Julius Raab, federal chancellor from 1953 till 1961 and thus a well-known figure. When Schärf died in office in 1965, the People's party once more turned to a former chancellor, Dr. Alfons Gorbach, who had followed Raab as chancellor. The Socialists picked the popular mayor of Vienna, Franz Jonas, as their candidate, in part perhaps because they hoped that his name might rouse memories of the deceased emperor. In any event, Jonas continued the series of Socialist presidential victories and was reelected after six years in office, defeating veteran diplomat Kurt Waldheim. The unhappy tradition of presidents dying in office continued with Jonas, who died in the spring of 1974. This time, the Blacks rallied behind the mayor of Innsbruck, Alois Lugger, while the Reds picked the rather nonpartisan foreign minister in the Kreisky administration, Rudolf Kirchschläger. The Reds' candidate was elected, and thus became the fourth directly elected president of the Second Republic.

We have mentioned presidential roles in the formation of Austrian governments. The president has the power to influence events as long as the situation is fluid and unclear; that is, as long as there is no clear-cut majority in Parliament. Under such circumstances the president can use his discretion; he can work toward the selection of his choice and he can try to persuade the parties to accept his viewpoint. But clearly the standings of the parties and their positions greatly limit his influence. In 1970, Franz Jonas approved a one-party minority government under Bruno Kreisky; Jonas might have insisted on a coalition had he so desired. But in 1971, when Kreisky obtained an absolute majority in the *Nationalrat,* the chancellor and not the president held trumps, and his view would probably have prevailed if there had been a disagreement. In practice, the continuation of a one-party Socialist government was never in doubt. In normal, clear-cut situations the president plays a role like that of a figurehead monarch. Only in emergencies or when parliamentary elections do not produce an obvious winner is he called upon to enter the political arena.

This may be democracy in its best tradition. However, the office of head of state generally presupposes nonpartisanship, and because independence and initiative are virtues not generally looked for in the very model of a modern Austrian president, one may wonder whether the president would really be able to perform the nation-saving task that might be expected of him during an emergency. There is plentiful evidence that in the serenity of being an "elder statesman" political activities are held to a minimum. When, shortly after the turn of the century, a Frenchman suggested that the best choice for president of France's Third Republic would be the most stupid person they could find, he certainly did not have a future Austrian situation in mind. But the parallel is not too far-fetched, although Austrian presidents need not be stupid, only innocuous. In practice, Austrian presidents since the Second World War are expected to be gentlemen, often adored father or grandfather figures, who represent the beauty and sweetness of Austria rather than partisan political activism. Emergency situations are hardly called for in a country which today has reached a remarkable degree of stability and economic wellbeing.

The figurehead presidency, especially after World War I, was an ill-concealed substitute for a defunct royal reign. The last surviving monarchy of the Holy Roman Empire is Liechtenstein, where the principality has survived because the transformation to a full-fledged democracy was made at the right time. With the dissolution of the Austro-Hungarian empire, Liechtenstein eventually established close ties with Bern. At that time a domestic upheaval occurred, even if most citizens were unaware of it. The governor and the three members of the *Landtag* whom the prince had appointed all resigned. Eventually *Fürst* Johannes named his nephew as the new governor, an action accepted by Parliament. Some of the procedural steps may well have been constitutionally illegal; however, prince and people were able to reach an agreement, and the Constitution of 1921 was the result.

Even though the prince lived six hundred miles away, abolition of the monarchy was never contemplated. The *Fürst,* who visited his little realm periodically, had been on the throne so long that he, like Franz Joseph of Austria, was an institution, part of the scenery. The 1921 constitution was officially proclaimed on October 5, Prince Johannes II's eighty-first birthday. When he died in 1929, he had been on the throne for seventy years and few would disagree with the memorial inscription in one of the local churches, which called him "John the good, father of his people, helper of the poor, friend of peace, protector of the arts." He was the kind of beneficent ruler that a twentieth-century monarch is supposed to be. John was followed by his seventy-nine-year-old brother, Franz I, who nine years later appointed his grandnephew as regent. The time was March 30, 1938, a few weeks after Hitler's Third Reich, by swallowing Austria, had become Liechtenstein's neighbor. Franz I died in 1938, and on July 26 the regent assumed the title of Franz Josef II and became prince of Liechtenstein, a position he holds to this day.

One major reason for this monarch's popularity is that he was the first to make the principality his permanent residence. He is thus familiar with the affairs of state and has an easy, personal relationship with Parliament and government. Although the constitution provides for shared governance, any disputes that might arise can be settled behind closed doors. The Constitution describes the prince as head of state and declares his person to be "holy and unviolable." This in itself is a reminder of an era long past. But other constitutional provisions make it clear that the constitutional hereditary monarchy indeed rests on a democratic and parliamentary basis. The *Regierungschef* and the four ministers are named by the prince in agreement with, and at the suggestion of, the *Landtag.* Thus Parliament in reality determines the members of the government. Events in 1970, 1974, and 1978 clearly show that there is a switch in government personnel whenever another party wins an election. Legal experts disagree as to whether or not the prince is obligated to conform to the wishes of the *Landtag,* and also as to what might happen if a minister were to lose the confidence of the prince but to retain that of the majority in Parliament. In reality, it is doubtful whether the prince would wish to oppose the democratically elected Parliament, except under the most unusual of circumstances.

Similarly, Article 9 provides that each law needs the approval of the prince, which raises the question of whether the right of veto exists. Until little over a decade ago, commentators were inclined to believe that the veto continued merely on paper and that the prince, for practical purposes, would refrain from using it. However, in 1961 the prince refused to give his consent to a new hunting law which had originated through a popular initiative and was approved by the people in a referendum. The *Fürst* regarded the measure as unwise, rejected it as undemocratic, and as being contrary to the interests of even those who started the initiative. The people accepted this judgment as within his authority as protector of the state, especially since the prince now asked the government to have a committee study the subject and come up with a better proposal. This was done and eventually a new and much better law was worked out, which was approved by all concerned. The entire episode added to the prestige of the prince and the royal veto, while sparingly applied, definitely remains a possibility.

This means that in practice the prince will recognize the wishes of the people, but that he also will not hesitate to use the veto when he feels the situation demands it. Article 10 enables him to take steps necessary for the safety and welfare of the state in emergency situations, and it was under this provision that he extended the term of the *Landtag* during World War II. The wisdom of not holding elections during these dangerous times is hardly in dispute today.

The prince also represents his country in relations with foreign states, but the *Landtag* must give its consent to treaties. He has the power to pardon or to commute sentences, with the proviso that such a measure may be taken only at the suggestion of the *Landtag* if it concerns convicted members of the government. Although Article 48 gives him the power to call, conclude, adjourn, or dissolve the *Landtag*, it is hardly likely that he will do so under ordinary conditions. However, there have been instances when the factions in Parliament were unable to work together and a deadlock resulted that was broken only through new elections. Under those circumstances, the *Fürst* will use his prerogative, just as he will initiate steps to get diverse interests to meet together if he feels that by doing so agreement can be reached. In all this, the prince is obviously much stronger than one might expect a twentieth-century monarch to be. Any danger of misuse of monarchical power is slim because of the attitude held by people and monarch alike.

To the rotating presidency of Switzerland, the figureheads in Bonn and Vienna, and the monarch in Liechtenstein must be added one more type of head of state, that found in Communist East Germany.

When the German Democratic Republic was established in 1949, Wilhelm Pieck became its president. He represented the old-timers in the Communist party. Born in 1876 of humble origins, he became a Socialist and, at the end of World War I, a Communist. He was instrumental in establishing the "Socialist" regime in the Eastern zone and became increasingly identified with Communist party affairs. Together with fellow Communist Walter Ulbricht and Socialist Otto Grotewohl, he helped bring about the merger of the two parties. When the DDR became a reality, the largely ceremonial position of president went to the aged Pieck, who held it unchallenged until his death in 1960. Real power was exercised by Ulbricht, whose position in the government was only that of deputy prime minister. But he also occupied the position of general secretary of the Socialist Unity party, and since the party dominated, Ulbricht was probably the most influential man in the German Democratic Republic.

After Pieck's death, it was decided not to fill his post. Instead a Council of State was established, which elected Ulbricht as its presiding officer. His official position now indicated what was already true in practice, that he was the most important person in the country. In 1963, Ulbricht was reconfirmed as president of the *Staatsrat*. When Grotewohl died the next year, Willi Stoph became minister president, which did not affect Ulbricht's predominance. The Constitution of 1968 did not recognize any position of head of state or its equivalent. Instead, it provided for the Council of State which, according to Article 66, "fulfills all fundamental tasks resulting from the laws and decisions of the People's Chamber." It is responsible to the People's Chamber for its activities.

The 1974 version varies slightly but apparently not significantly in this respect. It provides for the chairman of the Council of State to be elected for five years rather than four. He "directs the work" of the council, appoints and recalls ambassadors, receives envoys, and awards medals and titles instituted by the Council of States. The rights to represent the DDR in international law, and to ratify treaties, rights that he had under the 1968 Constitution, have now apparently passed from the chairman to the council as a whole.

The functions of the chairman of the council are thus largely ceremonial and closely resemble those of monarchs of the British pattern. As long as this role was combined with that of party chieftain, however, it was quite a different story as illustrated by Walter Ulbricht, who had returned from exile in Moscow in 1945 to take the lead in the building of Socialist Germany. In May of 1971, as a result of unpopularity with the German people, his party, and the Russians, he lost his job as party chief to Erich Honecker, the new number one personality in the Communist hierarchy of the DDR. Nevertheless, until his death in the summer of 1973, he held the ceremonial position. In the German Democratic Republic, as in so many other countries, this post seems to be reserved for old and faithful politicians as a sort of retirement reward. This raised some questions when, upon Walter Ulbricht's death, the chairmanship of the council passed to Willi Stoph, who was chairman of the Council of Ministers at that time and only fifty-nine years old. However, there were reports that he was in ill health. Since the real power had apparently shifted from the Council of State to the Council of Ministers, its new chairman, Horst Sindermann, together with party boss Erich Honecker, seemed to be among the most influential people in the German Democratic Republic.

15

The Governments

We will now deal with the real decision makers in the executive branch. In each country under discussion, they reflect the standings of the parties in the respective Parliaments. Except in the DDR, where elections are after all devoid of any real contest, the voice of the people is thus paramount in deciding the composition of the cabinet. This is particularly true of the German Federal Republic and of Austria, and to a somewhat lesser degree of Liechtenstein.

However, in Switzerland a multiparty system based on proportional representation in a stable society makes for a situation where party strength in the *Nationalrat* changes little. As a result party composition in the *Bundesrat* remains virtually the same. The Swiss system is not a parliamentary one, for the federal councillors, the members of the government, are chosen for four-year terms and cannot be removed by parliamentary votes of no confidence. An incumbent who wants to be reelected is usually assured of his post. It is around vacant positions that the political battle is waged, taking careful note of geographic balance as well as the necessities of the magic formula of four-party representation. If a political group can present a name that can command majority support in the Federal Assembly, well and good. If not, it may take several ballots and perhaps quite a bit of horse-trading before it is all over: the best man does not always win, nor is victory assured for the original party nominee. In 1973, three vacancies were filled by men who had not been the official choices of their parties. By what the *New York Times* described as a "stinging" disavowal, the three were elected by the necessary absolute majority on the first ballot, thereby defeating endorsed party candidates.

Once new members are named, the *Bundesrat* meets and decides who should head what department. Incumbents usually retain their portfolios, but it is by no means unusual for a more senior member to claim a recently vacated ministry. Rudolf Gnägi, who was chosen in December of 1965, headed the Transport and Energy Department for two years and then switched to the Military Department when the incumbent, Nello Celio, gave up that office to seek another portfolio. Even though each of the councillors has a specific area of duties, they work under the *Kollegialsystem* where they cooperate as colleagues for the benefit of the country. Each is an equal of the others, and important decisions are made as a group, thereby overlooking as much as possible previous partisan ties. But no matter how a member may have fought a particular decision within the *Bundesrat*, once adopted he must defend it in public.

When Parliament is in session, all members of the *Bundesrat* may attend. At least one of them always does, depending on the subject under discussion. Although the legislature does not have the power to terminate the ministers' term of office, its members can and do request information from the government by way of different devices, some of which may lead to heated debates and criticism of the administration.

The *Bundesrat* itself meets formally about twice a week. More important, however, is the close physical proximity of the governmental offices. Because they must see each other almost daily, personal ties and friendships are formed among the councillors, so that much of the actual business can be conducted privately and informally. The ministers are expected to lead unassuming, simple, middle-class lives, arrive at their offices at 8:00 A.M., and travel as little as possible outside of the country. The president in particular is not supposed to leave Switzerland during the year in office, although he personally represented his country at the Helsinki Conference in 1975. Perhaps the entire situation is best summarized by the legend that members of the *Bundesrat* travel third class on the railways, the reason being that there is no fourth class.

Switzerland is a rather unique situation. A certain amount of decentralization may be found in the German Federal Republic, although the West German *Länder* are larger than Swiss cantons, while their powers are more limited. But they do have some real power, which in turn weakens the national executive. The principle is maintained that the federation, the *Bund,* and the states are basically equal. The federal government is not superior to the states nor does it supervise the activities of the *Länder.* Detailed jurisdiction is stipulated by the *Grundgesetz.* However, if the *Land* does not fulfill its constitutional obligations, the federal government, with the support of the *Bundesrat,* that is, the majority of the other *Land* governments, can force the *Land* in question to perform its duties.

To say that important tasks and obligations are inherent with the state and therefore not within the competence of the federal government does not mean that the latter does not occupy a powerful position. Indeed it does, and this makes the federal chancellor who heads the government the most significant political personality in the Federal Republic. The first chancellor would not have been content with anything less. The Constitution stipulates that the chancellor "shall determine, and be responsible for, the general policy guidelines." He also "shall conduct the affairs of the federal government." He suggests possible ministerial appointments to the president, and is responsible for the overall business of government. Individual ministers, under his guidance, look after their own particular portfolios.

A chancellor is appointed immediately following a *Bundestag* election when new majorities may have developed. This does not mean that, once appointed, the chancellor is safe from removal for the next four years. The chancellor in the German Federal Republic is dependent on the *Bundestag,* and when he no longer has its support his days in office are numbered. The framers of the

Grundgesetz were well aware of the rather irresponsible way in which chancellors could be dismissed in the days of Weimar. They also had before them the examples of France's Third and Fourth Republics.

In order to prevent such a chaotic situation, Bonn provides that the only way in which a chancellor can be dismissed is for a majority of the *Bundestag* to vote for a replacement as chancellor and to request the president to name him and dismiss the old one, a request the president must honor. Merely voting against someone is not enough; the majority of Parliament must be willing to name someone else. This is known as the "constructive vote of no confidence," because it cannot be irresponsibly applied. Only once so far has this been attempted. In April of 1972, after the Brandt government had suffered a series of defections, the opposition proposed to replace him with CDU leader Rainer Barzel but failed to do so by a two-vote margin, thus saving Willy Brandt's administration by a razor-thin majority. The chancellor himself may ask Parliament for a vote of confidence, and if he cannot muster a majority of all elected members, he may ask the president to dissolve the *Bundestag* unless the legislature can name someone else who has majority support. Willy Brandt utilized this provision to hold elections a year ahead of schedule. He acted in full agreement with the other parties and it seemed to be a good way of overcoming the parliamentary deadlock. However, this solution went beyond the actual letter of the law and its long-range effect may be harmful in the future.

During the first twenty-five years of its existence, the Federal Republic has had only five chancellors, three of them members of the CDU and two Social Democrats. The first was the father figure Konrad Adenauer, who was seventy-three years old when he assumed the office. He had been active in *Zentrum* party politics, was unanimously elected mayor of Cologne by the city council in 1917 for a twelve-year term, and won reelection in 1929 by a one-vote margin. The Nazis dismissed him soon after they came to power. Adenauer had been harassed and repeatedly imprisoned during the Third Reich, so it seemed natural for the American conquerors to give him back his job in 1945. However, as Cologne came under British occupation, he was dismissed for supposed lack of energy and administrative incompetence. Even though this order was rescinded shortly afterwards, it did help establish the point that Adenauer was by no means a tool of the Allied powers, and subsequent events left no doubt on that score. Adenauer worked hard in the councils of the CDU, making the new party a progressive Christian force in which he, the pious Catholic, could work with Protestants. The Parliamentary Council which drew up the *Grundgesetz* was chaired by Adenauer, and when the first *Bundestag* met after the 1949 elections, Adenauer won the chancellorship with 202 votes in the 402-member body.

One of his major achievements was the change of status for West Germany from a former enemy to a valued friend and ally in the contest with communism, a task that was greatly enhanced by his friendship with such Allied leaders as John Foster Dulles and Charles DeGaulle. Another vital job facing the Adenauer administration was rebuilding the war-damaged country. To this day, there is talk of the *Wirtschaftswunder,* the economic miracle which transformed the Federal Republic into one of the world's leading economic powers and the German mark into one of the soundest of currencies within a short period of time.

The man chiefly responsible for this achievement was Adenauer's minister of economics, Ludwig Erhard. An academician who faced dismissal from his post rather than join the Nazi party, Erhard became active in Bavarian politics after the war and was Adenauer's economics minister in all four cabinets and vice-chancellor in the last two. While this seemed to make him Adenauer's heir-apparent, the old chancellor was in fact violently opposed to such a succession, first because it was next to impossible for him to harbor any thought of his own retirement, and second because he did not believe that Erhard had the necessary drive and initiative for the post. However, in 1963 Adenauer was finally persuaded to step down and at the age of sixty-six, Erhard took over as chancellor, continuing his predecessor's long-standing alliance with the FDP.

Erhard was not the most successful of chancellors. His party improved its position in the 1965 elections but so did its rival, the SPD, while its coalition partner, the FDP, lost quite heavily. In October 1966, there was disagreement between the government parties which could not be settled, and the Free Democrats withdrew from the administration. A crisis developed and the party councils of the CDU and CSU did not seem particularly interested in saving Erhard's political skin.

Members of the Christian parties in the *Bundestag* soon afterwards chose Kurt Georg Kiesinger, the minister president of the state of Baden-Württemberg, as their candidate for chancellor. That Kiesinger had joined the Nazi party in 1933 at the age of twenty-nine and remained in the Foreign Office during the war as liaison with Goebbels' Ministry of Propaganda has become a matter of considerable controversy. In any event, he won his party's nomination, and after unsuccessful negotiations with the FDP an agreement was reached with the SPD. Erhard resigned and on December 1, 1963, the *Bundestag* approved Kiesinger as chancellor, thus ratifying a situation created through activities of the various parties behind the scenes. A Kiesinger-Brandt coalition was now formed that excluded the FDP and thereby left parliamentary opposition in the hands of forty-nine Free Democratic deputies.

This administration began the rapproachement toward the East, the so-called *Ostpolitik* with which Willy Brandt in particular is associated, and which eventually was to earn him the Nobel Prize for Peace. Domestically, economic, financial, and penal reforms were instituted. Kiesinger as chancellor and Brandt as vice-chancellor and foreign minister cooperated with mutually beneficial results: thus Kiesinger's Nazi past seemed to become acceptable to some people through his association with a refugee from Nazi persecution, while Brandt's absence from Germany during the Hitler period and his service with the Norwegian armed forces became palatable to others because Kiesinger seemed to have confidence in him.

In any case, the activities of the Grand Coalition were overshadowed in 1969 by the forthcoming elections, in which Kiesinger and Brandt were rivals for the chancellorship. Despite early claims to victory, the CDU/CSU, while remaining the strongest single party in the *Bundestag*, lost some support among the voters. The Socialists, on the other hand, having shared power for the first time in a generation, gained more than 3 percent, while the FDP went from 9.5 percent to 5.8 percent. The real winners, therefore, were the Social Democrats, whereas the Free Democrats did not seem to benefit either from being associated with the CDU or being in opposition to the government.

The Free Democrats had never quite forgiven the Christian Democrats who dropped them after so many years of Christian-Liberal cooperation. Consequently, they swung their support to Socialist Gustav Heinemann the previous spring and assured his election as president. It soon became clear that this new alliance with the Socialists would be continued, and that the next government would be a coalition between the SDP and the FDP with Willy Brandt as chancellor and Walter Scheel as vice-chancellor and foreign minister. What had been unthinkable a few years earlier had thus become reality: the CDU was in opposition and the FDP had allied itself with the Socialists.

It was a relatively new experience for the Germans that government changes could be brought about peacefully and democratically by elections. Within a span of a few years, all three parties represented in the *Bundestag* had, at different times and in different combinations, cooperated with the other parties and played their part as members of the executive. This not only showed that they were willing to assume responsibility, but also that they could modify their own positions so that they could work together with their coalition partner. A country once known for its uncompromising, extremist political forces now regularly gave more than 90 percent of its vote to parties that were democratic, moderate, and pragmatic.

The small majority that the SPD/FDP government had in the *Bundestag* after the 1969 elections dwindled and disappeared, necessitating the 1972 elections at which the coalition received the overwhelming support of the voters. A year or so later criticism of the government mounted. Local election results showed a definite swing toward the CDU. Brandt was said to be tired of his job. Then it was discovered that one of his trusted advisors was actually a Communist spy. Brandt decided to take full responsibility for having trusted the wrong person. He resigned the chancellorship while still retaining the chairmanship of his party. The resignation demonstrated a high sense of responsibility and of moral values, setting standards which could not but strengthen the young democracy.

New top leaders emerged. The position of chancellor went to Finance Minister Helmut Schmidt. Walter Scheel, junior partner in the Brandt-Scheel coalition, was elected president and his place as vice-chancellor and foreign minister went to the chairman of the Free Democrats and former minister of the interior, Hans-Dietrich Genscher, thus continuing the Socialist-Liberal alliance. Two years later, in October 1976, the administration had to meet a determined challenge at the polls. After seven years in opposition, the Christian parties under the new leadership of Helmut Kohl attempted to regain power but failed by a few votes, getting 243 seats to 253 for the government parties, which were thus confirmed in office, probably for another four years.

Since the first elections were held after World War II, Austria has had five chancellors, the same number as the German Federal Republic, even though its democratic history started four years earlier.

On April 20, 1945, Dr. Karl Renner, who had been negotiating with the Russians, could state that they had asked him to form a provisional administration. This was accomplished a week later when a coalition of the three resurrected political parties was announced. The Americans, British, and French were not at all happy about the Renner government's dependence on the Soviet Union, and for a while refused to allow it any authority in their zones. In his memoirs, Harry Truman stated that there was no objection to Renner himself, but that his government had been established without consultation with the West and despite Western protests. Eventually, Renner was able to overcome the resistance and distrust of the Western powers, and after meeting with their representatives, he enlarged his government in order to answer the charge that it was based too much on the city of Vienna. On October 20, six months from the day Renner had first announced that he had been called upon to form a government, he was recognized by the Western Allies as well. He was given charge of the entire country, with the important proviso that all proposed legislation had first to be approved by the occupiers.

There was a free contest that November for the first time in fifteen years. It resulted in the emergence of the OVP and the SPO as the two major parties. Together they received 94 percent of the vote, leaving the Communists with a mere 174,000 out of more than 3 million votes cast. Consequently, the government was re-organized. Renner moved to the president's office; Leopold Figl, People's party leader, took over the chancellorship; Social Demo-crat Adolf Schärf became vice-chancellor. The Allies confirmed their recognition of the Austrian government, still subject to con-trol by the occupying powers.

One of the major problems facing that government was how to prevent the Russians from taking over local industries. The Aus-trians therefore proceeded in 1946 and 1947 with nationalization on a grand scale. Nationalization is usually a Socialist concept, but it became a national necessity in Austria and was carried out with full cooperation of the two parties, thus removing it from internal politics altogether. Further elimination of friction between the OVP and the SPO was achieved through the institution of *Proporz*. Every ministry and nationalized industry was headed either by a Black or a Red, according to a carefully planned and painstakingly negotiated scheme. Whatever party provided the person in com-mand, the other party named his deputy, thus giving rise to the joke that every government agency was headed by three people, a Black, a Red, and somebody who did the work.

The Figl-Schärf government continued in power until 1953, al-though some adjustments were necessary after the 1949 election improved the position of the Socialists in the coalition, because the People's party could no longer claim to be the choice of almost half the population. In terms of advantages within the coalition, the Socialists achieved much less in 1953 than four years earlier, even though this time they were in a far better electoral position. The first casualty was the chancellor himself, whom the Blacks blamed for their losses. Attempts were made to create a national coalition with the Independents but the Socialists would have none of it. Then there was talk of a "Small Coalition" between OVP and the third party. Eventually, all that happened was a renewal of the OVP-SPO alliance, but under a new leader, Julius Raab. Figl continued to play an important part in public affairs and was entrusted with the conduct of external affairs. The Socialists picked up two under-secretary posts; one of them in the foreign ministry went to Dr. Bruno Kreisky. In all these negotiations President Körner played an important role, and by no means confined himself to remaining quietly behind the scenes.

The most important task confronting the government, however, was to put an end to the Allied occupation. This was accomplished in 1955 with the signing of the State Treaty. After a decade of prolonged negotiations, Allied troops were withdrawn from all of Austria. In return, Austria "of its own free will" declared its permanent neutrality. In a sense, this was the high point for the coalition government; it certainly was the most important and the most pressing problem it had to deal with.

The 1956 elections showed great gains for the OVP, smaller successes for the SPO, and losses for the other parties. The Grand Coalition continued with Raab as chancellor and first Dr. Schärf and then Dr. Bruno Pittermann as vice-chancellor. The same political alliance was renewed after the 1959 elections. If 1959 showed the two major parties at almost equal strength, 1962 saw the Blacks gaining two seats at the expense of the Reds. Chancellor Raab had earlier faced serious problems, including disapproval of his actions by his own People's party leadership and conflicts with Socialist Vice-Chancellor Pittermann. Eventually Raab resigned and was succeeded by another OVP member, Alfons Gorbach, who led his party in the 1962 contest. Afterward it took several months to hammer out another coalition agreement, clearly indicating increasing difficulties between the two major parties.

The next elections in 1966 were fought under a different chancellor, Josef Klaus, who had replaced Gorbach as a result of intraparty squabbles. Negotiations between the Blacks and the Reds were started after the OVP achieved a parliamentary majority, but led nowhere. As a result, the OVP decided to govern alone. The Grand Coalition, begun as an emergency measure in the last days of the war, had finally come to an end after more than two decades.

If the Blacks were quite satisfied to govern by themselves without running rough-shod over the opposition, the Socialists in turn reformed their thinking and became advocates of a moderate welfare-state. Consequently, they widened their appeal to include the middle class and, under Kreisky's leadership, they were able to recoup their losses at the next election, and became the majority party both in terms of popular votes and in parliamentary seats. For the first time, Austria had a Socialist government. To be sure, 81 seats out of 165 forced them to rely rather heavily on the five *Freiheitlichen* who exercised the balance of power. Kreisky was able to obtain FPO support for his budget, for a plan to increase parliamentary membership from 165 to 183 and for an early dissolution of Parliament. The election results of 1971 were a clearcut victory for Kreisky in his attempt to obtain an absolute majority in the *Nationalrat,* an achievement he was able to duplicate almost exactly four years later. Receiving 93 out of 183 seats and slightly more than 50 percent of the popular vote in 1971 as well as in 1975, Kreisky was assured of Socialist control of government for the four years following each election.

The federal chancellor is officially appointed by the federal president, who must of course select someone who can command the support of the majority of the *Nationalrat.* While this gives the president some discretion when nobody's party has a clear majority, Kreisky's selection in 1971 and 1975, though not necessarily in 1970, was a foregone conclusion. Individual ministers are chosen by the chancellor and then formally appointed by the president. Dismissal of ministers is also a prerogative of the chancellor. To be eligible for ministerial office one must be eligible for election to the *Nationalrat,* although parliamentary membership is not required for executive office. Ministers may attend any public session of the *Nationalrat* and of its committees, even if they are not elected members of the legislature; if the sessions are held in private, however, they must obtain special permission to attend. On the other hand, in some cases the *Nationalrat* may demand their presence.

The government is charged with the usual executive functions. However, under Article 52 the legislators may bring up any and all matters; they are under no restrictions in their inquiries and they can freely express their views on governmental decisions and how these are carried out. Considering what was said earlier about the composition of the legislature and the way members are chosen by the high command of the parties, the real independence of lawmakers may be seriously questioned. This hands the administration more power than might appear on the surface. The ministers suggest legislation; given the expected support of Parliament, they usually have their way, although the Constitution specifically states that rejection of a government-sponsored measure does not necessarily have to bring about the resignation of the government itself.

The ministers are legally responsible for the conduct of their departments. Pelinka and Welan point out that the chancellor is *primus inter pares,* first among equals, not like the German chancellor, who seems to be developing into much more than that. In Austria, the chancellor presides over the cabinet; he is not superior to the other ministers, even though he appoints them; he is a colleague among colleagues; he is a chairman rather than the head of the government.

Legally, all this may be true and to the point. The political facts of life seem to indicate another reality. Anyone studying the parliamentary election campaigns of 1971 and 1975 will conclude that the contest was not between the SPO and the OVP but between the proven, confidence-inspiring Bruno Kreisky and the leader of the opposition party. On both occasions, the victory was largely that of the chancellor, who overshadowed his party and its program. Under these circumstances, he obviously dominated his subsequent administrations no matter what the legal and theoretical niceties might be. As members of the legislature are thought of more in terms of numbers of party adherents than as individuals, the personality of the chancellor becomes even more important, especially since he is also the national chairman of his party. Despite the differences explicitly and implicitly inherent in the two systems, one cannot help but compare the Austrian chancellor with the president of the United States who is, according to Clinton Rossiter, "a kind of magnificent lion who can roam widely and do great deeds as long as he does not try to break loose from his broad reservation."[1]

Liechtenstein's democracy dates back to the end of the First World War and the break with Austria, when the citizens themselves assumed some of the powers previously exercised by the prince or his appointed representative. Joseph Ospelt was the first head of government, under whose stewardship the new constitution was adopted. After thirteen months in office, he was followed by Professor Gustav Schädler, whose administration made the agreement binding the country economically to Switzerland. But there were serious problems to be faced. By the time the 1928 elections approached, the people had suffered from their nation's connection with a defeated empire, the crash of a reputable bank, and from damage caused by heavy flooding of the Rhine River. The government came in for severe criticism, perhaps not altogether deserved, for as the first independent government it lacked the experience to deal with these exceptionally difficult problems. As a consequence, the People's party lost the election and the Citizen's party under Dr. Hoop assumed power, which it was to hold until 1970. It took the Republicans in the United States two decades to overcome the Depression image, but it was twice as long before the People's party could obtain another majority in the *Landtag*.

Dr. Josef Hoop was chief of government until 1945, when he was replaced by Dr. Alexander Frick, who in turn was replaced by Dr. Gerard Batliner in 1962. As the pendulum swung to the Reds in 1970, Dr. Alfred Hilbe, who had served as deputy chief of government, became head of the administration. In 1974, the tide turned again, and now Dr. Walter Kieber moved from the position of deputy chief to chief of government, a position he held for four years, until an election defeat led to the appointment of Hans Brunhart as *Regierungschef*. Dr. Batliner was elected to the *Landtag* in 1974 and was its presiding officer during the following four years while his party had a majority, after which he became Parliament's vice-chairman. His predecessor, Dr. Frick, had also moved from the executive to the legislature and presided over the *Landtag* for several years.

Before 1965, the governmental structure and method of appointment were a little different from what they are today. Now the deputy chief is a full-time administrator, as is the chief himself, while the other three members of the administration serve on a part-time basis. There are a number of portfolios, distributed along the lines of a member's leanings and interests, with the bulk of the ministries going to the chief and the deputy chief. In Dr. Kieber's administration in 1974, he himself became responsible for external affairs, finance, agriculture and forestry, justice, and building construction. The deputy government chief looked after internal affairs, education, economic affairs, and traffic. The three remaining ministers divided among themselves the portfolios of culture and environment, social affairs and health, and youth, sport, and leisure. Similarly, in the Batliner government, only sanitary affairs, social administration, and building construction were in the hands of the three part-time ministers.

The *Landtag* now suggests the five administrators to the Prince. In a parliamentary session following the election, the majority party officially proposes the *Regierungschef* to Parliament, which then elects him. Then each party names two more ministers, and one of the minority members is designated as deputy chief of government. Since this procedure usually receives the unanimous support of the *Landtag*, it is obvious that the vote is preceded by carefully worked-out agreements. After the ministers have been voted on by the *Landtag,* their names are sent to the prince for his approval. Whether this is always automatic is a matter of conjecture. One can assume, however, that in all probability a princely veto of appointments would be possible under very special and exceptional circumstances.

The other Germany, the DDR, now commands our attention. Here the *Volkskammer* is elected without opposition; the parties and other groups represented each receive a prearranged number of seats and the members are certainly in no position to voice any dissent. The head of state never had real power and the post was abolished with the death of its one and only incumbent. Today the chairman of the Council of State performs whatever formalities and ceremonies are expected from a head of state. The *Ministerrat,* the Council of Ministers, is the center of authority, inasmuch as it is connected with the leadership of the SED, the all-comprising Socialist Unity party which in itself is Communist-dominated. Stalin for many years had total control of the Soviet Union in his capacity as first secretary of the Communist party, and this was long before he saw fit to assume the office of premier too. In the early 1970s important Soviet negotiations with Presidents Nixon and Ford and with British Prime Minister Harold Wilson were conducted by party boss Brezhnev rather than Prime Minister Kosygin. Similarly, in the DDR, the head of the party for all practical purposes governs the country. This made Walter Ulbricht easily the key figure in the German Democratic Republic.

Much has been written about Ulbricht's ability to survive first Stalin's mistrust and later the charges brought after Stalin's death against the dictator and his former associates. Ulbricht, with a few other trusted Communists, arrived in Berlin in late April of 1945. He had the task of leading the country according to the wishes of Moscow and immediately became one of the most prominent Communists in the Soviet zone. Ulbricht played a leading part in founding the Communist-dominated Socialist Unity party and in forming the "anti-Fascist democratic bloc" with the other parties which in this way in effect recognized the predominance of the Communists. When the SED elected its Politburo in 1949, Walter Ulbricht together with Wilhelm Pieck and Otto Grotewohl were among its members.

Grotewohl had been a Social Democratic leader in the Soviet zone and had worked diligently for the merger of the Communist and Social Democratic parties. High positions in state and party were his reward. When the DDR was established, Grotewohl became its prime minister while Ulbricht was one of the three deputy prime ministers. However, given party realities, this could not be regarded as any demotion for Ulbricht. Among the first international negotiations conducted by the newly formed state were talks with Poland, Czechoslovakia, and Hungary. In each case it was Ulbricht who led the East German delegations in visits to these countries and who worked toward closer relations in the fields of trade, culture, and technology. It was again Ulbricht who first put his name under a document recognizing the Oder and Neisse rivers as frontiers between the DDR and Poland, followed a month later by the formal signatures of the prime ministers of the two countries, with Grotewohl representing the DDR. When in 1951 the *Volkskammer* appointed a commission to draw up regulations for all-German elections, Ulbricht himself took on the chairmanship of the committee.[2]

In 1953, Ulbricht, though still deputy premier, was named first secretary of the SED. Together with Grotewohl and several others,

he visited Moscow in August. Important agreements regarding
improved trade relations and the ending of reparations were negotiated. Ulbricht's speeches were given the attention usually given
to one authorized to make policy statements, and when he pro-
tested against personality cult or advocated a confederation of the
two German states, the messages were not lost on the listeners.
Similarly, when in 1959 5 million American television viewers
were accorded the opportunity "to hear for the first time the truth
about the DDR and the policies of the two German states," it was
Ulbricht who presented the East German viewpoint.

When Pieck died and the office of president was discontinued,
the ceremonial functions of a head of state were also assumed by
Ulbricht. He was able to speak in whatever capacity seemed most
appropriate. He communicated with Adenauer on the desirability
of peace rather than conquest and aggression, and it was the first
secretary of the Central Committee of the Socialist Unity party
writing to the chairman of the Christian Democratic Union of the
German Federal Republic. Similarly, there are records of Ulbricht
corresponding, in the same capacity, with Willy Brandt as chairman of the Social Democratic party of the Federal Republic. As
party leader and head of state, he could use either position to
exercise leadership, receive foreign visitors, and make foreign
trips. There was no doubt that Ulbricht was the most important
and most influential personality in the DDR. The Central Committee of the SED regularly reelected him first secretary of the
party, just as the *Volkskammer* chose him to preside over the
Staatsrat. With no election contests possible and only one list before the voters, no change could be expected in Ulbricht's status
except by death or by removal from within the party leadership.

In fact, Ulbricht was removed from public life only when he
died in the summer of 1973. However, two years earlier he had
been reduced to not much more than a figurehead. Perhaps it was
his age; perhaps he had become less useful than he believed; in any
case his own collaborators as well as the leaders of the Soviet
Union turned against him. In May of 1971, Erich Honecker replaced him as first secretary of the Central Committee of the
Socialist Unity party. Ulbricht was made honorary chairman of the

SED and retained the chairmanship of the *Staatsrat*. He also remained a member of the Politburo, although he now was merely a shadow of his former self.

It is characteristic of communist systems that the letter of the Constitution and the actual realities of political life may be miles apart. The career of Walter Ulbricht clearly illustrates this point. Theoretically, the *Staatsrat* is subordinate to the *Volkskammer,* since Article 66 calls the Council of State an organ of the People's Chamber, holds the council responsible to the chamber, and requires the former to carry out the tasks assigned to it. Promoting "democratic activity in the construction of the advanced socialist society" and taking fundamental defense and security decisions are further duties assigned to the *Staatsrat.* While Grotewohl as chairman of the Council of Ministers was deputy chairman of the *Staatsrat,* the ministers were subordinate to the Council of State.

Grotewohl died in 1964 and was replaced by Willi Stoph. Like Honecker, Stoph represented a new generation. Both were born shortly before World War I and therefore in their early twenties during the first years of Hitler's regime. Both were ardent Communists almost from the beginning. Stoph entered the armed forces of the Third Reich and served on various fronts during the war. Honecker also stayed in Germany during the Nazi period, but spent most of the time in prison until the Red Army liberated him. Uneasy accommodation during those twelve years—prison, concentration camps, or exile—are in the background of many of the present-day leaders of the DDR.

Horst Sindermann is another example. Born in 1915, he also was old enough to have a Communist record before Hitler came to power, and as a result spent most of the Nazi epoch in prisons and concentration camps. Apparently a refined gentleman, he is able to combine communism with *Kultur,* was quite a success as head of the SED in Halle, and became Stoph's deputy and eventually his successor as chairman of the *Ministerrat.*

In October of 1972, a "law concerning the *Ministerrat*" was adopted and there is reason to believe that the *Staatsrat* is no longer part of the decision-making process, at least as far as important measures are concerned. The *Ministerrat* seems to have been strengthened, particularly in the economic sphere, which in turn has enhanced Sindermann's career. But the center of power remains the party.

Honecker, Stoph, and Sindermann belong to a generation that sooner or later will be replaced by people to whom Weimar and Hitler are merely part of history. Of the sixteen people who in 1974 were full-fledged members of the Politburo, six were born before 1910, six between 1911 and 1920, and four between 1921 and 1929. The ten candidates for membership for this important body were much younger, however: the oldest was born in 1907, the second oldest in 1921, and the remaining eight between 1927 and 1931. Thus, Werner Lamberz was four years old when Hitler assumed power and sixteen when the war ended. Since the Communists have been in power since 1945, more and more people will have spent their adult life under that regime. They are accustomed to a situation where one party dominates, where the ministers and other governmental officials are faithful servants of an all-encompassing state, and where the party is regarded as infallible and its decisions unalterable by anyone. Of the five countries we have been discussing, elections in the DDR alone are meaningless because one does not argue about articles of faith, and one does not want to change a leadership that is regarded as the best possible. Since democracy in the Western sense is largely unknown and not particularly admired, most of the East Germans seem content to leave matters as they are.

Notes

CHAPTER 2

1. See Gregor Steger, *Fürst und Landtag nach liechtensteinischem Recht* (Vaduz: Buch-und Verlagsdruckerei A.G., 1950), especially pp. 21–25.
2. Before that time, the emperor was elected whenever a vacancy occurred, and it was by no means a foregone conclusion that the crown passed from father to son. Until Albert II became emperor in 1438, only two Habsburgs had been in possession of the imperial crown, Rudolf I (1273–1291), and his son, who was first bypassed but who did become emperor in 1298 and who reigned for ten years.
3. The broad Viennese dialect "So hab i' mir des aber net vurg'stellt" is quoted in G. E. R. Gedye's excellent eyewitness account of the entire period, *Betrayal in Central Europe* (New York: Harper and Brothers, 1939), p. 351.
4. Arnold Brecht, *Prelude to Silence* (New York: Oxford Univ. Press, 1944), p. 41.
5. See Alfred Grosser, *Deutschlandbilanz* (Munich: Carl Hansler Verlag, 1970), pp. 59–60.
6. Preamble to the *Grundgesetz*.

CHAPTER 3

1. The 1968 version of the Constitution of the German Democratic Republic calls the regime a "Socialist state of the German nation"

and speaks of "the political organization of the working people in town and countryside who are jointly implementing socialism under the leadership of the working class and its Marxist-Leninist party." It is worth recalling that this wording was changed rather abruptly and with as little public notice as possible.

2. William H. Riker, *Democracy in the United States* (New York: Macmillan, 1953), p. 34.

3. From "New Program of the Communist Party," published in *Current Digest of the Soviet Press* (December 1961) and reproduced in Samuel Hendel, *The Soviet Crucible*, 2d ed. (Princeton, N.J.: D. Van Nostrand Company, 1963), p. 653.

4. Approximate translation by author.

5. Ulrich im Hof, *Von Bundesbrief zur Bundesverfassung*, Druck E. Löpfe-Benz (Rorschach, Switzerland: Buchreihe der Stiftung Schweizerhilfe, Fünfte Veröffentlichung, 1948), maintains the former; George Arthur Godding, Jr., argues the latter in *The Federal Government of Switzerland* (Boston: Houghton Mifflin, 1961).

CHAPTER 4

1. Joseph II became coregent with his mother, Empress Maria Theresa, in 1765 and sole ruler upon her death in 1790, a year after the outbreak of the French Revolution during which his sister, Marie Antoinette, queen of France, was executed.

2. There were thirty-nine members in 1817, but several of the small princely lines died out and a few others were absorbed by larger states. By 1866 there were thirty-three members. As a result, the total number of votes in the Plenum varied from sixty-nine to sixty-five.

3. Thus Liechtenstein, together with the other small principalities of Hohenzollern-Sigmaringen, Hohenzollern-Hechingen, the two Reuss', Schaumburg-Lippe, Waldeck, and after 1838, Hessen-Homburg, formed the sixteenth *Kurie*. There was one ambassador for all of them and he was frequently unable to express the views of his various clients. By the summer of 1866, six members remained in the *Kurie*, and its vote for Austria and against Prussia was important in bringing about the war and the dissolution of the confederation. Liechtenstein was active within the *Kurie* and instrumental in having the *Kurie's* vote cast in favor of the Austrian position, leading to Bismarck's scornful accusation that Liechtenstein had precipitated the war, a charge which appears to be quite an exaggeration.

4. Clinton Rossiter, *Constitutional Dictatorship* (New York: Harcourt, Brace and World, 1963), p. 73.
5. William L. Shirer, *Rise and Fall of the Third Reich* (New York: Simon and Schuster, 1960), p. 198.

CHAPTER 5

1. Ernst Deuerlein, *DDR—1945–1970* (Munich: Deutscher Taschenbuch Verlag, 1971), p. 41.
2. Author's translation of Ulbricht's remarks; Walter Ulbricht, *On Questions of Socialist Construction in the GDR* (Dresden: Verlag Zeit im Bild, 1968), p. 625, from a statement at the Fourth Session of the People's Chamber, December 1, 1967.

CHAPTER 6

1. Erich Machek, *Die Österreichische Bundesverfassung* (Vienna: Cura Verlag, 1968), p. 15.
2. It is typically Austrian that a British-born writer, Richard Rickett, who is now an Austrian resident includes among the most noteworthy events of 1919 the appointment of Richard Strauss as director of the Vienna State Opera. See his *A Brief Survey of Austrian History* (Vienna: Georg Prachner Verlag, 1966), p. 119.
3. Adolf Merkl, *Die ständisch-autoritäre Verfassung Österreichs* (Vienna: Julius Springer Verlag, 1935), p. 2.
4. The gentleman in question was absent because he had to go to the bathroom! When his vote was cast by a proxy, various constitutional questions were raised, resulting in the resignation of the presiding officer and his deputies. With no one legally empowered to call on Parliament to assemble, it was not too difficult for a determined chancellor to abolish Parliament altogether.

CHAPTER 7

1. Alfred Grosser, *Deutschlandbilanz*, p. 403.
2. *Parteien in Beiden Deutschen Staaten* (Bonn-Bad Godesberg: Friedrich-Ebert Stiftung, Verlag Neue Gesellschaft GmbH, 1973), p. 53. Translated by the author.
3. Arnold Heidenheimer, *The Governments of Germany*, 3d ed. (New York: Crowell, 1971), pp. 271–72.
4. *Introducing the GDR*, 2d ed. (Dresden: Verlag Zeit im Bild, 1969), p. 55.
5. Ibid., 4th ed. rev., 1974, p. 49.
6. Ibid.

CHAPTER 8

1. David Childs, *East Germany* (New York: Praeger, 1969), pp. 104–22.
2. *Thesen zur Politik der Partei der Arbeit der Schweiz,* adopted in June 1971 at Lausanne. Author's translation.
3. The figures used are taken chiefly from Erich Gruner, *Die Parteien in der Schweiz* (Bern: Francke Verlag, 1969) and Jürg Steiner, *Das Politische System der Schweiz* (Munich: R. Piper and Co. Verlag, 1971).

CHAPTER 9

1. William T. Bluhm, *Building an Austrian Nation* (New Haven: Yale Univ. Press, 1973). See especially Chapters 3 and 4 for an excellent discussion of the breakup of the coalition and political developments following this event.
2. Erich Gruner, *Die Parteien in der Schweiz.*
3. Ibid., p. 128.
4. From the program adopted at the party conference in Winterthur in 1959. Author's translation.

CHAPTER 10

1. *Christen und Kirche in der Deutschen Demokratischen Republik* (Dresden: Verlag Zeit im Bild, n.d.).
2. Bishop Waitz, according to Alfred Diamont, *Austrian Catholics and the First Republic* (Princeton, N.J.: Princeton Univ. Press, 1960), p. 68. Cited in Kurt Steiner, *Politics in Austria* (Boston: Little, Brown, 1972), p. 8.
3. Gottfried Heindl, in "Das Osterreichische Monatsheft," quoted in William T. Bluhm, *Building an Austrian Nation,* p. 111.
4. Pierre Raton, *Liechtenstein: Staat und Geschichte* (Vaduz: Liechtenstein-Verlag, 1969), p. 117.
5. *Introducing the GDR,* 4th ed., 1974, p. 49.
6. *Parteien in Beiden Deutschen Staaten,* p. 153.

CHAPTER 11

1. *Volksrecht-Partei, Kampfgemeinschaft der Arbeiter und Bauern* (which raises the question whether the German word *Bauer* is best translated as "farmer" or as "peasant"), and *Mittelstands-Partei.*
2. *Introducing the GDR,* 2d ed., p. 54.

CHAPTER 12

1. George H. Sabine, *A History of Political Theory,* rev. ed. (New York: Holt, 1955), p. 6.
2. Hans Tschäni, *Profil der Schweiz* (Zürich: Rascher Verlag Zurich, 1969), p. 108.
3. Erich Gruner and Beat Junker, *Bürger, Staat, und Politik in der Schweiz* (Basel: Lehrvermittelverlag Basel-Stadt, 1972), pp. 105–6.
4. Anton Pelinka and Manfried Welan, *Demokratie und Verfassung in Österreich* (Vienna: Europa Verlag, 1971), p. 83.

CHAPTER 13

1. The progress made by the SPD can be seen from the fact that in 1965 they had captured only one of the district seats in Schleswig-Holstein and five in 1969. However, in 1976 they were successful in only six districts.

CHAPTER 14

1. Article 54 III of the *Grundgesetz.*
2. Alfred Grosser, *Deutschlandbilanz,* p. 164.

CHAPTER 15

1. Clinton Rossiter, *The American Presidency,* rev. ed. (New York: Harcourt, Brace, 1960), p. 73.
2. The recommendations of the Committee were approved by the *Volkskammer* in the DDR but rejected by the Federal Republic, which wanted the elections supervised by the United Nations, a request regarded as illegal in East Germany. Needless to say, after a lot of argument, nothing was accomplished.

Glossary

Adenauer, Konrad (1876–1967). First chancellor of the German Federal Republic from 1949 to 1963, CDU.

Adler, Max (1873–1937). Austrian Social Democrat, associated with the party's left wing.

Adler, Victor (1852–1918). Long-time Austrian Social Democratic leader.

Aktion Demokratische Freiheit. Communist-backed party in the 1969 *Bundestag* elections of the German Federal Republic.

Aktuelle Stunde. Parliamentary procedure instituted in the *Bundestag* of the German Federal Republic since 1965, whereby a short debate on a current problem takes place immediately after the question hour.

Allied Control Council. The commanders of the four military powers that occupied Germany immediately after World War II. Purpose of the council was to coordinate Allied occupational policy, which never really materialized.

Alsace-Lorraine. Territory that frequently changed hands between France and Germany. It was German from 1871 till 1918, French till Hitler took it back, and French again after World War II. Bordered by the Rhine River on the east.

Altmann, Karl (1904–1960). Austrian Communist. In Renner's Provisional Government at the end of World War II, and from December 1945 till his resignation in November 1947, the only Communist in the Austrian government.

Anhalt.   Former German state. Became part of Sachsen-Anhalt, one
of the five states originally established in the Soviet zone of occupation after World War II. No longer in existence.

Anschluss.   The political integration of Austria with Germany, which
was prevented by the Allies after World War I but which took place
under Hitler in 1938.

Partei der Arbeit.   The Workers' party, the Communist party in
present-day Switzerland.

Arndt, Ernst Moritz (1769–1860).   German poet, noted for his patriotic songs, especially during the Napoleonic Wars.

Article 48 of the Weimar Constitution.   Provision which gave the
president emergency powers to suspend fundamental civil rights,
such as freedom from arbitrary arrest, inviolability of the home, etc.
The built-in safeguards proved insufficient to prevent Hitler from
taking over.

Ausgleich.   Arrangement of 1867 whereby Austria and Hungary became equal partners in the Habsburg empire.

Austro-Hungarian Empire.   New name given to the Austrian empire
after the *Ausgleich* (see above), indicating the equal status of Austria and Hungary, but not of any other part of the empire.

Bad Godesberg.   Site of the 1959 conference of the Social Democratic
party of the German Federal Republic, where the party adopted a
reform program.

Baden-Württemberg.   One of the states of the German Federal Republic. Its capital is Stuttgart.

Barzel, Rainer (1924–).   One of the leading politicians of the
Christian Democrats in the German Federal Republic. One-time
candidate for federal chancellor.

Basel.   Swiss canton, divided into two half-cantons: Basel-Stadt and
Basel-Land. Also, capital city of the former.

Basel, Treaty of.   Treaty of Independence of Switzerland guaranteed
in 1499.

Basic Law.   See *Grundgesetz*.

Batliner, Gerard (1928–).   Leading member of Liechtenstein's Progressive Citizen's party. Head of government from 1962 till 1970;
member and presiding officer of Parliament (1974–1978).

Bauer, Gustav (1870–1944).   German Social Democratic politician;
chancellor, 1919–1920.

Bauer, Otto (1882–1938).   Prominent Austrian Social Democrat; associated with the left wing of the party.

Bauern-, Gewerbe-, und Bürgerpartei.   Swiss political party, sometimes listed as Farmers' party, but now known as Swiss People's party (Schweizer Volkspartei).

Bavaria. See *Bayern.*

Bayerische Volkspartei. Conservative, church-oriented, Bavarian-based political party in Germany during the Weimar Republic.

Bayern. One of the states of the German Federal Republic. Capital is Munich.

Beck, Wilhelm (1885–1936). Liechtenstein politician, founder of the *Volkspartei,* who helped to bring about political changes following the collapse of the Austro-Hungarian empire.

Bern. Swiss canton. Also name of capital city of that canton, which is the capital of the federal government of Switzerland.

Bezirk. German local government unit. With the dissolution of the states in the German Democratic Republic, the *Bezirk* has become the major administrative entity in that country.

Bicameral. Legislature. Consists of two houses.

Bismarck, Otto von (1815–1898). Prussian statesman instrumental in the establishment of the German empire and its first chancellor (1871–1890).

Bizonia. Economic merger of the American and British zones of occupation in Germany after World War II, leading eventually to political unification too (after the French zone was added, it became Trizonia).

Blacks. Nickname given to church-oriented party in Austria. Also used in other countries including Liechtenstein where, however, the clerical connection is rather obscure.

Bolsheviks. Radical majority wing of the Russian Socialist party which in 1903 split from the Socialists. Successful in the quest for power in 1917 under Lenin's leadership, they took on the name of Communists.

Bolz, Lothar (1903–). Political figure in the German Democratic Republic, foreign minister from 1953 to 1965, and affiliated with the National Democratic party.

Bonn. University town in Germany on the Rhine River and birthplace of Beethoven. After World War II, capital of the German Federal Republic.

Bourbon. French royal family which governed at the time of the Revolution of 1789.

Brandenburg. Onetime German principality whose rulers in 1701 became kings of Prussia. Since then a province of Prussia. After World War II one of the five states in the Soviet zone. No longer in existence.

Brandt, Willy (1913–).   Social Democratic politician of the German Federal Republic, mayor of West Berlin (1957–1966), and chancellor from 1969 to 1974.

Breitner, Dr. Burghard (1884–1956).   Austrian surgeon and professor who in 1951 ran for president as candidate of the Independents.

Bremen.   North German port city, now one of the states of the German Federal Republic.

Brno.   City in Moravia (now Czechoslovakia) and site of the 1899 conference of Austrian Socialists.

Brugger, Ernst (1914–).   Member of the Swiss *Bundesrat* since 1970; president in 1974.

Brüning, Heinrich (1885–1970).   German politician, *Zentrum* party. Chancellor from 1930 to 1932. Migrated to American in 1934.

Bund.   Translated as league, alliance, confederation (see also Deutscher Bund, German Confederation).   Also indicates federal institutions, such as *Bundesrat*, the Federal Council.

Bundeskulturrat.   A federal cultural council set up in Austria in the mid-1930s after Parliament had been eliminated.

Bundesrat (Federal Council).   (a) Assembly of the representatives of the princes that made up the German empire (1871–1918). (b) Second house of the bicameral legislature of the present-day German Federal Republic, in which the states are represented on an unequal basis. (c) Branch of the legislature in Republican Austria in which the provinces are represented, but actually without much power. (d) The seven-member executive branch of the government in Switzerland.

Bundesrepublik.   The Federal Republic, official designation of the present West German regime.

Bundestag (Federal Diet or Parliament).   (a) The assembly set up by the *Deutscher Bund* after the Napoleonic Wars, based at Frankfurt-on-Main. (b) The elected parliamentary body which is the main legislative body of the German Federal Republic today. (c) In nondemocratic Austria in the mid-1930s an assembly in which the various councils, such as economic or cultural councils, were to be represented.

Bundesversammlung (Federal Assembly).   (a) In the Federal Republic a kind of electoral college consisting of *Bundestag* and representatives of the state Parliaments which meets for the purpose of electing a federal president. (b) In Austria, a joint meeting of the two houses of the legislature which takes place only on ceremonial (swearing-in of presidents) and extraordinary occasions (declaration of war or impeachment). (c) In Switzerland, joint sessions of the two houses of the legislature constitutionally provided for such matters as the election of members of the *Bundesrat*.

Bundeswirtschaftsrat. The economic council in nondemocratic Austria in the mid-1930s.

Burgenland. Eastern-most province of the Austrian republic which contains some Croatian minorities. Capital city is Eisenstadt.

Bürgerpartei (Citizen's party). As in *Fortschrittliche Bürgerpartei* in Liechtenstein.

Burgfrieden. "Peace within a castle," a medieval term which today means discontinuation of party strife, an attitude adopted by the European Social Democrats during World War I when they supported their national governments.

Cantons. Swiss political units somewhat equivalent to American states. At present there are twenty-two cantons, three of which are subdivided into half-cantons.

Carinthia (Kärnten). Southern-most of the Austrian provinces; the capital city is Klagenfurt.

Center Party. See *Zentrum*.

Central Powers. The World War I alliance of Germany, Austro-Hungary, Turkey, and other countries who were fighting the Allies, led by France, Britain, Russia, and later the United States.

Chamberlain, Neville (1869–1940). British politician and prime minister from 1937 to 1940, who negotiated the Munich Agreement and took Britain into World War II.

Chancellor (*Kanzler*). Policy-making government leader equivalent to prime minister. The official title in the German Federal Republic and in Austria is *Bundeskanzler* (federal chancellor), whereas the term *Reichskanzler* (imperial chancellor) was used from Bismarck to Hitler (1871–1945).

Christian Democratic Union (CDU). Major political party in the German Republic; held office from 1949 till 1969.

Christian Social Party. (a) Church-oriented, conservative party in Austria's First Republic, nicknamed Blacks, governed first under the parliamentary system in alliance with small anti-Socialist groups and later established clerical quasi-Fascist dictatorship. (b) In Liechtenstein, a minor and unsuccessful third party, the Greens.

Christian Social Union. Conservative major party in Bavaria today, in close alliance with the Christian Democrats.

Churchill, Winston (1874–1965). British politician and statesman and prime minister (1940 to 1945 and 1951 to 1955).

Cold War. A tense, almost warlike situation between countries (especially the United States and the Soviet Union beginning in the late 1940s), but without any actual military combat taking place.

Comecon. Communist-sponsored Council of Mutual Economic Aid, somewhat equivalent to the West's Marshall Plan.

Communists. Extremist, left-wing political party. (a) At one time outlawed in the Federal Republic, now free to compete but without much of a following and not represented in the *Bundestag*. (b) In Austria also without parliamentary representation since 1959. (c) In Switzerland, under the name of *Partei der Arbeit*, they usually win a handful of seats in national parliamentary elections. (d) In the German Democratic Republic, the major political force, now officially merged with the Social Democrats in the SED, which plays the leading part in all political and economic affairs.

Concordat. An official agreement or treaty between the Vatican and a particular country, usually on matters relating to the Catholic church in that country.

Confederation of the Rhine. See *Rheinbund*.

Coopposition. Situation in Liechtenstein where the two political parties participate in the same government but where the minority party in Parliament opposes and criticizes governmental activities.

Corporate, Corporative. Political or governmental institution in which representation is according to occupations, classes, or estates *(Stände)* and not political parties as expressed in elections.

Creditanstalt. Viennese banking institution which collapsed in 1931, marking the beginning of the Great Depression.

Crimean War (1853–1856). France, Britain, and Turkey waged war against Russia, primarily to stop Russian designs on parts of the collapsing Turkish empire.

Croatia. Slavic area on the Balkan peninsula, once part of the old Austro-Hungarian empire and now part of Yugoslavia.

Curzon, Lord (1859–1925). British statesman who in 1919 suggested the Curzon Line, the frontier between Russia and Poland, which became the basis for the border of 1945.

Danube Monarchy. The Austro-Hungarian empire, because it was centered around the Danube River (or *Donau*).

Dehler, Thomas (1897–1967). Politician and leader of the Free Democrats in the German Federal Republic; Adenauer's first minister of justice.

Demokratische Bauernpartei Deutschlands. The German Democratic Farmers party in the DDR, which supposedly looks after the interests of farmers; part of the Democratic bloc.

Demokratische Volkspartei. The Democratic People's party established in 1946 in the West German *Land* of Württemberg-Baden under the chairmanship of Theodor Heuss; later part of the Free Democratic party.

Denk, Dr. Wolfgang (1882–1973). Austrian surgeon who in 1957 unsuccessfully ran for the presidency as candidate of the two non-Socialist parties.

Deutsch, Julius (1884–1968). Austrian Social Democratic leader.

Deutsche Demokratische Partei (German Democratic party). Liberal party in the Weimar Republic, which it supported. Later renamed *Staatspartei*. Its public support fell from 18.6 percent in 1919 to 1 percent in 1932. Some of its surviving members helped establish the Free Democratic party after World War II.

Deutsche Demokratische Republic (DDR). The German Democratic Republic, official name of the East German regime, formerly the Soviet zone of occupation.

Deutsche Friedensunion. The German Peace Union for which Communist votes were cast in the West German parliamentary elections of 1961 and 1965.

Deutsche Kommunistische Partei (DKP). Since 1968 the official name of the Communist party in the German Federal Republic. A minority party without parliamentary representation.

Deutscher Bund. The loose confederation of German states that was established in 1815 at the end of the Napoleonic Wars.

Deutsche Staatspartei. Name assumed by the *Deutsche Demokratische Partei* in 1930.

Deutsche Volkspartei (German People's party). The successor of the National Liberals, provided the Weimar Republic with an outstanding leader in Gustav Stresemann (1878–1929).

Deutschösterreich. German-Austria, the name officially assumed by the newly established Austrian Republic immediately after World War I, denoting its German connections and heritage.

Dollfuss, Engelbert (1892–1934). Austrian Christian Social politician; chancellor from 1932 till his assassination by Austrian Nazis. Transformed his country from a parliamentary democracy into a quasi-Fascist autocratic state.

Druey, Henry (1799–1855). Swiss politician and leader of the liberal movement in the Waadt who helped write the 1848 Constitution. Member of the *Bundesrat*, 1848–1855; president in 1850.

Dual Monarchy. The Habsburg Austro-Hungarian empire after 1867.

Ebert, Friedrich (1871–1925). German Social Democratic leader, first president of Weimar Republic.

Eidgenossenschaft. Literally, "comradeship based on an oath," the official designation of the Swiss confederation to this day as an obvious reminder of the origin of the country.

Elector. One-time princely title *(Kurfürst)* whose holders in the Middle Ages were entitled to participate in the election of the German emperor.

Emperor *(Kaiser)*. Highest princely title, dating back to Roman times, which assumed a distinctly German character in the tenth century. This lasted until 1806 when German Emperor Franz II abolished the so-called Holy Roman Empire and assumed the title of emperor of Austria, which remained with the rulers of that country until the military defeat of 1918. In Germany, the title was resurrected in 1871 by the kings of Prussia, who were German emperors until 1918.

Enabling Laws. See *Ermächtigungsgesetz.*

Erfurt. Town in central Germany, now in the DDR. Prussia unsuccessfully attempted to assemble a German Parliament there after the failure in Frankfurt of 1849. Also the site of the Social Democratic conference in 1890 which adopted the Erfurt Program.

Erhard, Ludwig (1897–1977). Politician in the German Federal Republic, Adenauer's minister of economics (1949–1963), and his successor as chancellor (1963–1966).

Ermächtigungsgesetz. Enabling legislation passed by the German Parliament in 1933 giving Hitler sweeping powers, supposedly for only four years and with certain safeguards which were promptly discarded.

European Defense Community Treaty. A plan to integrate newly created German armed forces within a European army after World War II. Rejected by the French National Assembly in 1954.

European Free Trade Association (EFTA). Agreement in 1959 among countries not in the common market to establish a free trade area in Western Europe.

Fascism. Right-wing, totalitarian nationalist dictatorship, as in Hitler's Germany.

Federalism. Form of government where authority is divided between the national government and the component parts, such as states or provinces.

Ferdinand (1793–1875). Austrian emperor from 1835 until his abdication during the Revolution of 1848 in favor of his nephew, Franz Joseph.

Figl, Leopold (1902–1965). Austrian politician, OVP, and chancellor from 1945 to 1953, then foreign minister from 1953 to 1959.

First International. Workers' association founded in London in 1864 by Karl Marx.

Fischer, Ernst (1899–1972). Austrian Communist leader and member of the first government following World War II.

Five Percent Clause. Provision in the election laws of the German Federal Republic whereby a certain number of seats in the *Bundestag* are allocated according to the percentage of votes received by a given party. In order to be eligible a political party must receive at least 5 percent of the total vote.

Fortschrittliche Bürgerpartei. The Progressive Citizen's party, one of the two main parties in Liechtenstein. Nicknamed Blacks, the party provided such leaders as Alexander Frick, Gerard Batliner, and Walter Kieber.

Fourier, Charles (1772–1837). French Socialist philosopher.

Fraktion. Parliamentary grouping. Members of the same political party in the legislature get together in order to form an effective political unit and to be represented on committees and at conferences of parliamentary party leaders, etc. Where a minimum number of members is required for the formation of a *Fraktion* (fifteen in the German *Bundestag* or five in the Swiss *Nationalrat*), smaller parties may combine for the purpose of forming such a grouping.

Fraktionszwang. The obligation of a *Fraktion,* after discussion among its members, to vote as a block; party discipline.

Francois-Poncet, André (1887–). French diplomat and ambassador to Berlin (1931 to 1938). After the war he was high commissioner (1949–1953) and then ambassador (1953–1955) in Bonn.

Franz I (1853–1938). Prince of Liechtenstein from 1929 to his resignation in 1938, shortly before his death.

Franz II (1768–1835). The last "Holy" German emperor from 1792 till 1806, when he assumed the title of emperor of Austria.

Franz Josef II (1906–). Liechtenstein's reigning monarch since 1938.

Franz Joseph I (1830–1916). Emperor of Austria from 1848 until his death.

Frederick the Great. See *Friedrich der Grosse.*

Free Democratic Party. See *Freie Demokratische Partei.*

Free Imperial Territory. In the old German empire land that was subordinate only to the emperor and to no intermediary prince, bishop, and so on.

Freibrief. A document from the emperor assuring a free imperial territory of its status.

Freiburg (French *Fribourg*). Swiss canton in which two-thirds of the population speak French. Capital city has the same name.

Freie Demokratische Partei (FDP). The Free Democratic party in the German Federal Republic and since 1961 the only small party to be represented in the *Bundestag*. From 1949 until 1966, the FDP was associated in coalition governments with the Christian Democrats and since 1969, with the Socialists. Its leaders have included Theodor Heuss, Thomas Dehler, Walter Scheel, and Hans-Dietrich Genscher.

Freiheitliche Partei Österreichs (FPO). The Austrian Freedom party, since 1959 the only third party represented in the *Nationalrat*. Regularly obtains a handful of seats, but so far has never participated in any government. Present leader is Friedrich Peter.

Freisinnig. "Free thinking," one of the major Swiss political parties, also known as "Radicals." Strong liberal tendencies, and a major political force since before 1848.

Frick, Alexander (1910–). Liechtenstein politician and head of government from 1945–1962. President of the *Landtag*, 1966–1970.

Frick, Wilhelm (1877–1946). German Nazi leader and one of the original three Nazis in Hitler's first government; served as minister of the interior. Convicted for war crimes at Nuremberg and executed.

Friedrich der Grosse. Frederick II of Prussia, nicknamed "the Great" (1712–1786). He became king in 1740, built up the army, and waged a number of victorious wars.

Frommelt, Anton (1895–1975). Priest and important political figure in Liechtenstein, who was deputy head of government from 1934 to 1938.

Führer. Title of "leader" adopted by Hitler. After Hindenburg's death in 1934, official designation of Hitler as highest government official was *Führer und Reichskanzler*.

Geneva Protocol. In 1922, Austria and various members of the League of Nations worked out arrangements for economic assistance for Austria subject to Austria's financial and political commitments.

Genf (French *Genève*). Swiss canton where three-quarters of the population speaks French. Capital city has the same name. Seat of the League of Nations between the two World Wars.

Genscher, Hans-Dietrich (1927–). Prominent Free Democratic politician in the German Federal Republic and minister of interior under Willy Brandt. When Walter Scheel became president, Genscher succeeded him as vice-chancellor and foreign minister.

Gerlach, Manfred (1928–). Prominent politician in the German Democratic Republic. Represents the Liberal-Democratic party in the *Volkskammer* and the *Staatsrat*.

German Confederation. See *Deutscher Bund*.

German Democratic Republic. See *Deutsche Demokratische Republic* (DDR).

Gnägi, Rudolf (1917–). Member of the Swiss *Bundesrat* since 1966; president in 1971.

Goebbels, Josef (1897–1945). Leading member of the Nazi party. Minister of propaganda under Hitler and one of his closest advisors.

Goldenbaum, Ernst (1898–). Life-long Communist and a leading politician in the German Democratic Republic. Founding member of the Democratic Farmer's party, which he represents in the *Volkskammer* and similar official bodies.

Gorbach, Alfons (1898–1972). Leading Austrian People's party politician and chancellor from 1961 till 1964. Ran unsuccessfully for the presidency against Franz Jonas in 1965.

Göring, Hermann (1893–1946). Leading advisor of Hitler. Served as airforce chief.

Götting, Gerald (1923–). Leading politician in the German Democratic Republic, where he heads the Christian Democratic Union. Important member of the *Volkskammer* and the *Staatsrat*.

Grand (Great) Coalition. Alliance in a government of the two major parties to the exclusion of minor ones (i.e., the OVP/SPO governments in Austria from 1947 till 1966 or the Kiesinger administration in the German Federal Republic between 1966 and 1969).

Gredler, Wilfred (1916– .) Austrian diplomat. Elected to *Nationalrat* in 1971 but preferred remaining as ambassador in Bonn. Formerly parliamentarian of the Freedom party.

Grosse Anfrage. "Large" or major "inquiry" in the *Bundestag* of the Federal Republic, where thirty signatures of deputies can demand an oral answer to a pressing problem, to be followed by a debate. See also Kleine Anfrage.

Grossdeutsche Volkspartei. The pan-German People's party in Austria's First Republic, usually part of the anti-Socialist alliance with the Christian Socials.

Grotewohl, Otto (1894–1964). Leading politician in the German Democratic Republic. Social Democrat who helped found, and became cochairman of, the Socialist Unity party in conjunction with the Communists. Prime minister from 1949 until 1964.

Grundgesetz. The "basic law" according to which the German Federal Republic has been governed since 1949. Supposedly temporary until both Germanys were unified but is for all practical purposes the Constitution of the Bonn government.

Guilds. In medieval Europe, associations of craftsmen and merchants with considerable political and economic power.

Habsburg. Ruling family of Austria and one of the great royal families that dominated Europe until 1918; frequently (and for several hundred years) German emperors.

Hainisch, Michael (1858–1940). An originally "nonpolitical" land-owner who from 1920 till 1928 was president of Austria.

Hallstein Doctrine. Named after West German Foreign Office official Walter Hallstein (1901‑). Maintained that the Federal Republic was the only legitimate government of Germany and that any country that diplomatically recognized the German Democratic Republic was therefore unfriendly to Bonn. Discontinued by Willy Brandt as foreign minister.

Hamburg. Germany's major seaport. Historically a free, independent city and today one of the states of the German Federal Republic.

Hanusch, Ferdinand (1866–1923). Austrian Social Democratic leader, member of the imperial *Reichstag* and republican *Nationalrat*. Served in government immediately after World War I.

Haus der Abgeordneten. The House of Representatives of Austria's bicameral *Reichsrat* of pre-World War I, supposedly representing the people.

Häuser, Rudolf (1909–). Austrian trade unionist and Socialist politician. Vice-chancellor and social affairs minister under Kreisky.

Heimwehr. One of the quasi-military organizations in Austria's First Republic. Strongly anti-Socialist.

Heinemann, Gustav (1899–1976). Politician and statesman of the German Federal Republic. Held various government posts and in 1969 was proposed by Social Democrats for office of president, which he held until 1974.

Helsinki. Finnish capital and site of the 1975 Conference on European Security and Cooperation in which all five German-speaking countries and thirty others participated and which more or less recognized the existing European boundaries.

Helvetic Republic. Established by Napoleon in 1798 in an attempt to reorganize Switzerland into a centralized, unitary state. The plan was abandoned five years later.

Hermes, Andreas (1878–1964). Formerly leader of *Zentrum* party who became a prominent CDU member in the Soviet zone after World War II. He was removed from his leadership position by occupation authorities because of his opposition to land reforms.

Herrenhaus. The House of Lords, which together with the House of Representatives formed the *Reichsrat,* the Parliament in the last decades of imperial Austria.

Hesse. One of the states of the German Federal Republic. The capital is Wiesbaden.

Heusinger, Hans-Joachim (1925–). Leading member of the Liberal Democratic party in the German Democratic Republic, member of the *Volkskammer,* and minister of justice.

Heuss, Theodor (1884–1963). Liberal member of the German *Reichstag* prior to Hitler; leader of the Free Democrats and first president (1949–1959) of the German Federal Republic.

High Commissioners. Title assumed by the military governors of the three Western powers in 1949 as the Federal Republic was established and thus no longer constituted occupied territory.

Hilbe, Alfred (1928–). Liechtenstein politician of the *Vaterländische Union;* headed government from 1970 till 1974.

Himmler, Heinrich (1900–1945). One of Hitler's leading associates. In charge of the secret police and the concentration camps.

Hindenburg, Paul von (1847–1934). German army officer and field marshal in World War I. Elected president in 1925 and reelected in 1932. Appointed Hitler to position of chancellor.

Hitler, Adolf (1889–1945). Founder and *Führer* of Nazi party in Germany. Chancellor from 1933 till he committed suicide when war was lost.

Hohenzollern. Family name of the kings of Prussia, who from 1871 till 1918 were the emperors of Germany.

Holy Roman Empire of the German Nation. The *Heiliges römisches Reich deutscher Nation,* which was established in 962 and lasted until 1806. This was the First Reich; the Second Reich existed under the Hohenzollern; the Third Reich from 1933 to 1945.

Honecker, Erich (1912–). Life-long Communist who was imprisoned during the Nazi regime. Leading member of the Socialist Unity party in the German Democratic Republic and first secretary of the party.

Honner, Franz (1893–). Austrian Communist leader and member of the government immediately after the German defeat in 1945.

Hoop, Josef (1895–1959). Liechtenstein politician and head of the government from 1928 till 1945.

Imperial Council of Princes. See *Reichsfürstentag.*

Industrial Revolution. The introduction of machines and mechanical devices into the manufacturing process, which radically changed society. Begun in England in the second half of the eighteenth century, it eventually spread throughout Europe and the United States.

Initiative. A method whereby the population, through the collection of a prescribed number of signatures, originates a certain piece of legislation, thereby forcing Parliament to consider a particular proposal or to discuss repeal of an existing law.

International Atomic Agency. An international body established in 1957 to facilitate the peaceful use of atomic energy.

International Court of Justice. Established under the auspices of the United Nations in 1946 as successor of the League of Nations' Permanent Court of International Justice to bring about a judicial settlement of international disputes between states.

Iron Curtain. Term coined by Winston Churchill to describe the sharp, often unpassable dividing line that has separated the Communist from the non-Communist world since the end of World War II and which runs across the European continent "from Stettin in the Baltic to Trieste in the Adriatic."

Johannes II (1840–1929). Ruling prince in Liechtenstein from 1958 to 1929.

Jonas, Franz (1890–1974). Austrian Socialist politician, mayor of Vienna, 1951–1965, and president from 1965 till his death.

Joseph II (1741–1790). German emperor and ruler of Austria (at first with his mother, Maria-Theresa).

Kaiser. See *Emperor.*

Kaiser, Jakob (1888–1961). German politician and leader of Christian trade unions prior to Hitler. Prominent in CDU affairs in the Soviet zone of occupation immediately after World War II till he was dismissed. Went to West Germany where he became minister for all-German affairs under Adenauer.

Kaliningrad. The old German city of Königsberg in East Prussia, now part of the Soviet Union.

Kanzler. See *Chancellor.*

Kärnsten. See *Carinthia.*

Keller, Gottfried (1819–1890). Swiss author, novelist, poet.

Kieber, Walter (1931–). Liechtenstein politician and head of the government from 1974 to 1978.

Kiesinger, Kurt (1904–). CDU politician in the German Federal Republic. Minister-president of Baden-Württemberg from 1958 to 1966 and federal chancellor from 1966 to 1969. Headed the "Grand Coalition" of the CDU/CSU with the SPD.

Kirchschläger, Rudolf (1915–). Austrian diplomat and foreign minister from 1970 till 1974 when, as candidate of the Social Democrats, he was elected president of Austria.

Kleine Anfrage. Form of parliamentary inquiry in the *Bundestag* of the German Federal Republic. Takes fewer signatures than is necessary for *Grosse Anfrage* and the reply may be made in writing.

Kohl, Helmut (1930–). CDU politician in the German Federal Republic, minister-president of Rhineland-Palatinate since 1969, and his party's candidate for chancellor in 1976.

Kollegialsystem. A system whereby the ministers in a particular government work together as equals for the benefit of the country and are jointly responsible for the actions of the entire administration.

Kommunistische Partei Deutschlands (KPD). The Communist party, active in the Weimer Republic where even after the *Reichstagsfeuer* in 1933 it received one-eighth of the total vote. Prohibited by Hitler and revived after World War II, it elected fifteen deputies in the first *Bundestag* elections in 1949. After that could not meet the "Five Percent" requirement. Prohibited in 1956 for subversive activities. Since 1968 it is again functioning under the name of *Deutsche Kommunistische Partei*.

Königsberg. See *Kaliningrad*.

Körner, Theodor (1873–1957). Austrian Socialist leader, general, mayor of Vienna, 1945 to 1951, and from 1951 till his death, president of Austria.

Kreisky, Bruno (1911–). Austrian Socialist politician, foreign minister from 1959 to 1966, and since 1970, chancellor.

Kultur. An advanced stage of a culture; a civilization and its achievements in the realms of art, literature, and so on.

Kulturkampf. The struggle in the 1870s between Bismarck's Prussia and the Catholic church, during which the state attempted to curtail the activities of the church.

Kurie (plural, Kurien). Group of smaller states in the post-Napoleonic Federal Diet of the German League. One vote was shared by several states.

Lager. Camp, an appropriate name for the party groups in Austria during the First Republic.

Land (plural Länder). The states that make up the Federal Republic of Germany. Also, one-time political units in the DDR.

Landammann.   Highest local government official, an ancient title still
in use in some Swiss communities.

Landbund.   Agrarian right-wing political movement in Austria during
the First Republic.

Länderkammer.   In the beginning of the German Democratic Republic, the chamber representing the states in the bicameral legislature.
Discontinued after the disappearance of the *Länder.*

Landsgemeinde.   A gathering of citizens who meet to make local government decisions or to elect their local leaders. Example of direct
democracy, still practiced in a few Swiss cantons.

Landtag.   The state legislatures in the German Federal Republic. Also
the legislature in the principality of Liechtenstein.

Lausanne.   Capital city of the predominantly French-speaking Swiss
canton of Waadt (*Vaud* in French).

League of Nations.   The international organization established after
World War I, with headquarters in Geneva, Switzerland. In 1945
was superseded by the United Nations.

Left.   The term originated during the French Revolution when the
most radical elements sat to the left of the presiding officer in the
semicircular assembly. Today, leftists advocate an increase in social
legislation and social reforms. The extreme Left, the Communists,
favor one-party dictatorial regimes; the moderate Left, the Social
Democrats, are committed to a democratic welfare state.

Leipzig.   City in Germany, now in the DDR. Site of an important
victory by the anti-Napoleonic forces in 1813.

Lemmer, Ernst (1898–1970).   CDU politician who represented the
German Democratic party in the pre-Hitler German *Reichstag.*
After World War II he was prominent in Christian Democratic politics in the Soviet zone and eventually went to the Federal Republic,
where he occupied a number of ministerial posts.

Liberal.   A major European political movement which advocates a
maximum amount of personal liberty for the individual and rejects
both clerical and Socialist orientation. It is represented today in
Switzerland by several smaller parties as well as the *Freisinnig,* in
Austria by the *Freiheitlichen,* and in the German Federal Republic
by the *Free Democrats.*

Liberal Democrats.   The Liberal party in the German Democratic Republic, part of the Communist-controlled National Front.

Lower Austria.   *Niederösterreich,* one of Austria's provinces. Its capital city is Vienna, though Vienna is actually regarded as a separate
province.

Lower Saxony. One of the states of the German Federal Republic, newly created after World War II. The capital city is Hanover.

Ludendorff, Erich (1865–1937). Important military figure in Germany during World War I. Politically active in nationalist anti-Weimar movements after the war.

Lueger, Karl (1844–1910). Austrian politician who helped found the Christian Social party and who served as Vienna's mayor.

Lugger, Alois (1912–). Austrian politician; mayor of the Tyrolean capital of Innsbruck and in 1974 the unsuccessful People's party candidate for president.

Luzern. Swiss canton; also the capital city of that canton.

Magna Charta. The "great charter," an agreement forced on King John of England in 1215 by the nobles, assuring them of important rights. Though not a democratic document, it paved the way for further concessions.

Maier, Reinhold (1889–1971). In the Weimar Republic, a leading politician of the German Democratic and the German State party. After the war, active in the Free Democratic party. Minister-president of Baden-Württemberg.

Marignano. Site of important Swiss defeat by the French in 1515, which in effect ended Swiss militarism.

Marshall, George (1880–1959). American general and secretary of state who in 1947 initiated the European Recovery Program, known as the Marshall Plan.

Marx, Karl (1818–1883). German journalist and author who developed a particular view of history and consequently a program known as Marxism.

Marx, Wilhelm (1863–1946). German *Zentrum* politician and chancellor in the 1920s. In 1925 he was the unsuccessful candidate of the democratic parties for president.

Maximilian (1459–1519). German emperor and member of Habsburg family. Under him Switzerland permanently lost to empire.

McCloy, John (1895–). American high commissioner in Germany after World War II, who was instrumental in normalizing the relationship of the newly established German Federal Republic with the Western Allies.

Mecklenburg. One of the original five states in the Soviet zone of Germany after World War II until the *Länder* were discontinued in the DDR in 1952.

Mediation, Act of. Napoleon's compromise solution in 1803 after his attempt at making Switzerland a centralized state had failed.

Metternich, Klemens (1773–1859). Austrian statesman and thus leading German diplomat from 1812 until the Revolution of 1848 forced his departure.

Miklas, Wilhelm (1872–1956). Austrian Christian Social politician and president from 1928 until 1938.

Military Governors. Commanders of the occupying powers in Germany immediately following World War II.

Minister-President. In a number of states the title given to the first minister, otherwise known as prime minister, or in the Federal Republic and in Austria as chancellor.

Ministerrat. Council of Ministers, a term used in the DDR for the cabinet or government.

Morgarten. Swiss mountain range where in 1315 the Swiss mountain communities defeated the Austrian army.

Müller, Hermann (1876–1931). German Social Democratic politician. He was foreign minister in 1919–1920 and chancellor, in 1920 and from 1928 till 1930.

München (Munich). Capital of the Bavarian state in the German Federal Republic.

Munich Agreement. Hitler and Chamberlain, together with Mussolini of Italy and Daladier of France, met in Munich in September of 1938 and agreed to cede the Sudeten area of Czechoslovakia to Germany in return for a vague promise of "Peace in our time." Identified with "appeasement policy."

Napoleon Bonaparte (1769–1821). French general and emperor of France, from 1804 to 1814/15.

Nationaldemokratische Partei. The National Democratic party. (a) A right-wing neo-Nazi group in the German Federal Republic which in the 1960s won some seats in state parliamentary elections but lost them again soon afterward. Unable to place any deputies in the *Bundestag*. (b) One of the officially recognized parties in the German Democratic Republic which is allocated seats in the *Volkskammer* and given representation in high government positions.

National Front. The combination of all parties and mass organizations in the DDR.

Nationalrat. (a) The popularly elected Parliament of Austria, now consisting of 183 members. (b) The popularly elected Parliament of Switzerland, now consisting of 200 members.

Nazis. Members of Hitler's Nazi party, a popularly used abbreviation of Nationalsozialistische Deutsche Arbeiterpartei (National Socialist German Labor party).

NATO. The North Atlantic Treaty Organization, the Western defense alliance concluded in 1949 between Western European countries, the United States, and Canada. The German Federal Republic joined in 1955.

Neisse. A river in Eastern Europe. See *Oder-Neisse Line.*

Neuenburg. A Swiss canton (French, Neuchatel). Capital city has the same name. Largely French-speaking.

Neues Deutschland. The official party newspaper in the DDR.

Nobs, Ernst (1886–1957). Swiss Socialist politician and mayor of Zürich, who in 1943 became the first Socialist member of the *Bundesrat,* a position he held until 1951; president in 1949.

North German Federation (Norddeutscher Bund). The confederation of German states set up by Prussia in 1866 after they defeated Austria and excluded her from German affairs.

North Rhine-Westphalia. One of the West German states, newly created after World War II. The capital city is Düsseldorf.

Nuschke, Otto (1883–1957). Leading Christian Democratic politician in the DDR. For many years one of the deputies of the chairman of the Council of Ministers.

Oberland. The former *Grafschaft* Vaduz, one of the two districts of Liechtenstein.

Occupation Statute. Statement of a number of powers which the three Western Allies reserved for themselves in 1949 after the German Federal Republic came into existence. Ceased after the Federal Republic formally became part of NATO in 1955.

Oder-Neisse Line. Two East European rivers which became the borderline between Poland and the German Democratic Republic. This border only gradually received *de facto* recognition in the West.

Olah, Franz (1910–). Austrian trade union leader in the Second Republic, a prominent Social Democrat, and minister of the interior from 1963 till 1964. He was expelled from the party and accused and convicted for misappropriation of funds; he ran a separate party in the 1966 parliamentary elections which did not get anyone elected but took 150,000 votes from the SPÖ.

Ollenhauer, Erich (1901–1963). Leading Socialist politician in the German Federal Republic. Party chairman, 1952–1963, and chancellor candidate.

Olmütz Convention. In 1850, Austria with Russian help forced Prussia to abandon all plans for German unification under Prussian leadership.

Ospelt, Josef (1881–1962). Liechtenstein politician who headed the government from 1921 till 1922.

Österreichische Volkspartei OVP. The Austrian People's party, the

Blacks, one of the two great Austrian parties, successor to the Christian Socials. Governed from the end of World War II until 1966 with the Socialsts and during the following four years by themselves.

Ostmark.   An old name for Austria which the Nazis resurrected after the *Anschluss*.

Ostpolitik.   Policy toward the East; Willy Brandt's attempts to establish normal relations with the Communist East European countries, which entailed recognition of the existence of the DDR as an independent state and of the Oder-Neisse line.

Palatinate (Pfalz).   Area in the German Federal Republic situated west of the Rhine River. See *Rhineland-Pflaz*.

Papen, Franz von (1879–1969).   German politician, *Zentrum*, chancellor in 1932, paved the way for Hitler, in whose first cabinet he served as vice-chancellor.

Parliamentary Council.   Assembly meeting in Bonn in 1948/49 for the purpose of drawing up the *Grundgesetz*.

Patriotic Union.   One of the two major parties in Liechtenstein, the *Vaterländische Union*.

Paulus, Friedrich (1890–1957).   German general in World War II, who was captured by the Russians at Stalingrad and cooperated with them afterwards.

People's Chamber.   See *Volkskammer*.

People's Party.   See *Volkspartei*.

Permanent Court of International Justice.   The international court set up by the League of Nations and situated at The Hague in The Netherlands.

Peter, Friedrich (1921–).   Austrian politician. Leader of the *Freiheitliche Partei*. In the *Nationalrat* since 1966.

Pieck, Wilhelm (1876–1960).   Leading German Communist. From 1949 until his death he was president of the German Democratic Republic.

Pittermann, Bruno (1905–).   Austrian Socialist politician who served as vice-chancellor from 1957 until 1966 and was Party chairman for many years.

Potsdam.   Situated outside of Berlin and now in the DDR. Once the garrison town of Prussian kings. Meeting place of the leaders of the United States, Britain, and the USSR in July 1945 to decide the fate of conquered Germany.

President.   Highest official in the land. In Germany and Austria largely a figurehead position. In Switzerland, rotated yearly among members of the *Bundesrat*.

Progressive Citizen's Party.   See *Fortschrittliche Bürgerpartei.*

Proportional Representation.   An election system whereby the seats in the legislature are apportioned among political parties in proportion to the number of votes received (a party that obtains 25 percent of the total vote would be assured of about one-quarter of the seats). In some form or another and with certain modifications, it is in use in most continental European countries.

Proporz.   The Austrian name for proportional representation, especially as used during the coalition government during the first two decades after World War II, when the two major parties divided all top jobs in government and industry with one party holding the number 1 position and the other the number 2 spot, thus giving both parties a major say in running the office.

Prussia.   A major North German state which developed from the principality of Brandenburg, becoming a kingdom in 1701. Fought for control of Germany and formed all of Germany into an empire from which Austria was excluded. Still the largest German state during the Weimar Republic. At the end of World War II, the Allies completely dismembered Prussia, and it no longer exists today.

Pufendorf, Samuel (1632–1694).   One of the first who wrote in the area of international law.

Putsch.   Attempt by a small group of people to gain control of the government of a state.

Raab, Julius (1889–1964).   Austrian politician and minister of trade in 1938. From 1953 till 1961 he was chancellor, and in 1963 the unsuccessful candidate of the People's party for president.

Rechtsstaat.   A state or government based on justice and law.

Reds.   Nickname for left-wing parties, such as Socialists and Communists. Used especially in Austria to describe the Social Democrats and in Liechtenstein for the *Vaterländische Union;* both are contrasted to the other major party, the Blacks.

Referendum.   A form of democracy whereby the people participate in the decision-making process directly rather than through their elected representatives. Especially in use in Switzerland. May be compulsory, where approval of a majority of voters is required, as for changes in the Constitution, or optional, in which case a given number of signatures must first be collected before a particular question can be submitted to the voters for approval.

Regeneration.   Process in 1830 when many Swiss cantons "regenerated" their constitutions, that is, changed them in a more democratic direction.

Regensburg.   Ancient German city, now in the eastern part of Bavaria on the Danube River. From the middle of the seventeenth
century until 1806, it was the permanent seat of the German
Reichstag.

Regierungschef.   Head of government, the chief executive, highest
political government official in Liechtenstein.

Regierungsrat (plural, Regierungsräte).   The ministers or members
of the government in Liechtenstein.

Reich.   The empire, used particularly in Germany. See Holy Roman
Empire of the German Nation.

Reichsfrei.   Territory directly subordinate to the German emperor
that did not recognize any other monarch under him.

Reichsfürstentag.   The Imperial Council of Princes in the old German empire; a gathering of those monarchs who came directly under
the allegiance of the emperor.

Reichsfürstentum.   Imperial principality; land which in the old German empire came directly under the rule of the emperor.

Reichsrat.   The bicameral Parliament in imperial Austria, consisting
of the *Herrenhaus* and the *Haus der Abgeordneten.* In the Weimar
Republic it represented the states' governments on an unequal basis.

Reichstag.   The Imperial Diet or Parliament. Between the seventeenth century and the end of the First Empire, a gathering of representatives of all the component parts of the empire at Regensburg.
Between 1871 and 1918, the popularly elected representative body
of the German empire. During the Weimar Republic, again the representative body of the German people but with more power. Under Hitler the one-party mouthpiece of the regime.

Reichstagsfeuer.   On February 27, 1933, a month after Hitler had
become chancellor and a week before scheduled parliamentary elections, the *Reichstag* building was set on fire. There are strong indications that the Nazis may have done the deed; in any case, they
blamed the Communists and used the occasion to confiscate their
property, to prohibit their candidates from campaigning, and to
rally the German people against allegedly Communist-inspired ar-
son, anarchy, and chaos.

Renner, Karl (1870–1950).   Austrian Socialist politician. Chancellor
from 1918 till 1920, and president from 1945 till his death.

Republic.   Form of government ruled by more than one person, not
a hereditary monarch, and usually headed by a president. Established
after World War I in Germany, the Weimar Republic lasted until

Hitler came to power. In 1949, the Bonn Republic (or Second Republic) came into being. In Austria, the First Republic was established after World War I and ended with the Dollfuss regime in 1933/34. The Second Republic began in 1945.

Rheinbund. The confederation of the Rhine, established by Napoleon as a league of German states that did his bidding.

Rheinland-Pfalz. Rhineland-Palatinate, one of the present states in the German Federal Republic, with its capital in Mainz.

Right. The German word *Recht,* which means justice, law, legality. Also in contrast to the political Left, i.e., Nationalists, Conservatives, monarchists, opponents of Socialists and Communists.

Robertson, Sir Brian (1896–1974). British general who served under Montgomery in World War II and became military governor in the British zone of occupation and eventually British high commissioner.

Saarland. Land in the Federal Republic of Germany with Saarbrücken as its capital. Created after World War I and placed under the rule of the League of Nations till a plebiscite showed overwhelming support for the return to Germany. After World War II the French again favored internationalization but bowed to a referendum for return to Germany.

Sachsen-Anhalt. See *Anhalt.*

St. Germain. Town situated to the west of Paris, where in 1919 the peace treaty between the Allies and Austria was signed.

Salzburg. Austrian province; capital city has the same name.

Sarnerbund. In the early 1830s a league of several Swiss cantons which felt physically and ideologically threatened by the formation of the more liberal *Siebnerkonkordat.*

Saxony. Sachsen, a one-time component part of Germany, was one of the five *Länder* in the German Democratic Republic until the dissolution of all *Länder* into districts.

Schädler, Gustav (1883–1961). Liechtenstein politician, professor, and head of the government from 1922 until 1928.

Schaffhausen. Northern canton of Switzerland; capital city has the same name.

Schärf, Adolf (1890–1965). Austrian Socialist politician; Vice-chancellor, 1945–1957, and president from 1957 to 1965.

Scheel, Walter (1919–). Free Democratic politician in the German Federal Republic who was vice-chancellor and foreign minister from 1969 till 1974 and elected president in 1974.

Scheidemann, Philipp (1865–1939). German Social Democratic politician; chancellor in 1919.

Schellenberg. One of the two free imperial territories which were combined in the early eighteenth century to form the principality of Liechtenstein. Now the *Unterland*.

Schleicher, Kurt von (1882–1934). German general and Hitler's immediate predecessor as chancellor in 1932/33. He was murdered by the Nazis.

Schleinzer, Karl (1924–1975). Austrian politician, People's party. He was minister of defense and minister of agriculture in the 1960s, and his party's unsuccessful candidate for chancellor in 1971. Again his party's nominee for chancellor in 1975, he was killed in a car accident ten weeks before the elections.

Schleswig-Holstein. Province in northern Germany for which the war against Denmark was fought in 1864. Today, one of the *Länder* in the Federal Republic; capital city is Kiel.

Schmidt, Helmut (1918–). West German politician, Social Democrat. Minister of defense and of economics and finance in Willy Brandt's government, he became chancellor in 1974.

Schönerer, Georg von (1842–1921). Pan-German, anti-Jewish, "away from Rome" politician in the declining days of the Austrian empire.

Schreiber, Walther (1884–1958). One of the founding members of the CDU in the Soviet zone in 1945 who was expelled from leadership position in the party a few months later because of his opposition to Russian-inspired agricultural reforms.

Schumacher, Kurt (1895–1952). German politician, Social Democrat. Member of *Reichstag* before Hitler, he spent most of the Nazi period in concentration camps, then was a leader of the Social Democrats after World War II.

Schuschnigg, Kurt (1897–1977). Austrian politician and chancellor from 1934 till the annexation of Austria by Hitler in 1938.

Schutzbund. Quasi-military, pro-Socialist organization in Austria's First Republic.

Schwarzenbach, James (1911–). Swiss politician in the *Nationalrat* since 1967. A member of the "Republican and National Fraction," he supported right-wing, nationalist, antiforeigners programs.

Schweizer Volkspartei. The Swiss People's party, formerly the Peasants' (or Farmers') party; now holds one of the seven seats in the government.

Schwyz. One of the Swiss cantons; its capital city has the same name. Member of the original confederation which gave its name to the whole country.

Second International. International worker organization established in 1889. The "First" had been established by Karl Marx in 1864; the "Third" was established by Lenin in 1919 after the Russian Revolution and was dissolved during the Second World War.

Sedan. City in France; important Prussian victory in 1870 which resulted in the capture of Emperor Napoleon III.

Seipel, Ignaz (1876–1932). Austrian priest and politician during the Second Republic; Christian Social. He was chancellor from 1922 till 1924 and 1926 to 1929.

Seitz, Karl (1869–1950). Austrian politician, Social Democrat. He was president of the Constituent National Assembly in 1919 and mayor of Vienna from 1923 till 1934.

Siebnerkonkordat. Association formed in 1832 by seven Swiss cantons for the common protection of their Constitutions. The more conservative cantons replied by organizing the *Sarnerbund*.

Single Member Constituency. Election district from which one, and not more than one, person is elected in any given election. This means victory to the highest votegetter. Unless there are provisions for a run-off election between the top two if neither gets at least 50 percent of the total vote, the winning candidate may well be the choice of a minority of the electorate. The British refer to it as "first past the post."

Social Democrats. Among the oldest political parties in the German-speaking countries and still of major importance in Germany, Austria, and Switzerland. Originally workers' parties with radical Marxist programs, they have in the course of time become acceptable to non-working-class voters as they emphasized democratic commitments together with welfare-state programs.

Socialist Labor Party. Name given to the combined German Socialist groups in 1875 which formerly consisted of two distinct factions.

Sonderbund. A "separate league" formed by Catholic cantons in Switzerland in order to resist constitutional reforms. Defeated during the Civil War of 1847.

Sovereignty. Complete national independence of a country and freedom from any external control. Idea first developed by a Frenchman, Jean Bodin (1530–1596).

Sozialistische Einheitspartei. The Socialist Unity party of the German Democratic Republic and the governing party which was formed by combining the Social Democratic and Communist parties in the Soviet zone of occupation in 1946.

Sozialistische Reichspartei.   A small, semi-Fascist party that developed in the German Federal Republic in its early days and outlawed in 1952 because of its extremist and antidemocratic character.

Spiegel, Der.   A news magazine founded in 1947 in Hamburg. In 1962, the Adenauer administration accused the magazine and some of its editors of high treason. Arrests and searches took place, but the accused persons were eventually freed.

Staatspartei.   See Deutsche Demokratische Partei.

Staatsrat.   Council of State, since 1960 the highest governmental body in the German Democratic Republic.

Staatsvertrag.   State Treaty, name given to the agreement of 1955 between Austria and the four occupying powers resulting in the withdrawal of Allied military forces and complete restoration of Austria's sovereignty.

Stalin, Joseph (1879–1953).   Communist leader and dictator in the Soviet Union.

Stand (plural Stände).   Estate; grouping; social, economic, or political class.

Ständerat.   Part of the bicameral Swiss legislature in which each canton is represented by two representatives.

Ständestaat.   The "corporate state" which Dollfuss established in Austria in 1933 wherein various cultural and economic interests were to have an influence on the government in place of a representative democratic legislature.

Steiermark (Styria).   One of the Austrian provinces with Graz as its capital.

Stoph, Willi (1914–).   Important political figure in the German Democratic Republic. Communist prior to Hitler, he has held various governmental posts since 1945. Member and since 1973 president of the *Staatsrat*.

Sudetenland.   Mountain area of Czechoslovakia. Before 1918 it was part of the Austrian empire. Because of its 3.5 million German-speaking people, Hitler claimed the area in 1938 and was awarded it in the Munich Agreement.

Tagsatzung.   In early Switzerland, meetings of representatives from the various communities for consultation and decision-making purposes. Revised in early nineteenth century, the last one in 1848 proclaiming the new Constitution.

Thälmann, Ernst (1886–1944).   German Communist leader and presidential candidate in 1925 and 1932 who perished in a concentration camp.

Third International. Founded by Lenin in 1919 as Communist-dominated workers' organization after he had assumed power in Russia. Centered in Moscow and dissolved in 1943 as a gesture of goodwill toward wartime Allies.

Third Reich. Established by Hitler in 1933, the "third empire" of Germany lasted until 1945.

Thirty Years War. Religious conflict in Europe, 1618–1648, terminating with the Peace of Westphalia in which Catholicism and Protestantism established their right to exist.

Thüringen (Thuringia). One of the German states during the Weimar Republic. Also, one of the *Länder* when the German Democratic Republic was first established until all states were dissolved in 1952.

Torgau. German city on the Elbe River where in April of 1945 American and Russian troops linked up with one another.

Trizonia. Economic merger of the American, British, and French zones of occupation in Germany after World War II.

Tyrol. Austrian province; capital city is Innsbruck.

Ulbricht, Walter (1893–1973). For many years the leading personality in the German Democratic Republic. First secretary of the Socialist Unity party and president of the *Staatsrat*.

United Front. A political alliance formed in the German Democratic Republic among all existing parties, whereby competition is avoided and each party is allocated a specific number of seats in the *Volkskammer*.

Unselbständig Erwerbende und Kleinbauern (Arbeiterpartei): (Employees and Smallholders—Labor party). A third party that appeared on the ballot in Liechtenstein in 1953 but which had little electoral support.

Unterland. One of the two component parts and electoral districts in Liechtenstein. Originally the *Grafschaft Schellenberg*.

Unterwalden. One of the original three cantons of Switzerland. It is now divided into two half-cantons, *Nidwalden* and *Obwalden*.

Upper Austria (Oberösterreich). Austrian province with Linz as its capital.

Uri. One of the original three cantons of Switzerland.

Vaduz. Capital city of Liechtenstein. The surrounding territory, now the *Oberland*, was once the *Grafschaft* Vaduz, one of the two duchies which combined to form the present principality of Liechtenstein in 1719.

Vaterländische Union. The Patriotic Union, formerly the *Volkspartei*, one of the two political parties of Liechtenstein. They were commonly referred to as Reds.

Versailles. Palace of Louis XIV of France, situated southwest of Paris. The German empire was proclaimed here in 1871, and in 1919 Germany was forced to accept peace terms here in order to end World War I.

Vienna (Wien). Capital city of Austria, situated on the Danube River. Also one of Austria's provinces.

Volkskammer. The People's Chamber, the representative body of the German Democratic Republic.

Volkspartei. The People's party, a common name for democratic, usually somewhat conservative and non-socialist parties. During Weimar there were the nationalist *Deutschnationale Volkspartei,* the national-liberal *Deutsche Volkspartei,* the *Fortschrittliche Volkspartei,* which thought it necessary to emphasize its "progressive" character, and the forerunner of the CSU in Bavaria, the *Bayerische Volkspartei.* Today in Austria the former Christian Social party has become the *Österreichische Volkspartei,* whereas in Liechtenstein there no longer is a party by that name. But in Switzerland, the conservative and Catholic group is now called *Christlich-demokratische Volkspartei,* the Protestants have their *Evangelische Volkspartei,* and the agrarians are now calling themselves *Schweizerische Volkspartei.*

Waldheim, Kurt (1918–). Austrian diplomat, foreign minister from 1968 to 1970, unsuccessful candidate for the presidency in 1971, and secretary general of the United Nations since 1971.

War of Liberation. Following Napoleon's defeat before Moscow and his retreat from Russia, there was a general European uprising against the emperor, culminating in the Battle of Nations at Leipzig in October 1813.

Warsaw Pact. A treaty of "friendship, cooperation, and mutual assistance" concluded in 1955 between Albania, Bulgaria, Hungary, the German Democratic Republic, Poland, Romania, Czechoslovakia, and the Soviet Union, which is the Communist equivalent of, and reply to, the North Atlantic Treaty Organization.

Weber, Max (1897–). Swiss politician and Socialist member of the *Bundersrat* from 1951 until 1953, when he resigned, thus temporarily terminating Social Democratic participation on the Federal Council.

Weimar. City in central Germany, now in the DDR. Here after

World War I was drafted and signed the document establishing the Weimar Republic, which lasted from 1919 till 1933.

Wels, Otto (1875–1939). German Social Democrat and leader of the party in the *Reichstag*. He spoke against Hitler's proposed Enabling Act in March of 1933, cast one of the ninety-four votes against it, then had to flee the country immediately afterwards.

Westphalia, Treaty of. Terminated the Thirty Years War in 1648.

Wetzlar. German city in Hesse, seat of the Imperial Court of Justice from the late seventeenth century until 1806.

Wilson, Harold (1916–). British Labour party politician and prime minister from 1964 to 1970 and from 1974 to 1976.

Wirtschaftswunder. The "economic miracle" which transformed West Germany in a few short years from a defeated, severely war-damaged country into one with a booming economy and a strong currency. Much of the credit is usually given to Ludwig Erhard, Adenauer's minister of economics.

World War I (1914–1918). War in which Germany and her Austro-Hungarian and Turkish allies were eventually defeated by a combination of powers including France, Britain, Russia, and, after 1917, the United States. Peace with Germany was concluded at Versailles, peace with Austria at St. Germain.

World War II (1939–1945). War begun by Hitler's attack on Poland which was quickly followed by the Nazi conquest of large parts of Europe. The Russian army was able to defeat German troops in the east and American and British forces which had landed at Normandy in June of 1944 attacked from the west. Hitler committed suicide in Berlin, and what was left of the German armies surrendered unconditionally.

Württemberg. A German state until 1945. A few years later, after a plebiscite, combined with neighboring Baden to form the present West German state of Baden-Württemberg. The capital in Stuttgart.

Yalta. Russian port city in the Crimea. Meeting place between Roosevelt, Churchill, and Stalin in February 1945 for the purpose of determining postwar policies.

Zemp, Josef (1834–1908). Swiss politician who became the first Catholic Conservative member of the *Bundesrat* in 1891.

Zentrum. German Catholic-oriented center party. Important during imperial Germany when it first took a stand against some of Bismarck's anticlerical proposals and one of the major supporting groups in the Weimar Republic. After its members reluctantly voted for Hitler's Enabling Law, the party ceased to exist. A small party by that name reappeared after World War II, but the *Zentrum's* major offspring, with a broadened base, was the CDU.

Zimmerwald. Meeting place in Switzerland in 1915 of antiwar socialist groups, with Lenin advocating civil war by the workers against war-supporting bourgeoisie and monarchies and the formation of a revolutionary International.

Zollverein. The customs union which Prussia began after the Napoleonic Wars and which eventually involved all of the German states in a tariff-free area. The economic union paved the way for the political union that followed.

Zürich. Largest canton of Switzerland according to population. Its capital, of the same name, is the economic center of Switzerland.

Index

GH

N83KK

KOHN

A3
hw